PRAYER ON TOP OF THE EARTH

ON TOP OF THE EARTH

The Spiritual Universe of the Plains Apaches

Kay Parker Schweinfurth

University Press of Colorado

Published by the University Press of Colorado
5589 Arapahoe Avenue, Suite 206C
Boulder, Colorado 80303

The University Press of Colorado is a cooperative publishing enterprise supported, in part, by Adams State College, Colorado State University, Fort Lewis College, Mesa State College, Metropolitan State College of Denver, University of Colorado, University of Northern Colorado, University of Southern Colorado, and Western State College of Colorado.

The paper used in this publication meets the minimum requirements of the American National Standard for Information Sciences—Permanence of Paper for Printed Library Materials. ANSI Z39.48-1992

Library of Congress Cataloging-in-Publication Data

Schweinfurth, Kay Parker, 1932–
  Prayer on top of the earth : the spiritual universe of the Plains Apaches / by Kay Parker Schweinfurth.
    p. cm.
Includes bibliographical references and index.
  ISBN 0-87081-656-X (cloth : alk. paper)
  1. Apache Indians—Religion. 2. Apache mythology. 3. Apache Indians—Rites and ceremonies. I. Title.
  E99.A6 S38 2002
  299'.782—dc21
                                                                    2001007755

Design by Daniel Pratt
Typesetting by Laura Furney

The author and publisher make grateful acknowledgment to the Texas Folklore Society for permission to reprint "In the Beginning," pp. 17–18 in "Kiowa Apache Tales" by J. Gilbert McAllister in *The Sky Is My Tipi*, ed. Mody Boatright. Publication of the Texas Folklore Society No. 22, University Press, Southern Methodist University, Dallas, 1949.

11   10   09   08   07   06   05   04   03   02   10   9   8   7   6   5   4   3   2   1

Co-winner of the 2001 Colorado Endowment for the Humanities Publication Prize

The CEH Publication Prize was created in 1998 and the first awards were made in 1999. The prize annually supports publication of outstanding nonfiction works that have strong humanities content and that make an area of humanities research more available to the Colorado public. The CEH Publication Prize funds are shared by the University Press of Colorado and the authors of the works being recognized.

The Colorado Endowment for the Humanities is a statewide, nonprofit organization dedicated to improving the quality of humanities education for all Coloradans.

Contents

Illustrations

Preface

In preparing this study of the Apaches and their spiritual beliefs, I have incurred multiple intellectual and personal obligations. My longest-standing debt is to my mentor, William E. Bittle, who more than twenty-five years ago kindled my interest in Plains Indians and native religions. A foremost authority on the Plains Apaches and a seasoned Plains ethnographer, he supervised my doctoral dissertation on Cheyenne grandmothers, providing valuable insights into social structure and cultural institutions of Plains Indians, many of which are applicable to this study.

When in March 1989 I paid a visit to Bittle in Reno, Nevada, where he had retired from his professorship at the University of Oklahoma, I learned that he had permanently abandoned work on his Apache ethnography, an ethnography for which he had taken several sabbaticals to complete. When he said, "In my heart I know they [the Apache field notes] need to get in print, but I simply cannot do it now," I did not have to guess to what he was referring. His frail frame communicated it all. He was a man in failing health, and now, he acknowledged, his multiple medical problems, which heretofore had not interfered with his work, were daily sapping his creative energy. He offered me his field notes, which I took for the purpose of assembling an ethnography but on one condition—that he would edit the finished product. He was more than happy to agree and seemed greatly relieved to be freed of this long-term nagging responsibility. I flew home with 75 pounds of Apache field notes, and one month later he mailed me an additional 25 pounds.

With the entrustment to me of the treasured Apache notes, I was acutely aware that he was relinquishing a good portion of his life's work. Bittle was a gifted field-worker and a brilliant lecturer, but he was modest to a fault, never touting any of his achievements. Absent ambition for himself, he nevertheless had a solicitude for these research notes that was motivated by an intellectual imperative his health now prevented him from realizing. The solution was to pass the responsibility on to someone else, someone whose theoretical orientation and style of authorship he knew well.

From the time I left his house that day up to the present, I have never forgotten the moral and intellectual responsibility of the task I have undertaken. As a "Bittle-trained" Plains specialist, a native of Plains Indian country in western Oklahoma, and an experienced field-worker among Southern Cheyennes, a Plains tribe bordering the Apaches, I was eager to immerse myself in the Apache field notes. And so I began work on what became a decade-long project, a manuscript on the spiritual life of the Plains Apaches that, I can truly say, has become a labor of love as well as a stimulating learning experience.

The beauty of Bittle's meticulous field notes is that not only do they transport the reader so he/she can experience "being There," but they are also a good read. Bittle was a lifelong friend of many Apaches and was acquainted with the complexities of their culture—a message that comes through in the numerous direct quotes. Now that I have assumed the burden of authorship—the writing, organization, and interpretation of the research of someone who was There—my being There is necessarily derivative. In fact, I was there, but only briefly several times in the late 1960s and early 1970s as a student in the field school and since 1990 another several dozen times. Throughout the preparation of this manuscript, I was fortunate to have had Bittle's ongoing commentary and editorial advice via e-mail, U.S. post office mail, and telephone until the last few months before his death in November 1999.

My debts to the amiable Apaches are many. I am especially indebted to those no longer living who contributed significantly to this book, in particular the Apache self-appointed historians who are quoted and highlighted in the biographical essay. Others who made important contributions were Gertie Chalepah, Helen Blackbear, Mrs. Bigman, Apache Sam Klinekole, Claude Jay, Stewart Klinekole, Apache Ben Chaletsin, and Wallace Redbone. I also want to thank Bobby Jay, Alfred Chalepah, and Alonzo Chalepah for helping to fill gaps in the field notes and to identify persons in the collection of photographs. I am also grateful to Father Daniels of St. Patrick's Mission in Anadarko, the Reverend J. L. Treat of the Apache Baptist Mission, the Reverend Ann Holmes of the True Holiness Mission in Anadarko, and the Reverend Joe Prickett of the Baptist Mission for their observations and analyses.

I have benefited from the reading of this manuscript and commentary by two historians, Wayne and Anne Morgan, and anthropologist Martha Blaine. I am especially grateful to Joseph Whitecotton for a thoughtful critique and valuable advice on current theoretical perspectives and to linguist John Dunn, who carefully examined the Apache vocabulary and corrected the diacritics. Many thanks to ethnobotanist Julia Jordan, a member of the field schools in 1961 and 1964, for her "I was There" knowledge and her many photographs that captured the personality of the subjects. I am indebted to a variety of persons and institutions for photographs, in particular Deborah Baroff at the Museum of the Great Plains in Lawton, John Lovett at the Western History Collections at the University of Oklahoma Libraries, the Oklahoma Historical Society, Tom Kavanaugh at the William Hammond Mathers Museum at Indiana University, Dorothy Klippell for her husband's photograph of Connie Mae Saddleblanket, and the Smithsonian Institution for its treasure of century-old photographs.

For my wonderful family who filled all the gaps and offered judicious insights, I am truly grateful. And finally, although she had no direct part in the preparation of this manuscript, I am greatly indebted to Angie Debo, whose impeccable scholarship and tireless commitment to justice and integrity are an inspiration to all who delve into the history and culture of the American Indian.

Introduction

The Apache Indians, long identified as Kiowa Apaches because of their historical, although somewhat tenuous, association with the Kiowas, will in this book be predominantly referred to as Apaches or Plains Apaches. The tribe dropped the Kiowa designation in the 1930s to officially become the Apache Tribe of Oklahoma, thus imparting an identity more truly reflective of its Apachean cultural and linguistic heritage. The people today uniformly reject the appellation Kiowa Apaches and wish to be known simply as Apaches.

As Ray Blackbear pointedly stated, "We don't like to be called Kiowa Apache. If we are called [Kiowa] Apache, it kind of makes us feel like a part of them, which we are not. The white man just calls us Kiowa Apache, and we don't like it. Apache is what we call ourselves."[1]

Using the term *Apache* is somewhat problematic in that it is also a collective designation for the linguistic family of Apache tribes located in the Southwest and the Plains. Recognizing that this may be a possible source of confusion, I nevertheless defer to the tribe's wishes and use the name Apaches or Plains Apaches, except in segments of the text where Kiowa Apache is needed for historical accuracy—namely when the subject tribe needs to be distinguished from other Apache tribes and in segments that refer to specifically named Kiowa Apache research of earlier scholars. The Plains Apache designation appropriately applies to the historical period from 1860 to the present, the time period when the previously named Kiowa Apaches clearly have the best claim of all Apache tribes to the title "Plains Apaches."

The Plains Apaches, although numerically small, are of extraordinary interest ethnographically because they represent the easternmost extension of the Southern Athapaskan–speaking peoples of the Southwest who during historical times inhabited a true Plains environment. They are of further interest because they may be the only example of a Plains tribe that came from an identifiable non-Plains source, arrived on the Plains, and adapted to a Plains economy and social structure. Yet remarkably little information is available on the tribe in the ethnographic literature, and what does exist is brief and scattered in diverse and hard-to-find sources.

James Mooney, as early as 1898, identified and described the Apaches, but his erroneous assumption that they were culturally one with the Kiowas led to a prolonged hiatus in research on the tribe until the 1930s. The first research that treated the Apaches as a separate cultural entity was undertaken by J. Gilbert McAllister in 1933–1934. Relevant to the perspective of the current study are his publications on social organization, doctoring, and folktales. Articles emanating from fieldwork in the 1940s by Charles S. Brant confirmed the tribe's cultural separateness from the Kiowas and demonstrated its many cultural similarities to other Apachean tribes. Charles Brant also recorded an excellent autobiography of an Apache man born in 1878, wrote an article on peyote and several on culture history, and transcribed numerous field notes, all of which have been valuable sources for this book.[2]

In 1952 William E. Bittle, director of the University of Oklahoma's Anthropology Field School and Indian Studies program, began his fieldwork with the Plains Apaches. Over a decade and a half, he and his students worked arduously and meticulously to collect a wealth of primary materials on the tribe's culture and history, only a portion of which has heretofore been published. The most significant articles are by Bittle on linguistics, peyote, the Manatidie Dancing Society, and Apache early history, and one by Bittle and Morris E. Opler on Kiowa Apache death practices. Two masters' theses and one article by Bittle's students on ethnobotany, medicine, and peyote are also of note.[3]

The ethnographic significance of this book rests on three characteristics. First, it brings together in one volume old and new materials to produce

Of Apache consonants, *b, d, g, h, k, l, m, n, s, t, z* have approximately the same values as in English. Other consonants and their approximate values are:

dz = dz as in a*dz*e

š = sh as in *sh*ell

ž = si as in vi*si*on

č = ch as in *ch*ief

x = ch as in German a*ch*

Ɣ = no English equivalent, voiced velar fricative

X = no English equivalent, voiceless uvular fricative

ł = no English equivalent, voiceless lateral fricative made by expelling air from both sides of the tongue

ʔ = glottal stop sounded with a slight catch in the throat as in uh-oh. Some consonants, *t´, k´*, and *c´*, and all vowels may be glottalized. They are pronounced with the same catch in the throat.

Pronunciation Guide

Apache scholars have employed different methods to record the Apache language. McAllister and Brant anglicized all Apache words. Hoijer and Bittle, both trained linguists, used phonemic transcriptions, and a number of nonspecialists recorded Apache words that were not always accurate enough to allow respelling in a phonemic transcription. Rather than try to reconcile these differences, I cite word forms as I found them and provide a simplified pronunciation guide for words that are phonemically marked.

Essentially, the vowels—*a, e, i, o* (there is no *u* except in anglicized words)—have English values: *a* as in f*a*ther, *e* as in m*e*t, *i* as in s*ee*, and *o* as in m*o*w. All four vowels may have tonal markings. They can be pronounced with a high pitch indicated by an accent mark over the vowel (*é*) or a low pitch indicated by a grave accent over the vowel (*è*). Falling pitch is shown by (*ê*), and rising pitch is indicated by (*ĕ*). The vowel may be lengthened with (·) or nasalized, indicated by a subscript (*ę*) and pronounced like *en* in French *e*nfant.

the first book-length publication on the Plains Apaches. This assemblage of materials from Bittle's and Brant's voluminous field notes with the afore-mentioned articles and theses makes possible a fairly comprehensive view of the tribe's spiritual beliefs and rituals extending from at least the early 1860s to the present and probably, by extrapolation, from many generations earlier.

Second, this book, which is a social history, provides the non-Indian population with a rare insight into the all-embracing Indian spiritual world—a world of nature spirits, pan-Indian religions, and Christianity. Whereas considerable material on American Indian religion exists in print, much of it focuses on only one or two unique aspects, as the book on Koyukon sym-bolism by Richard Nelson or Edward Anderson's book on peyote do.[4] So in this book I have strived to give a concise but comprehensive picture of Plains Apache spirituality by touching on a variety of religious topics through time.

Finally, this book provides its readers with the collective memory of one Apache tribe through an abundance of firsthand accounts. Particularly valu-able have been the interviews with elders who were able to recall details of various stories passed down from previous generations and to remember ritu-als they had observed or participated in as children. These individuals, all deceased, were the primary repositories of the tribe's culture. They were people like Joe Blackbear and Tennyson Berry, born in 1878 and 1876, respectively, who were Brant's primary sources; and others like Datose, Susagossa, and Rose Chaletsin, three women born in the last two decades of the nineteenth century; and Ray Blackbear and Fred Bigman, two men born near the turn of the twentieth century on whom Bittle primarily relied. Their memories of the stories, medicines, and rituals were exceptional. All not only gave their consent but were anxious to have their stories and recollections published. They expressed concerns that many Apaches of the 1960s were uninformed about the old ways. In particular, they worried that their grandchildren would never have an opportunity to learn the old tribal lore and cherish it as they (the elders) had if it were not transcribed.

Personal Indian narrative is powerful and undoubtedly the best means to evoke understanding of and empathy for a different culture. Breaking down the traditional barrier between the researcher and the culture being observed avoids a message of aloofness and, done well, brings a people to life.

Early ethnographers operated in the historical context of colonialism, a period often referred to as the golden age of anthropology, when there were few political concerns. The rite of passage for the budding sociocultural an-thropologist in those relatively worry-free days was to select an isolated cul-ture to study, record the findings, fit them into some theoretical framework, and finally report the conclusions in an extensive ethnography written primarily for academic anthropologists but for others as well in the literate West. The conclusions of the ethnographer, almost without exception, remained forever unknown to the group that had been observed—often American Indians—and were accepted carte blanche by the non-Indian population.

The collapse of colonial rule, which gave political independence to sixty-six countries in the period 1948–1968,[5] and the slightly earlier empowerment of American Indians with legislation, beginning in 1924, changed forever the role of the ethnographer not only in distant lands but in America as well. Today's ethnographer can no longer speak with automatic authority for those unable to speak for themselves. Neither they, the Others, nor Us is willing to accept an ethnographer's assertions of another culture paraphrased in turgid academic prose.

A number of anthropologists, with Geertz in the forefront, have discussed the moral and intellectual complexity of the ethnographer's dilemma and offered various ideas on how to bridge the gap between the observer and the observed. So that all who are "Here" can truly experience "being There," Geertz suggests that the researcher concentrate on "evoking" the Others rather than "representing" them and on transcribing, in words spoken by the Others, what they think, not what the ethnographer thinks they think.[6] The most important benefit of this method, according to Stephan Tyler, is that "it frees ethnography from *mimesis* and the inappropriate mode of scientific rhetoric that entails objects, facts, descriptions, generalizations, etc."[7]

James Clifford recommends making coauthors out of persons interviewed and utilizing dialogic and polylogic processes rather than "giving to one voice a pervasive authorial function and to others the role of sources, 'informants,' to be quoted or paraphrased."[8] The benefit of the dialogic process, suggests Tyler, is its emphasis on "the cooperative and collaborative nature of the ethnographic situation in contrast to the ideology of the transcendental observer. In fact, it rejects the ideology of the 'observer-observed,' there being nothing observed and no one who is observer."[9]

Reconstructing a cultural history from oral traditions is a great deal more complicated than simply practicing, in Geertz's words, "ethnographic ventriloquism." It requires "putting oneself into someone else's skin" while being careful not to get into some inner correspondence of spirit with that person. No matter how information is elicited, it is an undisputed fact that the ethnographer "does not, and largely cannot, perceive what the informant perceives."[10] Claude Levi-Strauss agrees, calling the immediacy of the "being There" approach essentially impossible, "either outright fraud or fatuous self-deception."[11]

Hearing and recording what someone says are only the beginning. Getting it right requires paying attention to how the person tells it, grasping the cultural framework in which it is told, finding out about the person's relationships, ascertaining motivations, and remembering that not all persons available and willing to be heard are of equal value. Recognizing the great differences in individuals' perceptions and their ability to recall past events is one of the basic precepts of credible fieldwork. Some persons give information freely; others do not. As Bittle noted, "Modern Apaches draw from somewhat different sources when they provide information. They most certainly have reflected on their own belief system and subjected it to contemporary interpretation, and they have forgotten things and sometimes make incorrect statements."[12] Especially in the area of religion, one can expect some recollections to show inconsistencies because of the early exposure of Apaches to Christianity. It is also important to remember that the Apaches, given their long association with the Kiowas and the Arapahos and their modern discourse with the Mescaleros and other Apachean speakers, freely borrowed and shared ideas so that what is distinctive to this group of Apaches living in Oklahoma is no longer clearly identifiable.

Given the great variability in the reliability and perceptiveness of persons contributing information, the critical elements for a successful ethnography depend foremost on the integrity, skills, and sensitivity of the ethnographer. He or she, above all else, must avoid the slightest temptation to ask informants leading questions. Apaches today are particularly amenable and anxious to assist in the recording of their tribal history and lore, and a field-worker who wishes to elicit a particular answer can do so easily by phrasing a leading question.

Assuredly, the avoidance of leading questions, as one of the basic precepts of Bittle's field school, could never be guaranteed, but close monitoring was employed to control it. Questions researchers asked were included in the recorded notes and overall indicate very little bias. The critical aspects of gathering meaningful information depend on establishing a trusting relationship with persons most knowledgeable about the culture, interacting with them, and showing some facility in, or at least a desire to learn, basic skills in the native language. Attaining a fluency in Apache was a priority for Bittle, whose first years in the field were spent collecting linguistic materials to complete his Ph.D. dissertation. From the very beginning he was able to establish a unique rapport with the elders, as evidenced by the considerable trust and respect they always accorded him.

In 1953 Bittle reported that approximately 100 persons had a high degree of fluency in Apache, and another 100 had limited skills—estimates since calculated to have been rather high based on the fact that the language was declared moribund in 1981.[13] Some of Bittle's interviews were conducted in Apache. The elders who had retained the most knowledge about Apache culture, however, spoke English as well as, if not better than, Apache, so most interviews in the 1960s were in English. Some interviews by the field school were tape-recorded during the day and transcribed later, but recorders were not used if they seemed to intrude or inhibit a free flow of information, in which case the notes were transcribed from memory later. Many of Charles Brant's interviews were conducted in Apache using an interpreter, usually someone who had learned English in a mission or government boarding school.

As a starting point for a discussion of Apache spiritual life, I offer a definition of native religion as I understand it applies to the Apaches before their exposure to Christianity, followed by defining characteristics of the current syncretic (inclusive) religion that has been shaped by the spread of literacy and the availability of religious options. I have selected defining characteristics from a wide range of definitions used by anthropologists, sociologists, and others that are most pertinent to this study, and I have identified some of their progenitors.

1. The religious thought of native peoples in preliterate cultures is based on a living analysis and a detailed knowledge of the natural world that is adaptable to perception and imagination. It is not primitive or inferior but simply "prior" (Levi-Strauss).[14] It is analogical thought, expressed in metaphor or metonym, that pictures the natural world as analogous to the human world and perceives all living things, natural phenomena, and inanimate objects as beings endowed with consciousness or living souls (Godelier).[15]

2. Religious thought in native religions divides the world into the sacred and the profane (Durkheim and Eliade).[16] Preliterate cultures perceive purity and danger in many actions. They are pollution-prone, and they observe many taboos (Douglas).[17]

   As literacy spreads, these characteristics decline, and characteristics from the third category take on more importance, although they may have already been present in the native religion.

3. Religion provides meaning and offers explanations for anomalous events and experiences (Geertz),[18] gives comprehension and emotional support for human suffering and death (Geertz and Malinowski),[19] provides criteria to explain the discontinuity

between things as they are and as they ought to be (Geertz),[20] and answers a human need to explain the cosmos (Eliade).[21]

In the final analysis, one of the most important functions of every religion, whether inspired by nature or a charismatic figure, is to set the moral tone of society and guide people's decisions about appropriate and inappropriate actions. The required code of behavior is reinforced by an ever-present threat of sanctions that can range from a fear of ghosts to a fear of eternal punishment and that serve to enlist people's loyalties and bind them to the group.

The unifying thread of this book is "the symbol," which Irwin defines as an identifiable form that participates in a context of possible meanings, both presently and historically, and that also points beyond itself to express those meanings in a highly condensed and simplified manner.[22] Whether an eagle feather, the hoot of an owl, or a replica of the sun, a symbol can inspire a variety of effects, from convincing warriors of their invincibility to warning everyone of impending disaster. It can inspire courage in the very young, stimulate generosity in the entire tribe, raise the hunter's expectations for success, or bind people to each other. Symbols serve as both inspiration and reinforcement for the native religion of the past and provide a bridge to the all-embracing syncretic religion of today. Although a symbol may lose its sacred qualities and become more secular, its power is as likely to increase as it is to diminish.

At the heart of the narrative is Plains Apache folklore—the important stories and adventures from the remote past, trickster tales, animal stories, pedagogical tales, and humorous fiction. Although there is a great amount of variety, American Indian folklore basically falls into one of two categories— categories the Eskimo call old and young; the Winnebago, sacred and narrative; and the Pawnee, true and false.[23] The first of these—the old, the sacred, the true—are the myths of ancient time, a time when the world had not yet assumed its present form, which explained the origins of the cosmos and transformation of the beings that inhabited it. Special kinds of myths were the charter myths, which explained how a ceremony or a cultural practice came into existence,[24] and the memorates, which were stories of adventures taken as part of vision quests.[25]

The second folklore category—the young, the narrative, the false—is a catchall category for all other narratives, including recent stories and legends that are nonhistorical or unverifiable, explaining something about the group's past.[26] Trickster tales about talking animals with human traits can belong to either category, depending on their characteristics.

A final observation is to note the critical role Coyote played throughout the folklore in keeping Apaches in touch with reality. He helped them balance their lives in the natural world with the supernatural and was an example of what one can do using one's brain.

Methodologically, this book is a combined diachronic and synchronic study. It is diachronic in its focus on cultural change compelled by numerous life-altering circumstances Apaches experienced after their final military defeat in 1867, and it is synchronic in its descriptions of Apache beliefs, sacred symbols, and rituals.

Following a biographical essay about the seven self-appointed Apache historians and a brief chapter on Apache history, the first part of the book focuses on beliefs Apaches held about their sacred universe, symbols found in nature—plants, trees, birds, animals; number, color, and direction symbols; the significance of the tribal medicine bundles and their associated rituals; and the kinship system and its linkage to a great fear of ghosts. The second part discusses how Apache beliefs are incorporated into individual and collective rituals in chapters on doctoring, ceremonial dances, and pan-Indian religions. A final chapter discusses the displacement and alteration of aboriginal beliefs and rituals by Christianity. At the request of the Chalepah family, discussion of the Poor Owl Medicine Bundle has been omitted from Chapter 4.

Seven Elder Historians

The oral history of the Apaches goes back to Apache beginnings as a tribe. Through the millennia it has been the instrument by which knowledge of Apache culture and history has been transmitted to new generations, informing them about their world, its dangers, its benefits, and its wonders. After the tribe's final military defeat, its body of cultural knowledge began to decline from disuse, particularly in the spiritual realm, since Indian religion was prohibited. The words of the Apache grandmothers and grandfathers in this narrative attempt to recapture and preserve some of that lost knowledge. To understand how the seven primary self-appointed historians, whose knowledge is collected in these pages, could speak with authority on various aspects of their culture, a short background sketch of each follows. Others contributed also, but to a much lesser degree.

Connie Mae Saddleblanket, or Datose, was born in 1888. Her paternal grandmother was Kiowa, her maternal grandmother was Tewa, and her grandfathers were Apache. At age fourteen she married Homer Saddleblanket, who was half Apache and half Cheyenne and the adopted son of a well-

Datose, or Connie Mae Saddleblanket. Photo, Henry Klippell, 1961. Courtesy, Dorothy Klippell.

known Apache medicine man. She learned about vision quests and related matters from her Kiowa grandmother, who had been the recipient of a vision on Crazy Hill, and from her grandfather, a great storyteller, who shared his recollections about going on the warpath and fighting Indians and whites. Her father was an Apache doctor but did not go on a vision quest. She remembered well the War Dance and Scalp Dance from her childhood and was one of the elders who taught the young Apaches the old Blackfeet songs for the Manatidie revival. She attended the Methvin Institute for a year and a half. She was fluent in Apache and Kiowa, having been taught Kiowa by her grandmother. She belonged to the Apache Baptist Church and Native American Church. She died in 1968.

Louise Saddleblanket, or Susagossa, a full-blood Apache, was born in 1893. Her Apache name was Yellow Sunrise, a name her father gave her because it was the first thing one sees after a peyote meeting. Her brother was married to Connie Mae. She loved school. She attended Cache Creek Presbyterian Mission School, followed by the Methvin Institute, then enrolled in St. Patrick's Mission for three years, and finally returned to the Methvin Institute. At age eighteen she married Hiram Hummingbird, a Kiowa who attended the Methvin Institute; next she married Frank Charcoal, an Arapaho who attended Chilocco in Kansas; and her third husband, Emmet Tointigh, was a Kiowa, a Holiness preacher who quit and joined the Native American Church. In 1967 she was the only living Apache who had attended a Ghost Dance.

Ray Blackbear articulated the opinion of many Apaches when he said, "These things should be passed on. . . . To the grave is no place for it. Our young peoples should know of our language, beliefs, and history, of our generation. It should be put in writing." Born in 1903, Ray had an encyclopedic knowledge of Apache culture and stories that had been drilled into him by his Indian scout grandfather. Married to a Kiowa, Ray was fluent in that language, as well as in Apache and English. He attended Haskell and Cache Creek Presbyterian Mission School, both boarding schools, and then transferred to a public school in Boone, Oklahoma, where he stayed from 1912 to 1921. He was first a Presbyterian, next a Baptist, and finally a Methodist.

Joe Blackbear, born in 1878, was half Apache and half Kiowa. He was fluent in both languages but could speak only a little English, having attended school for just two years. He belonged to the Baptist Church and was a devoted member of the Native American Church. He knew endless stories passed down to him from his father who had been an Indian scout for General Scott of the U.S. Cavalry during 1874 and 1875. His father had two names—Lone Chief, because he scouted alone, and Blackbear because of his dark skin.

Susagossa, or Louise Saddleblanket, making fry bread, 1963. Photo, Julia A. Jordan, 1964.

Rose Chaletsin, born in 1893, retained, Bittle believed, almost better than anyone else a thorough knowledge of the old way of life. Rose had two Indian names. At age five she was given the name Raccoon because she ate a discarded "coon's" liver that made her ill. The name Mail Carrier was given to her by her great-great-grandfather who had captured a stagecoach containing a lot of newspapers and money. Rose attended a mission school for three years and was baptized a Baptist in 1908. She first married Alonzo Chalepah and later Ben Chaletsin, known as Apache Ben, both of whom were important tribal leaders. Alonzo attended Chilocco from 1897 to 1899 and was a member of the Methodist Church and Native American Church.

Ray Blackbear, 1961. Photo, Julia A. Jordan.

Apache Ben, who was half Lipan Apache and half Plains Apache, was a member of the Indian police and briefly held the title subchief. He was a member of the Cache Creek Presbyterian Church and the Native American Church.

Tennyson Berry, born in 1876, was one of the best educated persons in the tribe, having graduated from Chilocco and Carlisle (a four-year government school in Pennsylvania), which according to Ray Blackbear gave Tennyson the equivalent of a college education. He was a delegate to Washington in 1897 and to the Oklahoma Constitutional Convention in 1906.

Joe Blackbear, age 71. American Indian Exposition, Anadarko, Oklahoma. Photo by Pierre Tartoué, c. 1948. Courtesy, Archives and Manuscripts Division, Oklahoma Historical Society.

Rose Chaletsin, 1961. Photo, Julia A. Jordan.

*Tennyson Berry in 1913 by Bureau of American Ethnology photographer, BAE no.
2598-a. Courtesy, Western History Collections, University of Oklahoma Libraries.*

Fred Bigman with grandson Kenneth, 1963. Photo, Julia A. Jordan.

His fluency in English was especially helpful in recalling old stories and describing different aspects of Apache culture.

Fred Bigman, a full-blood Apache, was born in 1900 to very traditional parents. Fred was a fluent Apache speaker, one of relatively few left, and well-informed on the old ways of life. He attended government and public schools for, in his estimation, a total of about six years. He married Annie Somti, a Kiowa, who knew a lot about Apache medicines, knowledge she had acquired from Fred's mother. She attended Rainy Mountain Indian School from age four, and after an interruption because of sickness, she finished her education through the twelfth grade at Bacone School near Muskogee, Oklahoma. Fred worked in agricultural activities most of his life but never had a steady job. He was a peyote leader of some repute.

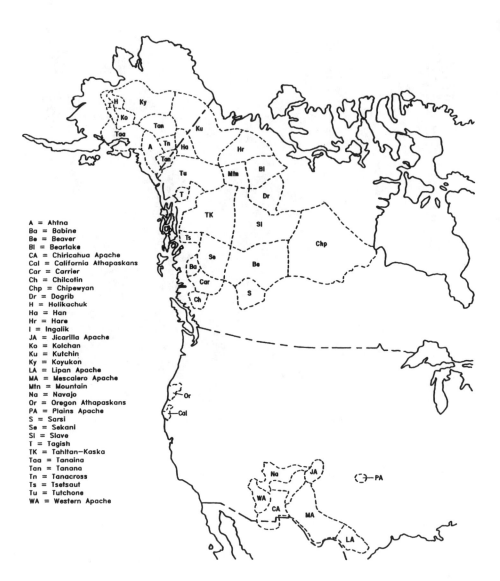

A = Ahtna
Ba = Babine
Be = Beaver
Bl = Bearlake
CA = Chiricahua Apache
Cal = California Athapaskans
Car = Carrier
Ch = Chilcotin
Chp = Chipewyan
Dr = Dogrib
H = Holikachuk
Ha = Han
Hr = Hare
I = Ingalik
JA = Jicarilla Apache
Ko = Kolchan
Ku = Kutchin
Ky = Koyukon
LA = Lipan Apache
MA = Mescalero Apache
Mtn = Mountain
Na = Navajo
Or = Oregon Athapaskans
PA = Plains Apache
S = Sarsi
Se = Sekani
Sl = Slave
T = Tagish
TK = Tahltan–Kaska
Taa = Tanaina
Tan = Tanana
Tn = Tanacross
Ts = Tsetsaut
Tu = Tutchone
WA = Western Apache

Distribution of Athapaskan-speaking peoples in North America. Adapted from Handbook of North American Indians, *ed. Sturtevant, vols. 6, 10.*

The Plains Apaches

Prehistory

The Plains Apaches are one of seven Apachean- or Southern Athapaskan–speaking tribes that migrated to the American Southwest and Southern Plains sometime between A.D. 1300 and 1500.[1] Linguistically related to the Northern Athapaskans of western Canada and Alaska and the Pacific Coast Athapaskans of California and Oregon, the proto-Apacheans probably separated from their base in the western subarctic forests of the Mackenzie Basin and moved onto the northwestern High Plains about 2,000 years ago. There they joined the Sarsi, the southernmost Athapaskan tribe at the time. Approximately 1,000 years later they left this location and the Sarsi in southern Alberta, Canada, and began their southward movement.[2] Ultimately, they would fan out across western Oklahoma and Texas, southeastern Colorado, much of New Mexico, central and southeastern Arizona, and adjoining areas of Mexico and differentiate into seven recognized Apachean languages and tribes: Kiowa Apache, Lipan, Jicarilla, Mescalero, Chiricahua, Western Apache, and Navajo. Although the routes they took, the length of time involved, and the processes of tribal separations are unknown, an ongoing dispute with widely differing hypotheses by Apachean scholars continues unabated and underscores the tentativeness of what actually is known about Apache prehistory.

Of the different issues, the approximate migration route is probably the most controversial. Some scholars believe archaeological data, linguistic analysis, and references in Spanish documents, although sparse, support an Apachean migration route via the High Plains just east of the Rocky Mountains. Others prefer a Rocky Mountain route through Utah or Colorado because of its ecological similarity to the Athapaskan homeland. Still others argue for an intermontane migration through the Great Basin based on the presence of numerous Great Basin traits in some Apachean groups.[3]

The mystery of Apachean prehistory is largely attributable to the political organization and culture of the proto-Apacheans. In the north they lived as hunters and gatherers, were organized in unstructured bands, lived in conical dwellings, wore skin clothing, made basketry but no pottery, used dogs and snowshoes for transportation, and practiced shamanism. Assuming that most of this culture remained intact upon arrival on the Southern Plains and in the Southwest, virtually none of it was of a nature that could be left behind for archaeologists to find, complicating a reconstruction of their past.[4]

With only ambiguous Spanish documentation of the tribe's identity and no definitive archaeological finds, much weight has been given to the science of linguistics to illuminate the tribe's prehistory. Given the fluidity of Apachean bands and tribes in the prereservation era and their later intermixing on reservations, however, it is not surprising that the linguistic analyses show inconsistencies and point to different conclusions.

Lexicostatistical data collected by Bittle support the position that Apacheans remained one group, or a closely approximated group, until approximately A.D. 1300, when their language differentiation began, and that in approximately 1500 the Kiowa Apaches separated from the eastern Apacheans, the Lipan and Jicarilla.[5] By breaking off from other Apacheans relatively late, the Kiowa Apaches were therefore able to retain a strong Apachean cultural base to which they added Plains traits.

Hoijer, whose earlier research agreed with Bittle, later reversed his position and argued that later lexicostatistical data showed sufficient divergence between Kiowa Apache and the other six Apachean languages to infer for the Kiowa Apaches: (1) a much earlier separation from other Apacheans in the north, (2) an independent migration onto the Plains, and (3) no ties to the southwestern Apaches. Although Hoijer believed his data might have been skewed in part by the twentieth-century grouping of New Mexico tribes on reservations apart from the Kiowa Apaches residing in Oklahoma, he believed nevertheless that the lexicostatistical differences were too significant to ignore. The attendant implications for the Kiowa Apaches, believed Hoijer, were an extended occupancy of the Plains and a Plains cultural base with only the Apachean language and a few Apache remnants still discernible.[6]

Hoijer's argument is supported by Davis's more recent research of historical records and comparison of Kiowa Apache cultural traits with those of the Kiowas and southwest Apacheans.[7]

Early History: 1541–1834

Although Plains Apache history prior to 1541 is almost completely unknown, the next three centuries—beginning with descriptions by Spanish chroniclers on Coronado's expedition and continuing into accounts by various other European explorers, civil authorities, and military officials—abound with descriptions that may refer to the Plains Apaches. But it is also possible that none of them do because unerring identification of the group is lacking. The major source of confusion has been the great profusion of specific names—Bad Hearts, Cataha, Cataka, Cattako, Cuttako, Gataea, Gattacka, Gutak, Katala, Kattekas, Padoucas, Quataquois, Quataquon, and Querechos—that were assigned, although somewhat ambiguously, to the group by LaSalle, Lewis and Clark, Harris, LaFlesche, LaHarpe, Beaurain, and others.[8] The frequently used general terms—Apache, Plains Apache, and Prairie Apache—are no clearer and could have applied to any Apachean-speaking peoples who ranged over the Plains and traded in the Pueblo area during this period. At times the group, numerically small compared to its larger, more powerful allies, was included in such labels as *affiliated groups*, *other tribes*, *wild tribes*, and even *etc.*

The earliest possible reference was recorded in 1541 by the Spanish of Coronado's expedition who encountered pedestrian bison hunters west of Pecos named Querechos, believed by most scholars to be Apaches but not Plains Apaches specifically. In a letter written in 1681 or 1682, LaSalle noted that the Gattacka were camped with the Manrhoet (Kiowas) south of the Platte River where they were trading horses with the Pawnees. In 1705 the same group was reportedly camped on the west side of the Missouri River above the Quapaws. LaHarpe in 1719 located the Quataquois and the Tawakonis on the south side of the Cimarron River near its junction with the Arkansas, and nearly 100 years later Lewis and Clark placed them between the heads of the two forks of the Cheyenne River near the Black Hills of Wyoming.[9]

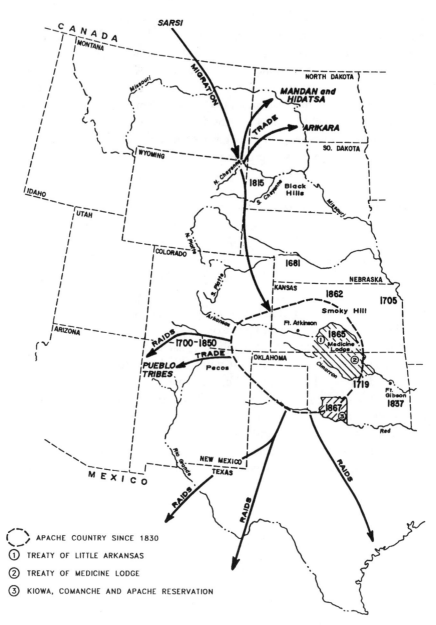

CANADA
SARSI
MONTANA
MIGRATION
NORTH DAKOTA
MANDAN and HIDATSA
TRADE
ARIKARA
Missouri
WYOMING
SO. DAKOTA
IDAHO
N. Cheyenne
1815
S. Cheyenne
Black Hills
Missouri
UTAH
N. Platte
COLORADO
1681
S. Platte
NEBRASKA
KANSAS
1862
Smoky Hill
1705
Arkansas
Ft. Atkinson
1865
Medicine Lodge
ARIZONA
RAIDS
1700-1850
TRADE
PUEBLO TRIBES
Pecos
OKLAHOMA
Cimarron
1719
Ft. Gibson
1837
1867
MEXICO
Rio Grande
NEW MEXICO
TEXAS
RAIDS
RAIDS
Red
RAIDS
RAIDS

APACHE COUNTRY SINCE 1830
① TREATY OF LITTLE ARKANSAS
② TREATY OF MEDICINE LODGE
③ KIOWA, COMANCHE AND APACHE RESERVATION

Apache migration and assigned lands.

Throughout much of this period a number of Apaches, Kiowas, and Comanches sporadically positioned themselves east of the Pueblos on the Rio Grande to hunt and gather on the Plains or trade in the Pueblo area as times and opportunities changed. A spectacular opportunity was offered by the seventeenth-century arrival of the Spanish and their livestock. The Indians cared for Spanish horses and quickly began to acquire riding skills. And soon, through a system of trading, raiding, and capturing in the wild, they were able to accumulate Spanish horses in sufficient numbers to revolutionize their pedestrian way of life on the Plains. Before the horse, they had hunted on foot, but with the horse they had much greater mobility, which allowed them to kill more buffalo, deer, and antelope. This in turn gave them more hides and skins, meat, and tallow with which to trade for blankets, pottery, maize, breadstuff, knives, axes, and, later, firearms and gunpowder.[10] By the early 1800s they had reached the height of their cultural fluorescence. The buffalo were still plentiful, essential trade goods were easy to obtain, and white threats to Indian lands had not yet become a pressing concern.

Years of Strife: 1835–1867

Events took a drastic turn in the 1830s as white encroachment on Apache lands began. From this time forward the free-roaming nonentity status of the tribe, which had prevailed for centuries, began to erode. Documentation of the tribe's whereabouts and activities began to appear in the *Annual Reports* of the Commission of Indian Affairs, and responding tactical moves by the U.S. military forces and U.S. Congress sought to displace and contain the tribe. This turbulent period, which led ultimately to the termination of Apache sovereignty and livelihood, was marked by (1) a precipitous reduction of hunting territory and autonomy extracted by U.S. treaties and military power, (2) devastating epidemics and deteriorating economic conditions, and (3) alternating periods of peace and war with other tribes.

Small in size, never numbering more than 400 or 500, the Apaches almost always camped near or allied themselves with a numerically larger tribe for defensive reasons. Although they most often associated with the Kiowas on the Plains, they showed great independence in their movements and loyalties and sometimes allied with the Cheyennes, Arapahos, or Comanches while breaking with the Kiowas. But even in periods of shifting loyalties their relationship with the Kiowas never deteriorated to a hostile one.

The U.S. government, in its thrust to reduce Indian lands and sovereignty, often provoked intertribal hostilities. In the treaty signed with the

Kiowas, Apaches, and Tawakoni at Ft. Gibson in 1837, the government promised the tribes presents in exchange for the right of American citizens to cross tribal lands and gave tribes living south of the Missouri River and west of the states of Missouri and Arkansas unlimited access to the three tribes' hunting grounds.[11] Ominously, this last directive induced exploitation by other tribes of a hunting area populated with what would soon be a dwindling supply of buffalo. Signing for the Apaches were Iron Shoe, One Who Is Surrendered, and Walking Bear.[12]

After the treaty was signed, the Cheyennes and Arapahoes quickly overran and exploited the Kiowa, Apache, and Comanche hunting area, reigniting serious altercations between the two groups. A peace was negotiated in 1840 by the Kiowas, Cheyennes, Comanches, and Apaches, with Leading Bear (presumably the Walking Bear of the 1837 treaty) speaking for the Apaches. The Arapahoes joined the peace accord the following year. For the remainder of the century, alliances among the Southern Plains groups would shift, but all would remain at peace with each other.[13]

Throughout this period the economic condition of the Apaches became increasingly precarious as the supply of game diminished, European diseases took a heavy toll, and periodic drought ravaged grasslands for the horses. As early as 1847, U.S. Superintendent of Indian Affairs David D. Mitchell, in a letter to Commissioner Orlando Brown, sounded an alarm about the decreased game available to the Southern Plains tribes:

> The ultimate destiny of these prairie tribes looks gloomy in the extreme. It is admitted by every one who has any knowledge of the buffalo regions that these useful animals are rapidly decreasing. From time immemorial, the buffalo has furnished the Indians with food, clothing, and shelter from the inclemency of the weather. Should they continue to decrease, the time is not far distant when the Indians will be compelled to change their mode of living, or perish for want of subsistence.[14]

Compounding the tribe's marginal existence were two particularly brutal epidemics that swept across the Southern Plains. Smallpox in 1839 took a heavy toll, and in the summer of 1849 cholera decimated entire families, killing as many as half of the Southern Plains Indians. The sudden onset of cholera and the speed with which it killed so panicked the Apaches and Kiowas that some took their own lives.

Economic conditions continued to deteriorate, and again in 1852 Superintendent Mitchell reported: "Notwithstanding the vast number of emigrants passing and repassing through their country, but little change has been effected in their condition; but the change thus far has been, as it ever has been, against the 'poor Indian.' Vast quantities of their game . . . have been destroyed. Their limited forests have been laid waste, and loathsome diseases . . . scattered among them."[15]

Particularly troublesome to Apaches during this period were the eastern tribes located on the fringes of the Plains who continually raided and trespassed on the Apache hunting range. Of these various enemies, the Apaches regarded the Pawnees as the worst and conducted periodic hostilities against them.[16]

Sometimes the results were disastrous, the most notable an attack on the Pawnees in the spring of 1853 by Apache, Kiowa, Cheyenne, Arapaho, Brulé Sioux, and Crow warriors. For many hours the battle raged on indecisively as the Pawnees continued to hold their ground. Finally, the impasse was broken when mounted Potawatomis, armed with new rifles, joined the Pawnees and in a quick, decisive action overpowered the attackers. Humiliated in defeat, the Plains warriors were forced into a hasty retreat.[17]

In the summer of 1854 a massive war party of Cheyenne, Arapaho, Apache, Comanche, Kiowa, Sioux, Osage, and Crow warriors resolved to revenge the 1853 defeat by the Pawnees and halt the eastern tribes' incursion into their lands. They assembled on the Pawnee Fork at the crossing of the Santa Fe road and headed north, but before they could reach the Pawnees they were routed by a well-armed but numerically inferior hunting party of Sauk, Fox, and Potawatomis.[18]

The U.S. government continued to draw up treaties with the Indians, reducing their territory and autonomy, but sometimes so few members of the tribes were represented at the signings that the treaties were ignored, and those who did attend often misunderstood the terms to which they had agreed. One such treaty was drawn up in the summer of 1853 with the Apaches, Kiowas, and Comanches at Fort Atkinson in Kansas. Unfortunately, the treaty had only one provision most Indians comprehended and on which some agreed—that which permitted the government to establish roads and routes across their lands. Other provisions were vehemently opposed or totally misunderstood by the Indians; they included: (1) the construction of military establishments, depots, and other posts on their lands; (2) the cessation of Indian "warlike incursions into the Mexican provinces, and all depredations upon the inhabitants thereof"; and (3) the return of all Mexican captives taken after the date of the treaty.[19] The Indians, only recently encouraged by the U.S. government to engage in hostilities against Mexicans in the Southwest and Mexico during the Mexican War, did not understand the change in policy and were reluctant to abandon profitable activities. They had no intention of returning captives, whom they needed to increase their own strength and numbers. But after the government agreed to issue annual rations to the three tribes, the treaty was signed, first by representatives of the Comanches and the Kiowas and then by four Apaches—Poor Wolf, Poor Bear, Prairie Wolf, and The Cigar—each adding his mark. Although some parts of the treaty were adhered to by some Indians, very little changed.

As Apache destitution grew more acute, raiding became an increasingly important means of maintaining livelihood. Apaches accelerated their raids on other tribes' horse herds and attacked white and Mexican settlements south into Texas and wagons on the Santa Fe Trail, targeting anything that could save them from starvation. In 1860 William Bent, the U.S. agent for Indians on the Arkansas, warned that "a desperate war of starvation and extinction is . . . imminent and inevitable, unless prompt measures shall prevent it."[20]

Two smallpox epidemics struck in 1862. The second one, in May and June, killed approximately seventy Apaches—one-sixth of the tribe, not counting the many smallpox deaths earlier that year.

Then came the first of three treaties that, in quick succession, would end Apache independence forever. The 1862 treaty between the government and the Cheyennes and Arapahos took away the two tribes' title to all lands except those between the South Platte and Arkansas Rivers. By extension, the treaty also applied to the Apaches who had been adopted by the Arapahos. The treaty was short-lived, however, because Kansans wanted those lands and pressured the government to remove all Indians to the south.[21]

On October 14, 1865, Major General Sanborn, heading a government peace commission, signed the second treaty, the Treaty of Little Arkansas, with approximately one-third of the Cheyennes and Arapahos, assigning the two tribes to a reservation on lands between the Cimarron and Arkansas Rivers and sharply curtailing their hunting rights in the Smoky Hill country between the Arkansas and Platte Rivers.[22] On the seventeenth, the Apaches signed an amendment to the treaty that brought them under the same terms to which the government had agreed with the other two tribes and officially established a confederate relationship between the Apaches and the Cheyennes and Arapahos.[23]

From this gathering we have one of the few recorded speeches by an Apache in the prereservation period, that of Poor Bear, who articulated poignantly his people's sense of despair, humility, and desire above all else to be cooperative:

> My people are so small that my talk does not amount to much. Those about me are all relatives of mine. I always want to follow the White road and do what is right. I am pleased that you are all here, that you

have come here from Washington to make peace. Neither I nor my people wish to do wrong, we always looking for what is right, and do not wish to be responsible for what is done to others. . . . My people are part of them north and part south, and I go from one to the other. I don't want to do anything that is wrong, and therefore do not want to speak much. I am done.[24]

Congress failed to ratify the Treaty of Little Arkansas, and settlers began moving onto reservation lands. Some Indians attempted to abide by the treaty, but the Cheyennes, not represented at the signing, refused to give up any rights to the Smoky Hill country and continued, with others, their plunder and harassments. An outcry across the nation called for an end to the "Indian menace on the Plains" by whatever means.[25] Raids and skirmishes, which early had been limited in scope, progressed to battles and massacres. By the spring of 1867 a full-fledged U.S.-Indian war was in progress, and negotiations had already begun for a new treaty.

The Treaty of Medicine Lodge was drawn up and signed by representatives of all Southern Plains tribes in October 1867 on Medicine Lodge Creek in Kansas. Comanches, Apaches, Kiowas, Cheyennes, and Arapahos ceded all former lands and accepted government annuities and lands in southwest Indian Territory, later named Oklahoma. Apaches were reunited with the Kiowas and Comanches and assigned a reservation "bounded on the east by the ninety-eighth meridian, on the south and west by the Red River and its north fork, and on the north by the Washita from the ninety-eighth meridian up to a point thirty miles by river from Fort Cobb, and thence by a line due west to the north fork."[26]

A Vanquished People

The Medicine Lodge Treaty did not quickly quell the conflicts, but it markedly decreased their frequency and scope. Some Indians continued sporadic fighting, but the Apaches, reputed to be more cooperative and obedient than other Indians, generally accepted the terms of the treaty and headed south to confinement on their reservation and an alien way of life.[27] Some, however, joined Comanches and Kiowas on raiding parties and forays into Texas and Mexico until all fighting ceased.[28]

The government was committed to changing all Indian economic, religious, and educational institutions and formulated policies to persuade or coerce the Indians to change to the white way. All Indians would become sedentary agriculturalists, Christianity would replace pagan beliefs and rituals, and formalized education would teach Indian children to communicate in the English language and acquire skills necessary to live in a white civilized

Kiowas, Apaches, and Comanches at Agency headquarters, November 1907. (1) Quanah Parker, Comanche chief; (2) Apiatan, Kiowa chief; (3) Lone Wolf, Kiowa headman; (4) Apache John, Plains Apache chief; (5) Ca-va-yo, Comanche headman; (6) Pah-ko-to-quodle, Kiowa headman; (7) George Hunt, Kiowa interpreter; (8) Mo-ziz-zoom-dy, Apache headman; (9) Sonte, Apache headman; (10) Arrushe, Comanche headman; (11) Eschiti, Comanche subchief; (12) San-ka-do-ta, Kiowa headman; (13) Otto Wells, Comanche interpreter; (14) Delos Lonewolf, Kiowa; (15) Tennyson Berry, Apache interpreter; (16) Pe-ah-coose, Comanche; (17) Eustace Merrick, Comanche; (18) Klinekole, Apache; (19) Max Frizzlehead, Kiowa; (20) Ko-mah-ty, Kiowa; (21) Henry Tse-lee, Apache; (22) Lt. Stecker; (23) John Hendricks, U.S. Indian Bureau attorney. Phillips Collection. Courtesy, Western History Collections, University of Oklahoma Libraries.

world. All such policies lacked not only benevolence but economic and cultural insight as well.

First and foremost, farming for the Apaches was not only undesirable but impossible. Apaches were not adequately informed or technically prepared to manage farms. Not only did they lack the regimentation necessary for farming, but most had no desire to be farmers. Given the vagaries of dryland farming on Apache reservation lands, subsistence could only be marginal at best. The only cultivation that was sporadically successful was the occasional vegetable garden, which even in consecutive years of good rain could not produce enough to furnish the tribe's nutritional needs.

Stock-raising programs were similarly ineffectual because of inadequate financing and insufficient grazing lands. When starvation threatened because of the poor quality of the government cattle issue, Apaches resorted to butchering the tribal cattle herds or stealing ponies and cattle from neighboring tribes to use for food.[29]

Disease and serious illness mainly attributable to malnutrition, overexposure to the elements, and poor hygiene accounted for a high fatality rate throughout the reservation period. Critical medicines were in short supply, which meant anyone who became seriously ill was lucky to recover. Malaria, typhoid, respiratory infections, and intestinal disorders were chronic problems, and as contact with the white population increased, the incidence of tuberculosis, syphilis, and infectious diseases rose precipitously.[30]

After an agricultural economy failed to materialize on the communal reservations, the government resolved to transform Indians into individual farmers. Apache land was allotted in severalty in 1900 and again in 1906 and 1908, and surplus reservation lands were opened to white settlement. Two hundred and six Apaches were given individually held trust lands that were uniformly 160 acres apiece, with the exception of the eight persons who received allotments under the terms of the 1908 act.[31] As hunters who had always lived and hunted cooperatively, living and farming individually were impossible. Some continued planting crops, but most finally gave up. The government's decision to make the Apaches individual farmers came at a time when subsistence farming by white individuals was giving way to large-scale, single-crop enterprises. Lack of tools, poor soils, and unpredictable climatic conditions also hindered intensive cultivation of the soil. Crop yields were so low that even efficient white farmers could not subsist on one-quarter sections of land.

To prevent starvation, Apaches were permitted to lease their uncultivated lands to white farmers and stockmen. The government passed legislation permitting alienation of inherited land in 1902 and the sale of allotments by allegedly competent Indians in 1907.[32] The system of leasing, which averted an immediate crisis, caused an extreme fractionalization of land that pauperized succeeding generations. As income from leases began to be divided among increasing numbers of heirs, it became insignificant.

The quality of Apache life steadily deteriorated in the first three decades of the twentieth century as all avenues to economic independence were gone and all signs of Apache culture were officially suppressed. The Indians were wards of a government that attempted to solve Indian problems with policies of assimilation. Welfare programs kept Apaches above the starvation level but failed miserably in solving the long-term problems of high unemployment, job discrimination by the non-Indian community, an abnormally high school dropout rate, and a high level of poverty with its attendant poor nutrition, meager living conditions, social problems, and compromised health care. Although economic conditions improved during World Wars I and II, when the U.S. economy experienced full employment, for the rest of the twentieth century and into the next millennium the cycle of poverty remained unbroken.

The most onerous and demoralizing effect was the prohibition on all forms of Apache religious ceremonies from 1887 to 1934, in particular the Kiowa Sun Dance, Medicine Bundle ceremonies, the Dancing Societies, the Ghost Dance, and the peyote ceremony—all of which amounted to a religious holocaust. The Sun Dance ceased, the Medicine Bundle rituals gradually died out, and the Ghost Dance continued in secret but only sporadically until approximately 1915. The Dancing Societies continued for a while but weakened as the Christian churches denounced the paganism of the dances. Not banned was the War Dance, which outsiders judged to be secular and entertaining. The Apaches performed it for hire as early as the 1890s and still perform it today.[33] The peyotists fought the government legally and in 1918 won an Oklahoma charter for the Native American Church, which permitted the use of peyote within a religious context.

On the positive side, however, planned and chance events offered members of the tribe opportunities for independence and self-expression. The three most important were beneficial legislation, military service, and revivalistic movements.

First, favorable legislation signaling a real turning point in the government's attitude toward Indians began in 1924 with the passage of the Indian Citizenship Act, offering Indians U.S. citizenship. The very important Indian Reorganization Act of 1934 followed, giving tribes the right to organize and to draft their own self-governing constitutions. This goal was not realized for many years because a large amount of lead time was required to inform tribes about the legislation, and many tribes were unable to understand the legislative process and draft a constitution before World War II broke out in 1941. By then the government's attention was centered on the war effort. The Johnson-O'Malley Act, also of 1934, authorizing states to administer educational, medical, and welfare programs on reservations, and the Indian Self-Determination and Education Assistance Act of 1975, encouraging Indian oversight of such programs, were significant as a stated ideal, but even this legislation, for example, has not yet helped the high school dropout and absenteeism rates.

The Indian Claims Commission Act of 1946, giving tribes time to file cases against the government, benefited the Apaches, who received a settlement in 1976, but that benefit was minimal. Each Apache received $1,700, which many of them spent in a day.[34]

The American Indian Freedom of Religion Act of 1978, giving all American Indians the inherent right to the free exercise of their traditional religions,[35] was a right the Apaches had been granted in a state charter in 1918 and a national charter in 1955 in which they were permitted to use peyote in a religious context. The national legislation confirmed a freedom they already had but that many local authorities had been selectively denying.

Finally, in 1996 Congress enacted the Native American Housing and Self-Determination Act, which allows tribes to make their own decisions concerning housing. Two years later the tribe applied to the U.S. Department of Agriculture–Rural Development for and received a loan of $974,728 toward a $1,047,575 housing project for very-low- and low-income elderly tribal members. The complex has twenty-four units of rental assistance and a community center.

Second, the opportunity for military service during America's twentieth-century wars boosted morale. During the two world wars every able-bodied Apache donned a military uniform to proudly represent the United States. The resulting revival and official recognition of martial skills had an uplifting effect on the entire tribe. During World War I, the women performed Apache Scalp Dances using captured German helmets as they turned out in full force to honor their returning warriors; and after World War II, with the women's Scalp Dance incorporated into the War Dance, both men and women honored returning warriors in full regalia. A swell of patriotism rippled through the Apache community again during the Korean and Vietnam conflicts with a high percentage of Apache participation and the requisite farewell celebrations and homecoming dances that were celebrated both individually and collectively. According to Meadows, as a result the frequency of and attendance at powwows increased and soon "produced declines in the attendance at Native American Church and Christian church activities."[36]

Twentieth-century wars had also provided much-needed employment for Apaches, but when the wars were over, little employment was available—especially in rural areas—and many veterans sought employment through relocation, a federal plan designed to move Indians to urban areas and provide job training and employment. But the program was only minimally successful because few Indians wanted to leave their rural families permanently, and the cultural adjustment to the city was simply too great. Bittle observed that only "acceptable" Apaches applied—that is, those who did not belong to the more conservative families—and Indians who did relocate generally returned home within a year.[37]

Military service was the impetus for the third positive wave of activity, the revival of one of the defunct warrior societies. Apaches had fought and survived as warriors, and the exposure and defeat of enemies in America's wars awakened their strong dormant warrior tradition. The returning veterans had not been Plains warriors, but their grandfathers had. Defeating enemies, whether on the Plains or abroad, helped maintain a kind of social order and served a higher tribal good. Reviving a traditional ceremony with its warrior and sacred symbols was one way to say "I am proud to be Apache." Alonzo Chalepah, the grandson of Alonzo Chalepah and Rose Chaletsin (formerly Chalepah), maintains that the purpose of the revived Manatidie, discussed in Chapter 9, has been to celebrate Apache heritage.[38]

The tribal ceremonial dance, alternately called the Manatidie and the Blackfeet Dance, has become a source of great tribal pride, and it is the primary institution that unifies the tribe. After its revival the Blackfeet Society functioned as one group, but in 1963 it split into two separate groups— the Redbone Apache Blackfeet Society and the Chalepah Apache Blackfeet Society, each of which has separate benefits and performances. The Redbone Blackfeet Society is made up of Apaches living in the Washita area, and the Chalepah Blackfeet Society consists of Apaches from Boone and Cache Creek. The Manatidie's perceived importance was summed up by an elder: "If we didn't have the Blackfeet Society, I'm not sure there would be an Apache tribe today. It's really what's holding us together."[39]

The tribe's survival appears assured since the population decline in the early part of the twentieth century reversed itself significantly by 1950, and during the rest of the century the population increased. Although the tribe has always been considered small, its numbers have fluctuated widely because of epidemics, intermarriage, and inaccurate counts when Apaches went on extended visits to other tribes during a count. Indian Agency records, usually considered accurate, indicate that the population of 332 in 1880 dropped to 241 in 1892 and to 173 in 1909 but rose to 400 by 1949.[40] Bittle estimated in 1970 that based on the previous one-quarter blood quantum criterion there were about 300 Apaches and an additional 25 full bloods.[41] The population began to increase considerably in the 1980s, especially after 1987 when the qualifying blood quantum for tribal membership was lowered to one-eighth, so that by 2001, according to the Oklahoma Indian Affairs Commission, there were 2,000 on the tribal rolls.[42] Today, any descendant of an original allottee qualifies for membership.

Ironically, as tribal membership has increased, the number of fluent Apachean speakers has fallen incrementally because of death, so that as of March 2001 only two fluent Apachean speakers were still living. The elder is

Alfred Chalepah, born in 1911, father of Alonzo Chalepah, who diligently records Apache words the elders remember and encourages other Apaches to learn the language. Carrie Redbone, the other fluent speaker, is in her late seventies, and she lives in Hobart, Oklahoma. To date, a 1,500-word Apache dictionary has been compiled, but its use is limited because it does not reflect the complexity of Apache verbs.[43] Reviving the culture by bringing the language to life is an important but difficult goal to achieve because so much has been lost. Locally, Alonzo Chalepah is confident it can be revived and is encouraged by the ten or twelve persons who attend weekly language classes. Michael Krauss of the Alaska Native Language Center states that the language can and must be recovered.[44] But motivating families to speak Apache at home is difficult.

The self-reliance required to escape the cycle of poverty is slowly developing in spite of an untrusting white population and continuing shortsighted government policies. Alonzo Chalepah states that it is discouraging that the multiple health and social problems do not improve but continue to worsen: "Five of every ten Apaches have diabetes, six of every ten have heart problems, and six of every ten [have] alcohol problems. Nutrition is part of the problem. Economically, we can't afford healthy food."[45]

The Plains Apache Culture

Plains Apaches possessed not only the material culture of all nomadic Plains tribes but their economic, social, and political structures as well. They were economically dependent on the buffalo, used the dog and the horse travois, lived in tepees, used hide receptacles, worshiped tribal medicine bundles, stood their ground in warfare when the situation was hopeless, counted coup (considered it more honorific to touch rather than kill an enemy), owned heraldic tipis that were passed to succeeding generations, and used a generational kinship classification. Their shield groups and Dancing Societies were fewer and less important than those in other Plains tribes, and the Plains scaffold burial was not customary. They attended Sun Dances and Ghost Dances of other tribes, most commonly those of the Kiowas, but never held or sponsored one themselves.

Two areas in which the Plains Apaches shared characteristics with other Apacheans, in addition to the obvious one of language, were the origin stories in the folklore and eschatology. In the origin stories, all Apache tribes had similar stories about the escapades of the twin culture heroes, Fire Boy and Water Boy. Although the specifics varied from one tribe to another, the twins destroyed monsters, determined proper roles for the different species, and brought order to their universe. Also common to all Apacheans was the story of the hand game at the beginning of time between good and evil animals to determine whether the universe would have eternal darkness. In the Plains Apache version, the prize in the hand game, survival and governance of the universe, went to the humans and the animals who defeated the monsters. The Kiowas, with whom the Plains Apaches most closely associated, did not have the twin culture heroes or stories about the hand game. But the beloved Coyote stories all Apaches shared were remarkably similar to stories about the Kiowa trickster Sendeh, which indicates substantial borrowing between the Kiowas and Plains Apaches. The entertainment and pedagogical nature of the trickster stories enabled them to be more readily shared than stories relating to the origin of culture.[46]

In the area of eschatology, all Apacheans shared characteristics clearly entrenched in Plains Apache culture: an excessive fear of contamination by the dead, a fear of ghosts of dead relatives who might appear as an owl or a whirlwind, a hasty burial, destruction of the deceased person's belongings, self-mutilation by the deceased's close relatives, fumigation of relatives involved in funeral rites, and suppression of the deceased person's name.

Religion in all Apache tribes was a combination of individually inspired shamanism and the learned tribal ritual of priestcraft. Most Apache rituals were inspired in individual vision experiences, but some were taught to others if the power source gave its consent. The sacred Medicine Bundle ceremonies were nonshamanistic, the ritual being passed on to succeeding generations. Both the passive dream experience of Apacheans and the contrasting active vision quest on the Plains were experienced, leaving open the debate over which was more common.

The Apaches are one of eleven nomadic Plains tribes from fundamentally distinct economic backgrounds and culture areas who quickly adopted a fairly uniform pattern of social and political organization and adjusted to the habits of the buffalo and the use of the horse. These changes, which were more dramatic and rapid for some tribes than for others, collectively defy a predictable time depth of Plains culture for the Apaches.

The Apache Universe

Spirit Beings

A mystical kinship with the land and the natural environment was the very essence of Apache sacred life. All of nature, Apaches believed, abounded with spirit beings that were intimately linked to the preservation of their existence. Spirit beings were perceived as sources of supernatural power, and when the need arose, supplicants could invoke the spirits to assist in the hunt, bring good health, change the weather, or, more important, influence matters of life and death. Spirits took on various forms and most often appeared within or about a sacred place in nature—a rock, a tree, a lake; in the atmosphere—the wind, the thunder; throughout the bird and animal kingdoms; and in the four tribal medicine bundles, which were primarily collections of sacred items found in nature. Persons sought supernatural power by praying to the spirit embodied in the particular object or element; for example, the spirit of the tree, the spirit of the whirlwind, the power of the medicine bundle. Actually, according to Fred Bigman, "they used to pray to anything—the moon, the sun, Mother Earth, or to a tree. They pray to the things that they can see. They pray to the water, to a good stream of water."[1]

According to Joe Blackbear, prayers to mythical heroes were common-place after a dream: "In the old days, when you dreamed of something good, you prayed it would come true. You might pray to Running-Under-the-Water or to Fire Boy or Water Boy. Good dreams would be things like getting a horse or somebody giving you something. If you dreamed about sickness or death, it was bad and you prayed it wouldn't come true."[2]

Ever cognizant of nature's powers, all Apaches, maintained Rose Chaletsin, understood the importance of courting and not offending the nature spirits: "In the old days they prayed to the moon, stars, and clouds. They go talk to them and make signs. If a moon has a ring around it, that's a bad sign . . . somebody is going to get sick. So they talk nice to the moon."[3]

Rose Chaletsin, for one, disavowed the existence of an important being and maintained that Apaches "didn't know God or Jesus, just lately. In the old days, they prayed to anything. . . . They don't know what they pray to."[4]

Susagossa affirmed the nonexistence of a God concept in her family: "I hear them prayers my mother pray. I never heard her say God, Jesus. She pray, and sometimes she shed tears. All she said was, 'Pity us, carry us on, supply our needs.' And she pray for her children, pray for her kinfolks. 'Help us to live long time so we can be worth more as parents and have good luck.'"[5]

Susagossa attributed her initial concept of a Creator God to the teach-ings of Christianity: "The church is where I learn God and Jesus. Pray out loud. That's where I learn how to pray. . . . For a while I didn't know what God was. I learn from the preacher what God is. I was so surprised to hear these things. How many things he done. He make this world. So that's where I learned about God."[6]

Others believed, as Datose did, that the old people had always prayed to the "Man-Up-There." "[My grandfather] used that peace pipe to pray with. He hold it up, let it touch the ground, and pray. Before he learn about Jesus, he talk to the 'Man-Up-There,' say 'Pity me. Take my prayer so I can learn about you.' . . . [The old people] pray like him. They say, 'Man-Up-There.'"[7]

This spirit, which some called Great Spirit, was ascribed various powers and roles or sometimes none at all. Ray Blackbear believed the Great Spirit was the Creator of all things: "In the old days and the old time, you didn't pray to Jesus but to the Great Spirit, Creator of all things. But since 1900 Jesus is in the prayer, the Son of God. After 1900 they mention Jesus in respect to the white man's ways. . . . You pray for everything to God, the Holy Spirit, and you put in 'for Jesus's sake.' Now you pray to two things, but in the old days it was one."[8]

28

The Apaches' increasing use of God as a substitute for Great Spirit or Man-Up-There, and their lack of differentiation between a missionary-taught God and an aboriginal one, were coincident with the growing pervasiveness of Christianity. To what degree their concepts of a Supreme Being were rooted in or altered by Christianity can never be known, especially considering the long time frame for recollection. Many Apaches saw parallels in the Christian and Indian deities and expressed uncertainty as to whether they were one and the same. Stewart Klinekole, among others, assumed they were:

> I ask them [the old people] how they learn to pray like now. They say, "We learn that from white people." When Indian pray, he get on his horse and stand straight west. He spreads his arms out and lifts his face. Calls to God, "Pity me."
>
> I hear one old man ask blessing for food. . . . He raised his right hand up, then touch the ground. Then he rubbed his hands together and patted himself here [chest and abdomen]. It's for Father [Sky], Mother [Earth], and me. Then he started praying for food. Just like Catholic priest; that's the way he ask blessing. This man say, "Everyday I want to live like this. My children, grandchildren, give me good life."[9]

Ambiguity surrounding the deity concept was also discernible in Ray Blackbear's comment: "Some of the Bible like our way, like the Great Spirit, not supposed to see him. You see him in the sun, the eyes of God. Some call us sun worshipers, but we worship through the sun."[10]

Although aboriginal concepts of a Supreme Being ranged widely from a vague unnamed spirit with no specific role to a Creator Deity referred to as *Dàxí àšé*, "Our Father"; *Nuahkolahe*, "Earth-He-Made-It"; Great Spirit; or "Blue-White Man";[11] important differences existed between Apache and non-Indian concepts of a Supreme Being. Foremost, the Apache concept did not embrace the high degree of omnipotence and omniscience non-Indians attributed to their Christian God. The Indian Great Spirit was simply one of many Apache spirits and, although perhaps given more importance by some, could not be interpreted as being absolute. Apaches who believed in a Great Spirit maintained contact with it primarily ad hoc in solitary prayer and did not concentrate spiritual communication in a weekly group worship.

The Christian God was defined by centuries of a long-standing literary tradition that engendered a unified creed for Christian denominations to adopt, whereas the Apache concept of a Supreme Being, regardless of whether its origin could be traced to Christianity, was defined only by an oral tradition that, because it was not written down, allowed for great flexibility in beliefs. Apache spirituality was highly individualized. It was constantly being shaped, reshaped, and reinforced by one-on-one experiences, and it gave individuals the freedom to formulate diverse concepts, which authoritarian Christian religion did not. Apaches treasure their religious autonomy, and they could not be expected to quickly and wholeheartedly embrace beliefs of a religion that took that autonomy away. But when the U.S. government made the practice of Indian religion illegal, Christianity was poised to fill the vacuum, and bit by bit the traditional Apache beliefs began to modify.

Ancient Time

At the center of Apache spirituality was a belief in the shared intellect of humans and animals that, in practical terms, meant humans and animals could communicate with each other and consciously affect each other's lives. The special symbiosis between Apaches and animals was rooted in a rich body of myth that went back to "ancient time," a mythological age in which all living beings were united. The humans and the animals lived by the same rules and conversed with each other in the same language. The anthropomorphic animals possessed human intellects that enabled them to make right or wrong choices and act responsibly. Their good deeds were rewarded, their bad deeds punished. After a series of individual failings, accidents, and just plain bad luck, the animals lost their human natures and abilities to converse verbally with humans. They erred and as punishment were allocated the distinguishing physical and behavioral characteristics of animals living today.

The rapport of humans and animals was reinforced by a strong oral tradition in which the extraordinary events and circumstances of ancient time were preserved in story form. This archive of myths and stories, although always entertaining, was also important pedagogically. In particular, the trickster, or Coyote, stories had strong moral lessons that reminded everyone of what behavior was acceptable and what was not. All of these stories were sacred and could only be told at night and during certain times of the year. Telling them in the daytime assuredly brought bad luck, although what kind was unclear. Tennyson Berry stated confidently, "You will get the itch if you tell the Coyote stories at the wrong time."[12]

Rose Chaletsin warned: "It has to be nighttime to tell Coyote. If you tell them in the daytime you'll go blind. I say I don't tell no Coyote stories in the daytime."[13]

Gertie Chalepah remembered the nighttime storytelling sessions, with Apaches gathered around the fire, that often lasted well past midnight:

> We used to listen to Apache John tell stories. We sat on the floor on a
> quilt. I put my head on my grandma's knee when I laid down. . . . He

[Apache John] said we always have to say *hà h* at the end of his stories or he'd quit. He'd tell us Coyote stories and stories of the old days. He said you can only tell Coyote stories at nighttime, not in the day. We sure liked to listen to him. Sometime his stories scare us. If we don't say *hà h*, then he know we're asleep and he quit telling stories.[14]

Stories of past real events, as well as those of ancient time, were relished by all—whether the old, who never tired of hearing them again and again, or the young, who acquired from them knowledge about tribal customs, survival skills, friends, and enemies. Stories capitalizing on the experiences of the elders of the tribe were especially effective in teaching the importance of courage, respect, and generosity to the young.

The personality of the storyteller played a key role in the level of expectation and enjoyment. An imaginative narrator could keep his or her listeners' attention by repeating incidents, telling different versions of the same story, changing characters and settings, and, for special effects, adding gestures, thumping the drum, or singing a group of songs. As the ages and moods of the listeners changed, so did the details of the stories.

The most sacred were the origin myths, which explained not how the earth was created but how order and structure were brought to an already existent Apache universe. They explained the origin of fire, the sun, the stars, humans, and the assignment of animal characteristics that were essential to an ordered universe.

The principal character in the stories was a being credited with performing culturally beneficial deeds so that Apache civilization could begin. He defeated the monsters. He brought the fire. He placed the sun in the sky. He established natural laws for separate species and essentially brought order out of chaos. Humanlike, he played the role not of creator but of one who rearranged and transformed what was already existing. Coyote, the ubiquitous trickster, was perfect for this role, and in most of the origin stories, it was he who by theft and trickery accomplished the tasks needed to prepare the world for human beings. He often had assistance from companions, but he did not need to summon help from the supernatural or any outside power. Rather, he depended solely on his intellect and wits to accomplish noble deeds.

In the most enduring of the creation stories, "The Hand Game," Coyote had the starring role. Set in ancient time when animals and humans still bonded with each other, the story, told by Ray Blackbear, centered on a hand game played between the monsters and other beings to determine who would rule the world. Coyote, using his wits and with aid from Beaver, was able to bring about the demise of the monsters and save the universe for all other beings, the animals and the humans:

THE HAND GAME

In the beginning, all of these people and animals spoke one language. They all understood each other. There were monsters and other people. The other people were animals and human beings both. The monsters were going to take over the whole world, but the other people didn't want them to. They decided to have a hand game, and the monsters played against the other people. They decided that whoever won the hand game would take over the world.

They began to play, and the people were losing the game. They just couldn't beat the monsters. Finally, the people had just four sticks left. They gave the sticks to Turtle. He had a special song that he sang, and he hid the sticks. But the monsters guessed where they were. Then they gave the sticks to Jackrabbit. He also had a special song that he sang, and he hid the sticks. But the monsters guessed again where they were. Then they gave the sticks to Frog, and he sang his special song. But the monsters guessed again. Finally, when they had only one stick left, they wanted to give it to Coyote.

But Coyote didn't want to play against the monsters if he was going to lose. Coyote just couldn't be a loser. So Coyote ran off up the river bank. The game was being played on a bluff over a river, and the monsters were sitting right on the edge of the bluff.

Coyote met Beaver and said, "Say, brother, we're about defeated by the monsters." Beaver asked why, and Coyote told him what was happening and asked for his help.

Beaver said, "Take some moss and make it into two ropes like braids. Put it around your neck, and when you go back to the game, start singing your song. When you come to a certain point in the song, squeeze the moss braids and water will spill out, fall over the cliff, and make the river below choppy. Waves will wash up against the bluff and cut it away."

Coyote went back to the game. The people had only one stick left. Coyote sat down and began to play. At a certain point in his song, he squeezed the moss, and water spilled over the edge. Waves began to wash up against the cliff. Coyote did this again and again, and finally all of the cliff gave way, and the monsters fell in and drowned.

Then Coyote looked over the edge of the bank and said, "Now you monsters aren't going to be on earth any more. You are all dead. The only way people will know you existed is by your bones, which they will find."

And that is where the bones we find come from. Those bones are from these prehistoric monsters . . . something like dinosaurs.[15]

The origin of human beings was narrated in two very different myths. The first, common to Apachean tribes of the Southwest, was narrated by

Solomon Katchin and recorded by McAllister in the 1930s as a beginning segment of a version of the hand game story. Its striking similarity to the Christian version may or may not be significant. The story is atypical in that it lacks character roles. It tells of the molding of humans from the earth:

IN THE BEGINNING

In the beginning, when the earth was put here, it was soft. It was like walking on soft rubber. At this time everything was in darkness; there was no day. Out west in the Panhandle of Texas there was a big bluff over which water was running, making a river. Since the earth was soft as quicksand, it was washing away rapidly. That was how it began.

Gradually, the earth began getting hard and grass started to grow. Then trees began to spread out from the rivers. There was more moisture then, so everything grew bigger than now. Plants were similar to the ones we have today, except sage. It grew as big as trees then.

In the springtime everything looked green; it looked pretty, and around the creeks something smelled sweet. In the fall everything dried up.

It was dark then, since there was no day, but big stars gave a little light. In this dim light the creeks looked white and the sage looked white.

Somebody was moulding mud in the shape of humans. Many were being so formed: men, women, young ones—all kinds. These forms were told to speak, and right there the Apaches learned to talk. All these people talked differently and couldn't understand each other.

In this time of continued night when they had snow, the people put sticks under their feet so they could walk on the snow. The Apaches didn't know very much then.

There was one place that looked as if smoke was coming from it. The people went over there and found deer. They killed them and had to dig them out of the ice.

The people were accustomed to living in the dark and didn't mind it. They didn't know about light. It was like living in the nighttime with only starlight.[16]

The next story about human origins, narrated by Ray Blackbear, tells how Thunder Man, or Lightning Man, destroys Nísjé, the monster, and saves Lucky Boy and his sister to become the first human beings:

LUCKY BOY AND NÍSJÉ

Lucky Boy had a mother, a father, a sister, and a grandmother. He went down to the spring one morning and found some groceries. He brought them back to the camp and said, "Hey, look what I found at the spring." The people were out of food at that time, so they ate it and were happy about it.

A couple of mornings later his father said, "Lucky Boy, go to the spring again. You may find some meat." Lucky Boy went down to the spring again and found some meat.

The next morning his father said, "Hey, Lucky Boy, go find some groceries." Lucky Boy went down and found some and brought them back.

The next morning his father said, "Hey, Lucky Boy, go find some meat." Lucky Boy went again and found some.

But pretty soon the father got curious and suspicious. He said, "Something to this. You don't get food for nothing." So he sneaked down there and saw Nísjé. Nísjé was carrying a bundle of food on his back, and he dropped it by the spring so that Lucky Boy would find it.

Nísjé said, "It sure is taking them a long time to get fat."

The father went back to the camp. He said, "Nísjé is fattening us up to kill and eat us. We're going to run far away so that he can't find us."

So he didn't send Lucky Boy down there again. They all got ready to move off. But before they left, something told Lucky Boy to get his baby moccasins and put them under the grass mat that lies in front of the tepee door. This something told him that this would help him. So the family took off running.

Nísjé found out the next morning that they had all gone away. He looked in the tent and said, "They got wise. But they won't get away." He started out after them, but when he got a hundred yards from the tepee he heard a baby crying. He went back to the tepee but couldn't find anything. Again he started off but heard the baby, and again he went back. Then this happened once more. On the fourth time he tore the tent up looking for the baby, and he found only the shoes.

So Nísjé said, "So this is it." And he ate those moccasins and then began to chase the family again.

The family was still running along, and finally the grandmother said, "I'm too old. You go on. I'll wait for Nísjé and let him kill me." So she sat down and waited, and pretty soon Nísjé got to her. He killed her and ate her.

A little later the mother said, "I'm too tired to go on. I'll sit down and wait for Nísjé and let him kill me."

Soon Nísjé came up to her. Nísjé said, "Where are the rest of them?"

The woman said, "They've gone."

Nísjé said, "I'll get them." Nísjé killed this woman and took just one or two bites out of her. Then Nísjé went on.

But soon the father said, "Go on, children. Go as far as you can. I can't go any farther. I'll wait for Nísjé and let him kill me." So he sat down, and Nísjé came upon him and ate the man. The others ran on.

Pretty soon the dog said the same thing, and he sat down to wait for Nísjé. When Nísjé came, the dog began to run around in circles. But Nísjé caught him and killed him.

The boy and the girl were left, and they ran along a creek bed. They started to cry. Then they heard a noise like someone chopping wood. The boy said, "Maybe that person will help us."

So they came up on Thunder Man, who was chopping wood. (This may have been Thunder or Lightning, I'm not sure.) Thunder Man was in the form of a man. Thunder Man said, "Hey, what are you crying for? What makes you run?"

The boy said, "That Nísjé is chasing us, and he's killed everybody else on earth and wants to kill us."

Thunder Man said, "He's not that bad."

"Yeah," said the boy, "He's ferocious and mean and dangerous."

Thunder Man said, "He's not that bad. Hide behind that boulder. I'll take care of him."

Nísjé came up and began sniffing around. "Hey!" he said, "Where did those two children go?"

Thunder Man said, "I didn't see anyone. I don't know."

That's how lying began, right there with Thunder Man.

Nísjé said, "If you don't tell me where they are, I'll do this to you." And Nísjé bit a rock and broke it apart.

But Thunder Man said, "Yeah, if you don't go away I'll do this to you." Thunder Man threw his ax and split a tree in half. Nísjé said, "Go ahead." And Thunder Man turned loose on Nísjé and killed him and scattered him all over.

Then Thunder Man said, "From now on you won't be on earth. You won't live. You'll just be remembered by people."

All human beings came from this brother and sister.[17]

The Apache cosmos was still a world of total darkness until, in a non-Coyote story narrated by Solomon Katchin, a bird, an insect, and some animals stole Light.[18] Ant stole Light from the house of two women and passed it in turn to Swift-Hawk, Jackrabbit, Buffalo, and finally Terrapin, who sequestered it under his shell. One of the women, who was Chief of the Day, asked Thunder to knock Light out of Terrapin. Thunder hurled a powerful lightning bolt that created the characteristic marks on Terrapin's shell but, alas, failed to free Light. Later, Terrapin opened his shell and released Light to create the day. To celebrate, the animals ran from east to west, which explains why the sun follows that path every day. Afterward, Terrapin shut his shell, causing night to fall.[19] From that time on, Apaches used the shell of a terrapin to ward off thunder, and the two women, who lost Light to Terrapin, went to live on the moon, šà (which is both sun and moon in Apache). One became the "woman in the moon," and when the moon changed, the other woman could be seen pulling a travois across the moon.

Now the greatest need of the cosmos was fire, kǫ in Apache, to keep the people warm. Two different versions of the fire-theft myth told how kǫ, or Light, was stolen by Coyote, passed along to a succession of three or four animals, and finally handed over to the people. The first myth, told by Ray Blackbear, follows:

How Coyote Stole Fire for the People

At the beginning, after the hand game between the people and the monsters, the nights were very dark. There wasn't any fire to light up the night. But Coyote said, "There's a way to light up the night. We've got to have fire."

Then Coyote said, "I want four good runners [he chose just three]. I'm going to go and get fire, and then we'll have fire on the earth." So Coyote chose Rabbit, Fox, and Deer, and he stationed them at intervals along a path. Coyote and Fox went to the end of this path, which ran under the ground. When they got down there, there was fire all around them. Coyote went over to look at the fire.

The people down there recognized Coyote, and they said, "That's Coyote. He's up to no good. Watch out for him or he'll trick us."

Coyote said, "I'm just looking around. I'm cold, and I wanted to get warmed up."

Then the people said, "Oh, all right. Go warm up by the fire."

Then Coyote told Fox, "I'm going to go over to the fire and stick my tail in there. When it catches fire, I'll give it to you and you run out with it."

Pretty soon all of the people were singing. Coyote was watching, and pretty soon he stuck his tail in the fire, and it caught on fire. The people saw this, and they said, "Look out, Coyote, your tail is on fire."

But Coyote just said, "I don't care. I'm having a good time."

He handed his tail to Fox who ran as fast as he could. The people chased him, but they couldn't catch him. When Fox reached Deer, he gave the burning tail to him, and Deer ran on. The people chased Deer, too, but they couldn't catch him. When Deer got to Rabbit, he handed the burning tail to him, and Rabbit began to run. The people were still chasing, but they didn't catch Rabbit.

Then Rabbit finally brought fire here and gave it to the people. The Indians always say that there is fire under the earth and that this is the way Coyote got fire for the Indians.[20]

Another version of the fire-theft myth, not recounted here, is similar except that (1) the animal characters were Black-Hawk, Jackrabbit, Prairie Chicken, and Turtle; (2) the gift of fire was transmitted by burning coals rather than Coyote's burning tail; and (3) from the fire, Coyote not only made the sun but also fire rocks to be an infinite source of fire for all people.[21]

Cosmic Spirits

Of all the Apache spirit beings, the one most closely approaching the status of a Supreme Spirit was the male sun. The giver of light and life, the sun, šà, was the central focus of the Apache world, and its great height in the sky increased its divine aura.

The Apaches collectively celebrated the ritual primacy of the sun at the Kiowa Sun Dance, held every one to three years, in which they sought spiritual renewal in prayers addressed to the sun. According to Joe Blackbear, some prayed individually to the sun at nonceremonial times throughout the year:

> Sometimes they made sacrifices. There is a story of a man who was hunting turkeys. He prayed to the sun to help him. When he saw some turkeys, he asked the sun to help him get them. The turkeys walked right toward him. When he shot at one it fell over dead, but there wasn't any bullet mark on it. He took out the heart and put it on the ground for the sun. He left the guts for "Owl Poor" [one of the sacred medicine bundles].
>
> One time I noticed that my grandfather's cousin had four scars on his arm, right in a row. I asked what they were. He told me that one time he liked a certain girl but that she would not talk to him. He went up on a hill and cut off four strips of skin from his arm. He used a needle to stick under the skin, and he cut the skin loose with a knife. He put the pieces of skin down and prayed, "You are the sun, and I want you to help me. I give you my skin."
>
> Several days later he met the woman he wanted coming from the creek with water. He asked her to marry him. She said it would be all right if he married her, but she would not just go with him.[22]

The female moon, šà, as opposed to the male sun, šà, exhibited waxing and waning characteristics that corresponded closely with the female reproductive cycle. Apache women believed the menstrual cycle most likely began with the "new moon . . . that's [the] time woman have her blood, or maybe with full moon," and they calculated the length of pregnancy by the number of moons. "A woman says, 'I got monthly. Next new moon I didn't have no monthly.' She keeps track. Maybe nine or ten moons that baby come. It comes with the moon."[23] Some believe the woman with a travois in the moon is holding a new baby.

In the all-night peyote ceremony, the moon had ritual significance as a symbolic focus. The central altar, which held the sacramental peyote, was an earthen mound shaped in the form of a crescent moon that cupped the central fire on the west and opened on the east. The crescent was mounded high in the summer to deflect the heat toward the east entrance and low in the winter to foster even circulation of the fire's warmth.

The moon was also important as a harbinger of the weather and sometimes sickness. Rose Chaletsin and Joe Blackbear gave their interpretations of the weather forecasts from the moon. A ring around the moon meant cold weather. Nothing around the moon meant it would be warm. The crescent moon, resting on its back, predicted dry weather, and tilted on one end the crescent was said to be spilling out water, a forecast of rain.[24] Susagossa added: "Up in the sky there is a white cloud that is long, and it is called like 'buttermilk.' When it gets straight up it is going to be cold, and when it lays on its side it is going to be warm."[25]

Compared to the spirits of the sun and moon, the stellar spirits were accorded less significance. Although Apaches had a rich knowledge of the stars and constellations and had names for the prominent ones, they most commonly used the stars as an indicator of direction, time, and changes in the seasons. The relative movement of the stars in the sky was recognized as critically important in providing a reliable map for the hunter, scout, or warrior. Susagossa explained,

> When they [the Apaches] were roaming around at night, there was a certain star, twinkling star, and then they would look for the Dipper and go by that for their direction. They would go by the stars to travel East, West, North, South. The morning star came about four o'clock, and then they would have to go to the mountains because they were afraid to travel in the daylight when they were raiding.[26]

In the stellar myths, earthly customs and certain beings of great importance to the tribe were commonly transformed into constellations and accorded supernatural status—for example, the running of the buffalo that provided the basic sustenance of the tribe, and the ritual smoking of the pipe that made events sacred and sealed a contract. Susagossa elaborated: "That great big old white streak across the sky, the Milky Way, they say it was the buffalo making all that dust. There's another place up there, they tell me. It's like a curve. They say there's a lot of men up there smoking a pipe, and they pass it on to each other till all have smoked it."[27]

Perhaps the best-known astral myth was that of the origin of the Pleiades, called sǫ́ǫ̀·dás-žò in Apache, or "stars lying in a circle." The Apache myth, narrated by Tennyson Berry, was about hunting, the principal economic activity of Apaches, in which six boys and a girl, who were the hunted, not only escaped from the bear but ascended to an abode in the sky to become immortal as a constellation:

THE SEVEN SISTERS

A long time ago, there was a big camp of Indians. The leader of this camp had two daughters; one was a young lady and the other was a small girl. They were camping close to timber, like the old Indians did. This chief and his wife always fixed up their oldest daughter every morning, combing [her hair], washing and painting her face. Finally, the father noticed that she wandered daily around in the timber and that when she came back in the evening, the paint on her face was gone.

So the father said, "Say daughter, why is it that although I always paint your face, you come back every evening unpainted?"

The daughter said, "Well, maybe I get hot during the day and wash the paint off."

But the father didn't believe this. So one day when the girl went off into the timber, the father followed her and spied on her. He watched her in the timber, and after awhile a big bear came along. It was her sweetheart. The girl had always wished that she would meet some young man in the timber, and finally she met one there. But the man she met was a bear in human form, and he finally changed back into his bear shape. And then the girl still had to stay with him.

The father went back and told the people in the camp what was going on and about the bear in the timber. In the morning the people got ready to hunt the bear. But the father didn't tell them about his daughter.

The next morning, all of the people went into the timber, and finally the bear came along, and the people killed him. The leader said, "We want to skin him well because my daughter will want to keep the skin as a remembrance." So they killed and skinned the bear and tanned his hide. Then the chief gave it to his daughter.

Now this camp, where these people lived, was a winter camp, which they had pitched near the water. Six young men in the camp went out on the warpath, and they had been gone for nearly a year. While the young girls were playing on the river near a sandy place, one of the girls asked the leader's young daughter to get her older sister to play bear because she knew how to act like a bear. So the young girl went to her older sister and told her that these girls wanted her to play with them.

The older sister said, "No, I don't want to do that." So the little girl cried and begged her to act like a bear. So finally the older sister said, "All right. I've been telling you I don't want to do this, but you won't listen. I'll play with you, but it won't be good."

Now, she had this bear hide that had been given to her by her father. The girls built a little playhouse near some growing fruit. Whenever the little girls would try to get some of the fruit, the girl acting like a bear would run out of the playhouse and would chase them. When she caught them she would shake them hard. The first and second times that this happened, everything was all right. But the third or fourth time the girl caught them all, turned into a bear, and tore them up and killed them.

The others ran for the camp, but the girl chased them. When she came into the camp she killed everyone she met, including her mother and father. Her little sister hid in the playhouse and was spared. The girl came to the little house and said, "Hey sister, you come out here." The little girl obeyed and came out.

"Well, now you see what I've done; what I told you would happen did." The little sister didn't have much to say. "You go down to the creek," said the eldest, "and bring me some water." So the little girl went down to the stream, carrying a skin bag.

Meanwhile, Bear-Girl was lying in her tent. When the little girl returned she said, "Here is your water, sister."

The older girl said, "This isn't good water. It's dirty and it smells bad. Throw it out and get me some more."

It was about this time when these young fellows who had been on the warpath returned. When they came back they noticed that there was no smoke in the camp, so they waited until nightfall. Then they discovered that all of the people were dead, so they just waited around the stream to see what would happen. They waited to see if anyone would come down to the stream.

In the morning, when the little girl came back again, one of these men said, "Hey little girl, can we talk to you?"

The little girl said, "No, you'd better not. My sister is pretty mean. She killed everybody but me."

They told the little girl to come back later and they would tell her how to get rid of her sister. The little girl said, "You had better be careful or she will kill all of you, too."

So she went back to take the water to her sister, and when she came into the tepee she gave the water to her sister. The sister said, "Hey, I smell a human."

The little girl said, "Well, maybe you smell all of those people that you killed."

"No," said the older sister, "I don't think so. But I'll tell you what I want you to do. I'm getting hungry, and you'll have to go out and kill a rabbit for me to eat."

So the next morning the girl went back to the watering place and told the men what she had to do. "She told me to kill a rabbit," said the little girl, "but I don't know how I'm going to do it."

But the men said that they would kill one, and they did. Then they said, "You take it to her and tell her you killed it. If she doesn't believe

66

you, you set the rabbit up straight, and then take this little stone ax and hit the rabbit, and then she'll have to believe you." So she took it back to the tipi.

The older sister said, "Say, sister, you didn't kill this. I smell some other humans on it who must have killed it for you."

"No," said the little girl, "I killed it. I'll show you how I did that."

"Well, go ahead," said the eldest sister.

So the little girl set this rabbit up and threw the Indian hammer at the animal and hit it on the back of its head. The eldest sister didn't say anything about that and pretended that she believed it. Then the little sister went back again to get water. She was getting to know these boys, and she wasn't afraid of them anymore.

"Say," they said, "We're going to tell you how to kill your sister. You go around the camp and pick up all of the needles that the people had. Get a whole bunch of them. Then you put them right alongside of the place where she's laying and put them at the door of the tepee. Make sure the points are all sticking up. Her heart is right under her paws, and when she chases you and those needles stick into her, she'll die." So the little girl went back and did all of this.

The eldest sister said again, "Get me some water. But be careful you don't touch my legs or you'll hurt me."

The little girl had a stick in her hand, and she said, "Oh, you're always so particular about your legs. I'm going to hit you." So she hit her two or three times.

The older sister growled loudly like a bear and began to chase her little sister. When she came to the door, she stepped on the needles and fell. Then she stopped to pull out the needles, and then she ran again. But she got more needles in her paws and had to stop again.

The boys on horseback rode into the camp and shouted to the younger sister, "Hurry up and get on."

The eldest sister was still trying to get the needles out. When she finally had gotten them all out, she yelled, "I'll get you. I know where you are going, and I'll find you."

The young men with the girl on one of the horses rushed off. The young girl, though, looked back and saw her sister following them. "Look out," she shouted, "she is still coming."

So the men beat their horses harder and tried to get away. They ran their horses down a long hill. All of these men had arrows. One of the young men said, "Well, when she gets too close, I'll shoot one of my arrows into the sky." But they kept on running, keeping ahead of Bear-Girl.

Finally, their horses began to wear out, and they realized that they couldn't go much farther. They began to cry. They came to a little bluff and were almost past it when a voice cried out, "Hey, where are you going? What are you crying about? Come here." All of the men heard it. Then this voice said, "Come on up here on the top of this bluff. What's the matter?"

The boys stopped, and they told their troubles to the man. One of them said, "Look, you can see her coming right over there."

Then the voice said, "Don't worry. She'll never get you."

Then the hill began to grow up higher and higher.

When the sister got very close, she began to talk and said, "You can't get away from me. I'll get you." Then she made a jump toward the top, but the hill kept growing and she couldn't reach it. She tried again and again, and finally, on the fourth time, she saw she could never reach that far, so she decided to let them go.

But the men were very high up on this bluff. They were talking among themselves, trying to decide what to do. Finally, one of them said, "Well, let's turn into stars." The others agreed.

Then one man said, "One of you shoot an arrow into the air, and that fellow will fly into the sky. Then the next one will shoot an arrow, and so on. The little girl will shoot an arrow last." So each one shot an arrow, and they were finally all gone. Then the little girl shot the last arrow, and she was gone. And that is the way they turned into stars—those six boys and a little girl. But we call those stars all together "the Seven Sisters."[28]

The next great task was to bring order and purpose to the animal kingdom. Fire Boy and Water Boy accomplished this in a myth that is actually an assemblage of slightly different and shortened stories McAllister recorded in 1933–1934.[29] The myths have expanded, contracted, merged, disappeared, and replaced others on a continuing basis.

The Fire Boy and Water Boy myth is one of the best-known boy hero myths in American Indian mythology, told throughout the Plains from Canada to Texas.[30] In fact, the myth in which boy twins perform heroic deeds and other exploits attributable to a culture hero enjoys such widespread popularity that Radin has called it "the basic myth of North American Indians."[31]

The myth recounts how a mysterious stranger (Sun in the version that follows and a monster in another) kills Fire Boy and Water Boy's mother at their birth and releases them from their mother's belly, a release analogous to the release of light, or life, from darkness. The stranger then throws one of the twins into the river, or darkness, and the other one into water's opposite, the fire, or light. The symbolic polarity of the twins is resolved with their subsequent union in a number of mischievous deeds that bring order to the chaos of nature. The myth, narrated by Ray Blackbear, follows:

FIRE BOY AND WATER BOY

From the very beginning when the Indians were at peace with the world, when there was no war, just hunting, living, and enjoying the summers and the winters, enjoying marriage . . . when everyone liked and enjoyed life, a man and a woman camped out by a stream. They camped there by themselves, way off from the others. The man hunted meat every day, and the woman prepared the meat and the tallow.

The woman was pregnant at this time. The man said, "Wife, there is some evil on this earth. It's here with us. Whenever I go away, someday, sometime, and you're left in the tent, you'll hear a voice talking to you. You'll want to look at the place where the voice is coming from, but don't do that. Just ignore the voice and go on about your work." The woman wondered about this.

One day when the man had gone off to hunt, the woman heard a voice. It said, "Hey, look at me. Take a peek."

But the woman didn't look, she just went on working. This happened every day for a long time. And each time the woman just went on working.

Finally, one day she got curious, and she took her needle and poked a little hole in the tepee. She looked outside the tepee and looked at the voice.

Then the voice said, "I thought you'd look at me sometime." So the voice [who was the Sun] took the woman and cut her hair off and split her down the middle. He opened her up and took out the twin boys who were inside. He threw one of them in the river and he threw the other one in the fire. Then he cut off the woman's head and placed it right at the front flap of the tepee so that it was looking out. Then Sun went away.

When the man came home that night, he saw his wife's head and went inside the tepee. Inside, he saw the rest of her body, all cut up into little pieces. He said, "I told you so. I told you not to look at the voice, but you wouldn't listen to me. I warned you. You couldn't resist the voice, and this is what has happened to you."

While he was looking around inside the tepee, he found his son alive in the fire. He picked up the boy and carefully washed him off.

The father took real good care of Fire Boy, and the boy grew up. When the man went off to hunt, he said to Fire Boy, "Just stay around the camp." Then he'd go off to hunt, but he always hurried back.

One day while the man was gone, the boy went down to the river. His twin was living there in the water, and he was all right, still alive. Fire Boy would yell to him, and Water Boy would answer. They played together all of the time and had a lot of fun.

One day Fire Boy said, "Dad, make me two hoops and two javelins." Fire Boy didn't tell his father about Water Boy.

Later Fire Boy said, "Dad, make me two sets of arrows." The father got suspicious about this and thought that Fire Boy was playing with someone else.

One day when the man came back from hunting, he saw Water Boy's wet tracks there in the tepee. He knew they didn't belong to Fire Boy. He asked Fire Boy, "Son, tell me, who do you play with while I'm gone?"

Fire Boy lied. He said, "I don't play with anyone while you're gone."

But the father asked again, and finally Fire Boy confessed. He said, "I play with my brother, Water Boy."

The father said, "Bring him up here to the camp, and we'll take him in, and he can live with us."

Fire Boy said, "No, I'm afraid of him. He's mean. He has long fingernails, and he will scratch me."

But the father said, "I'll make you a leather jacket to protect you. Now go down to the creek. I'll pretend to go away to hunt. You play the javelin and hoop game with Water Boy, and when you have both thrown your hoops, get into an argument about who won the game. Make Water Boy lean down to look more closely at the hoop. I'll be waiting, and when he leans down, you grab him, and then I'll come, too."

Fire Boy did as he was told. He played the game with his twin, and when they had both thrown the javelins, he argued about who had won. Water Boy leaned down to look at the hoop, and Fire Boy grabbed him. Then the man came running up and said to Water Boy, "Don't be mean."

But Water Boy replied, "You threw me in the water when I was a baby."

"No," the man answered. "It wasn't me who threw you in the water. It was someone else." They argued, but the man finally convinced Water Boy.

In those days there were no laws of the elements. Nothing was regular. If you walked under a tree, it fell on you right away. If you tried to jump over a creek, the creek would get wider as soon as you jumped, and you would fall in. This father told the twins about this and told them not to walk under trees or try to jump across creeks. But the boys ignored his warning, and they went ahead anyway.

The boys attached feather plumes to their scalp locks. Then they went out to walk in the woods. They came to a tree, and there were a lot of skeletons under the tree where the tree had been killing people. The plumes reached out toward the tree, and the tree fell on the plumes and broke all to pieces.

Then the boys said, "Now tree, this is the way you are always going to be. You aren't going to fall on people anymore. People are going to use you to make fire and get warm. They're going to burn with you and cook with you."

Now today that's what people use. We're using wood that way now. There is no mean wood anymore.

The boys came to a river, which started getting wider. The plumes again went out toward the river. Then the boys said, "Now rivers, this is the way you are always going to be. You aren't going to get wide when people try to jump across you anymore."

When they got home they told their father about what they had done. The father said, "I told you boys, don't you do those things. What makes you always try?" He didn't understand his boys were smart to do things.

Next he told them, "Don't do these bad things. And don't go over there. There's a horse standing over there. He's bad. Just when you get close to him he looks at you, his eyes sparkle like lightning, and he'll kill you with his eyes."

So the boys played around, and finally one of them said, "Say brother, let's go see that horse." They went to see the horse, but they hid from him.

One of the boys said, "I know how to get that horse. Let's turn into moles and go under the ground. We'll go under the horse to the edge of the pond where the horse comes to get his drink."

The boys turned into moles and went underground to the edge of the pond. When the horse came to get his drink, the boys threw a rock in the water. Where the rock fell in the water a ring appeared. The ring turned into a rope and roped the horse. The horse jumped up and down and tried to get away, but the boys held him down. They got his bad eye out, and now he can't kill anybody anymore. And they gave him a good eye to see [with]. And they said, "We got rid of your bad eye. You've got good eyes now. From here on people are going to use you. They are going to ride you, and you are going to be useful to people."

The boys went back to camp and told their father about the horse.

The father said, "What makes you all do things when I tell you not to?"

But this horse, he got gentle. Now people are using horses. And that's why we have good horses.

The father said, "You are both very bold. But up in the canyon there is a high bank. On this bank lives a buzzard, and he makes a waving motion with his wings. Anyone walking along the canyon is fanned by his wings, and they drop dead. Then the buzzard waits until they rot, and he eats the meat."

Fire Boy said, "Brother, let's go visit the buzzard."

But Water Boy said, "No, Father warned us not to go there."

But Fire Boy said, "No, that is nothing."

So they went, and the buzzard looked down on them. But the twins climbed up the bank and told the buzzard to look down into the canyon to see something. When he looked down Buzzard said, "What? I don't see anything."

Then the boys pushed him off the cliff. They told him that he would always be bald headed and that he would eat nothing but rotten meat from then on.

When they got back to camp, their father made them two hoops to roll along the ground. But he warned them, "Always roll these hoops into the wind or across the wind. Never roll them with the wind."

But the twins didn't believe this warning, and they ignored it. When they went out Water Boy said, "Hey brother, let's roll these hoops with the wind."

Fire Boy said, "Why not, brother?"

So they rolled the hoops with the wind, and the hoops started rolling so fast that they wouldn't stop. Every now and then the hoops would slow down and totter and look like they were going to fall. Then the twins would almost catch them, but when they got near the hoops rolled off again just as fast as before. Pretty soon the hoops rolled over a hill. When the boys found them, the hoops had fallen on the top poles of a tepee, and they were hanging there.

An old woman came out of the tepee and said, "Who's down there? Come on in, grandchildren."

The boys said, "Our hoops are caught on the top of your tepee."

The old woman said, "I'll get them off for you. Come on inside my tepee."

So the boys went inside the tepee. When they got inside they saw little pouches of skin hanging from each one of the poles. The old woman went over and untied four of the pouches, and then she went out of the tepee. It got very smoky inside the lodge. The old woman knew this and thought that the smoke would kill the two boys. When she went back in the boys were still alive, so she untied four more of the pouches. Then she went out again.

Water Boy said, "Brother, I'm not going to be able to hold out much longer."

Fire Boy said, "Just say this word 'sicana.'" (This word is used when you want something to go away, like a tornado.)

Water Boy said this word, and the smoke raised up and retreated from just the area where the boys were sitting.

The old woman came back in and untied four more pouches. It got smokier in the tepee, but the area where the boys were sitting was still clear of smoke. The old woman didn't notice this.

Then she came back in with a big pot. "What's the matter with you boys?" she said. She didn't understand why the smoke hadn't killed them. She opened the top flaps of the tepee, and the smoke all went out.

Then she put the pot on the fire and put the boys into it and boiled them.

Fire Boy couldn't stand the water very long, so he said, "Say brother, I can't hold out much longer."

Water Boy said, "Brother, say that word again." When Fire Boy said it, the water withdrew from just the area where the boys were sitting.

The old woman was stirring the pot with the boys in it. But the boys hung on to the spoon and went round and round inside the pot.

Finally, the old woman took the boys out of the pot, but she was suspicious of them because they were still alive. She said, "I'm dealing with boys who have more power than I have." So she took the hoops off the top of the tepee and gave them back to the boys. The boys went home.

When the boys got back to their camp, they told their father what had happened. The father said, "Oh, I forgot to tell you about that woman. She eats people."

Then he told them about tornadoes and told them never to mess with them: "They are the most powerful things on earth."

Fire Boy said one day, "Brother, see that funnel out there. Let's go over and see it."

"Why not?" said Water Boy.

But when they got near the tornado it picked them up and carried them off, and no one ever saw them again.

Some distance away, an old lady found a clot of blood. She picked it up and said, "This is good. It is some kind of a blessing. I'll fix it with my corn." She boiled the clot of blood and the corn all together. But when she dropped the clot into the mush, she heard a baby crying. She reached in there and found a baby. That's all that I know, but the old lady raised that baby, and he performed many miracles.[32]

Coyote the Trickster

The wily, intelligent Coyote, who was credited with accomplishing beneficial deeds for humankind, was especially beloved as the unpredictable trickster whose greed and maliciousness often led to some evil end. In this role, Coyote tricked and got tricked. His envy of others' abilities fed his insatiable desire to be something or have something he could not be or have, and when he ignored the boundary between acceptable and unacceptable behavior with disastrous results, he was a lesson for all. A capricious and whimsical character, he was often cast as the utter fool. He imagined himself a lady's man and was forever trying to steal someone's daughter or wife. A master of deception, Coyote was frequently punished for his bad deeds by being killed, only to miraculously revive and appear in the next story.

A favorite Coyote story in which Coyote pays a heavy price for deception is narrated by Ray Blackbear:

COYOTE JUGGLES HIS EYES

Coyote was watching this porcupine one day. It might have been a coon. This porcupine took his eyes out of their sockets and threw them up into the air. Then he would turn his head up and catch them again at the sockets. He did this over and over.

Coyote said, "I'd like to learn that trick. Hey, brother, you teach me that."

But Porcupine said, "No, I won't teach you anything. You're crazy. Go on away."

Coyote said, "No, I'm good and honest. I never cheat. Teach me that one trick."

But Porcupine still said, "No, you go on your way." Coyote begged him to teach the trick, so Porcupine finally said, "Yes, I'll teach you the trick. But don't ever do this trick near a plum bush. Don't ask me why, just don't do it there." Coyote agreed not to, and Porcupine taught him the trick.

Coyote started doing this trick and then started thinking, "I've got to find out about this plum bush." So he went over under a plum bush and threw his eyes into the air. But they didn't come back down. They just hung up there and turned into plums. Coyote ran around and couldn't see. He said, "I wish I hadn't done that."

Then he went stumbling along and came to some people's tents. These people saw he was in trouble. A young girl came over and said, "Poor Coyote. What happened to you?"

Coyote said, "I got sore eyes, but I'll be all right."

The girl took him in the tent. The whole family was eating there. Coyote wanted this girl and thought of a scheme to get her. While he was eating, he pretended to choke on some meat. He just choked and gagged. The people said, "What's the matter?"

Coyote said, "I'm choking. Send the girl to the creek to get some water." So the girl ran out. But Coyote said he couldn't wait for the water, so he ran down toward the creek. He was still pretending to choke. He met the girl and said, "Boy, I like to have died choking."

The girl gave him some water, and he drank it. Then Coyote said, "Your father felt sorry for me and gave you to me to marry. He said I could take you with me."

The girl said, "All right, if that's my father's wish."

So they both went up the creek. After a while they sat down to rest. Coyote said, "I'm tired. Look in my hair for lice."

The girl did this, and she rubbed his head and he got sleepy. When she moved her hand close to his eyes to look for lice, Coyote said, "No, look in the back of my head." So the girl did. This happened three times. Finally, Coyote fell asleep. Then the girl looked at Coyote's eyes and saw they were full of maggots.

"Boy," she said, "He's dying. I've got to get rid of him." She reached out and got buffalo manure and piled it under his head. Then she went off and hid on the other side of a ravine.

Coyote woke up and missed the girl. "Hey," he said. "Come on back. I see you."

The girl said, "You can't see me. You've got worms in your eyes."

But Coyote said, "No, no worms. I can see plain."

The girl said, "You better come and get me."

Coyote said, "Yeah, I can see you."

So he started toward her. But he fell off the high bank and was killed. The girl went home and told her father what had happened.

Her father said, "Beware of that Coyote-Man. He's very tricky."[33]

Coyote's most important attribute as trickster was his total self-reliance. He played an exemplary role by solving, attempting to solve, and creating problems for others by using his brain, his wits alone. In a culture infused with the supernatural, Coyote, through metaphor, kept people in touch with reality and reminded them that power that comes from self-knowledge and self-reliance is as important as power from the supernatural.

Sacred Symbols and Colors

Apaches utilized the circle in almost every physical and artistic endeavor. The circle was a symbol for the Apachean world. The sun, the paths of the sun and moon, the horizon—all were duplicated numerous times and ways in the tepee, the camp circle, the shield, and the dance. The circle symbolized wholeness, unity, and equality. All who sat in the camp circle or danced in the circle reaffirmed their equality and cooperation with each other, qualities essential for survival on the Plains. More important, the circle was sacred. It was a visible sign of being in harmony with nature and the supernatural.

Equally sacred was the number four, a symbolic replication of the circle. It represented the four cardinal directions and, by extension, totality and unity. Rituals, whether for the individual or the group, lasted four days. A vision quest, in which an individual sought supernatural power in nature, ideally lasted four days, as did the Sun Dance of other tribes in which Apaches participated. Parts of rituals were repeated four times, for example, the passing of the pipe or the cadence of dancers who were often in groups of four. In postcontact times the number seven gained some significance, no doubt because of the influence of the seven-day week of the Gregorian calendar, but it never attained the importance of the number four.

Ray Blackbear emphasized the importance of the number four: "[You] had four days to get better or die after you have been treated for something. Children were warned three times and were punished on the fourth time. Four peyote meetings were given in hopes of curing someone. Many things happen four times in peyote meetings, everything four times. It's supposed to prevent bad luck."[34]

Of the four directions, east and west were the most important because, Ray Blackbear declared, "in the Indian's way of thinking, east is where the sun comes up, and the west is where it goes down."[35] The door of the tepee always faced east, as did the opening of the big circle in the Sun Dance and the circle in the peyote ceremony. All ritual movements followed the path of the sun going clockwise, or sunwise.

The ritual importance of the sun reverberated in the tribe's widespread ceremonial use of the colors red and yellow, which interchangeably represented the "setting sun" and the "rising sun." For dances and the warpath, special designs in the sun's colors were commonly painted on men's and women's faces, with red predominating on men's bodies. Ray Blackbear's description was more specific:

> The men paint up special occasions. There'd be red paint, and they use a little yellow. They use that yellow paint on their hair where the part is. Some put just a little red mark on both ends of the part. They paint their cheeks red. Maybe three red marks across their cheeks. Maybe two red and a yellow—just any way. They do this especially for dances and for warpath. . . . They would paint their bodies as well as their faces when they went on warpath.[36]

Black had no supernatural role except that it was the color of the handkerchief medicine men wore as a badge of their craft. The black handkerchief, perceived as imbued with mysterious power, was used as a medium in curing and legerdemain. Black was primarily used for outlining designs on clothing, tepees, and other paraphernalia.

Supernatural significance was associated with white, or the absence of color, especially in the animal and bird kingdoms. White animals and birds were regarded with awe and fear, some equated with a ghost, and the use of white fur and feathers always commanded honor and respect.

Materials for the frequently utilized red, yellow, black, and white were easily accessible from close-by areas. Ray Blackbear, Rose Chaletsin, and Datose specified sources for the different colors. Near the tribe's present Oklahoma location, yellow and white clays were found at Sulphur Springs and red clay at Indian Canyon and in the creek bank at Red Point. Black was made from the charcoal of common trees—predominantly elms and blackjack oaks—and the color green was made by mixing the crushed leaves of the black walnut with white clay. With the advent of off-reservation stores near the end of the century, all colors became available in powder form.[37]

Apache designs expressed in bright colors their oneness with nature. Shields, tepees, parfleches, and clothing were decorated with symbols of nature. The patterns, in their ultimate simplicity, were a tribute to the cosmos—the sun, the moon, the stars, the expanse of sky overhead—and to animals vital to Apache sustenance. The designs, which were visionary in origin, subsequently became family or individually owned.

Joe Blackbear explained the sacred process involved in determining a shield's design:

> In the old days a man might dream and learn how to make a certain kind of shield. The shield has a certain kind of meaning. They used to believe something spoke to them and told them how to do it. Then when the person got old, he could give the shield and the story of it to someone.
>
> If you had a certain kind of shield and the knowledge to make it, no one could copy it without your permission. They said if you didn't get permission you would have a kind of curse on you. They believed that a shield was holy and that the power that taught you to make it would protect you. It would make the arrows miss you. . . . The power that helped you to make the shield [was the power] you prayed to when you went on the warpath. If your shield got pierced and you were hurt, they said you didn't understand and follow the instructions that your power taught you or that the person gave you who transmitted the shield to you.[38]

Ray Blackbear elaborated:

> Shields are painted like the rainbow or the sun. Maybe like the moon, with a ring around it. It represents the sun or the moon. Some people have got feathers on the shield. They are painted all kinds of colors. . . . Sometimes in the middle it's dark, any man could paint it that way, it's dark and it represents the nighttime. Around that it would be light that would represent the sky. That's what these Apaches use. One or two feathers hung from the middle of the shield and two or three more hung at the bottom.[39]

McAllister believed painted tepees, sometimes referred to as heraldic tepees, were common in early times, even though as late as 1935 he reported that only one painted tepee had been used as recently as "fifty years ago" (or 1885). He continued, "These tepees were painted in a definite manner with a design such as a panther, a bear, the rainbow, etc., according to the visionary experience. These tepees belonged to families and were never destroyed at

Tsáyadítl-ti, or Whiteman, head chief in 1893, and Dävéko, powerful medicine man and master of legerdemain whose power came from the snake, owl, and turtle. Photo, James Mooney, 1893–1894, Bureau of American Ethnology. Courtesy, Smithsonian Institution (neg. no. 2588-a-1).

the owner's death but were inherited in the male line. There was something sacred about them, probably because they were the result of supernatural experience."[40]

Joe Blackbear described several reminiscences of painted tepees to Brant fourteen years later. In both, the role of visions was critical for determining the design:

> Old man Taho's grandfather had gotten a vision of this tepee when he was out fasting and seeking power. Old man Taho told the people there, "You know, this tepee was given to me when I was married so that my children would grow. Now that they are grown up, I will make another one for my daughter who is getting married."
>
> Old Man Taho sought permission from the other old people to duplicate the tepee, and when the older people consented, the women began sewing the new tepee. They bought some yellow powder in town and also a red powder. They painted a red square on the south side of the tepee right near the smoke hole. They painted the entire tepee yellow except for that red square. They did it by mixing the yellow powder with water and rubbing it on with rags. In the old days they used clays for paints. The yellow stood for the yellowish color in the sky at sunrise and sunset.[41]

Joe Blackbear also recalled a blue tepee design that Dävéko, the medicine man, learned through his medicine. According to the story, Dävéko erected a tepee and painted it blue, and one day, while inside the tepee, he let the fire go out.

> The wind made the tepee strike against the poles, sounding like thunder, and the sparks flying up from the smoldering fire looked like lightning. He called the tepee "Blue Tepee." He named his stepson after it, "Blue Clouds." Dävéko's medicine was the Thunder, and he learned to make this tepee from it. . . . The blue color represented the sky. He believed God was up there in the blue sky and his children would be under it.[42]

The most important tepee belonging to Dävéko was a heraldic tepee inherited from his father, who was also a medicine man. The tepee had been inspired in a dream Dävéko's father had following a four-day Tlintidie dance. The tepee was solid black, except for red smoke flaps and a wide red band running down the middle of the front and the back. It was accented by a blue-green crescent moon, points up, near the top of each band. The father died after he got so old that "his skin peeled off," and his tepee went to Dävéko, who later passed it on to his stepson, Apache Sam Klinekole.[43]

53

Apache Sam Klinekole, Dävéko's stepson and doctor who inherited many of Dävéko's medicines. Courtesy, William Hammond Mathers Museum, Indiana University.

Water, Thunder, and Whirlwind Spirits

Of all the elements in the natural world, water, *kóó* in Apache, was the most revered. Whether in the form of spontaneous rainfall, which was considered a spiritual gift, or an already existing source, water was sacred and embodied a live spirit. According to Ray Blackbear, "Water is alive. It has a mind and spirit of its own, so you have to show the proper respect for it. They [Apaches] don't like tap water. It's artificial. They like water that comes from live springs, where you see water bubbling up, or from a river. Ever[y] thing grows with water. You put water on tomatoes, potatoes, and from that, that water's got spirit, you see. It's got life in it."[44]

Water, as springs, lakes, and rivers, brought healing and purification. The most sacred water in the Apache world was that from the mythological Devil's Lake, where one of the tribe's sacred medicine bundles was alleged to have originated. Because of like associations, Susagossa, among other Apaches, believed other lakes had healing properties where "people would visit to worship, say prayer, so they could live a long time and their children and grandchildren would live a long time."[45]

Zodlton, a group of cold water sulphur springs near the present Apache location in southwestern Oklahoma, was believed to have healing attributes that improved general health and cured various minor illnesses that were accompanied by fever or rashes. The prescription for healing, articulated by Ray Blackbear, was: "Go and dive in water four times. You do that enough days, and you get your health back."[46]

Zodlton's spirit was manifest in several ways, which added to its overall mystique. First, it had physically rejected Apache gift offerings, which Susagossa attributed to jealousy: "They [the Apaches] kinda worshiped water in the old days and would put a bracelet or ring in the water. And the next time they'd go down there, it would be thrown out. Whatever is in there is kinda jealous and won't keep it."[47]

Second, Zodlton's spirit had been observed floating around the springs as a mysterious light. The phenomenon was described by Helen Blackbear: "We'd seen that light coming. And then when it got to the end of the mountain, well, it'd just float over them trees, and it got on the west side of that mountain. And then it got on the south side and just went on in the creek. We'd see it every time it rains, when it rains steady for so many hours."[48]

Thunderstorms, or water in a turbulent form, were not welcome, and certain precautions were employed to keep them at bay. Commonly, people appealed to a horse to send the storm away, but at other times, according to Rose Chaletsin, "When storm came, old people pray and hold peace pipe to Mother Earth and talk to cloud. Cloud goes away."[49]

Thunder, the roar of storms, was a profound reminder of divine and fearful power in Apache beliefs that was reproduced frequently in ritual contexts with repeated rumblings of the drum. Thunder and its associated bird, the thunderbird, and associated animal, the horse, were important sources of supernatural power that could be summoned during a storm.

Another kind of storm, the whirlwind, was deemed unduly powerful and produced great fear in those who encountered it. The small spiral turbulent wind, which appeared with varying frequency on the hot Plains, "was a ghost capable of paralyzing a person," asserted Susagossa.[50] Its association with death is discussed in Chapter 7. In the following Coyote story, told by Ray Blackbear, the lesson of the whirlwind is "Don't aspire to be something you were not meant to be. Don't cross boundaries":

COYOTE AND WHIRLWIND

Coyote was going along a creek through some timber. He came to an open place and saw two pretty girls there. They were really Whirlwind, transformed into the shapes of pretty girls. This Whirlwind appeared as twin girls. Coyote stood there watching them, and they went round and round, dancing and skimming over the top of the ground.

Coyote kept watching. Then he got lured over to them. He said, "Hello, girls. What are you doing?"

The girls said, "Go away, Coyote. We're just free. We do what we want."

Coyote said, "That's just like I am. I'm free. I've got lots of time. How about going around with me?"

But the girls said, "No, you might not like the way we go. You might not like what we do."

But Coyote said, "No, I want to join you. I'll like what you do."

The girls refused and said, "We doubt that you'd like this."

Coyote said, "I'm honest. I'm like you. I'll do anything that you do."

The girls still refused and said, "No. You won't like the way we live."

Coyote said, "That's not right. I'm free. I go and come as I please."

Finally the girls said, "If you insist, come on." So one of the girls got on each side of Coyote, and they gave him a whirl.

Coyote liked that. He said, "That's fun. But let's go faster."

The girls said, "You had better stay here."

But Coyote insisted. So the girls whirled him even faster. Coyote got pretty excited. He said, "Boy, that's the way I like to live, reckless."

The girls said, "We'll give you more." They wanted to teach Coyote a lesson.

Coyote said, "Give me all you've got." So the girls agreed. They took him on a tremendous whirl through the timber and then just dropped him and left him. Coyote was all bruised and broken.

The girls cried out, "Come on, Coyote, let's go again."

But Coyote said, "No, you go on away."

The Indians say, "You should never fool with a whirlwind. It's dangerous."[51]

56

Sacred Fire and Tobacco

The sacred fire, kǫ, was the terrestrial counterpart of the sun. As an essential element for cooking and warmth, it served as a magnet for daily family and tribal activities. As a symbol of life and its renewal, it was the sacred focus of all rituals. All important political decisions regarding the settling of disputes, the timing of raids, the fate of prisoners, or the moving of camp were made around the fire.

The sacredness of fire was symbolically transferred to the pipe, and smoking the pipe was an important accompaniment to prayers invoking the supernatural. But Rose Chaletsin declared: "Some Indians here, they don't smoke, but they respect it. Like me. I don't smoke, but sometimes I do. When I want to pray, I smoke Durham or corn smoke and pray to the earth, sky, sun, moon. You pray for long life."[52]

In important ceremonies and councils, the smoking of the pipe by all participants gave decisions communal legitimacy. All who made and agreed to promises were morally bound to honor them. According to Ray Blackbear:

> Tobacco is supposed to have power, the power that made it grow, the unseen hand. It has more power than other plants because it is used by chiefs. Every time you smoke, you have to make a prayer. It's only used in ceremonies and councils. He [the chief] will make an invocation while packing the pipe, take a puff, move the pipe to the east and up, then puff, and to the left, to the right and back. Then he passes it to his left, and each one takes four puffs. When the tobacco runs out, they pass it back. He empties the pipe in one spot where all can see it's all burned. While he's talking he refills it and passes it on. Then it starts there again. It may run out two, three times. The pipe went around just once. Pipe could be red or black.[53]

Sweat Lodge

Fire, kǫ, and water, kóó, sacred elements necessary for survival, combined in ritual contexts to produce heightened spiritual experiences—most notably in the sweat lodge, where water was thrown over heated rocks to produce steam. Men routinely took sweat baths to maintain good health, although in an earlier time participation sometimes had specific religious purposes—for example, to bless one of the sacred medicine bundles or perhaps communicate with Owl.

Susagossa described the construction of the sweat lodge and preparation of the supplicants:

> We go down to the creek and gather willow trees. We get about sixteen of them. Of course, we clean the limbs and leaves off—just use the stick

alone. We put about six sticks on each of two sides and two on each of the other two sides. Make a hole in the middle and then bend the end sticks over and tie them together with strips of willow bark. . . . Then they put canvas or something heavy over it—make it real dark and with no air going out. They had a fire hole outside, and they put some hard rocks in it and put the cottonwood bark over them and make a fire to make the rocks as hot as they can.

About six men can go in. They are almost naked. A woman could go in if she could stand it. They use it if they have rheumatism. . . . They raise the front door and bring the hot rocks in and put them in the hole in the middle. They want it to be as hot as they can get it. . . . They have a bucket of water in there, and they put a dipper of water on the hot rocks. They protect their eyes and their faces, but they want their bodies to sweat as much as possible.[54]

Rose Chaletsin vividly described the men's tolerance of steam in the sweat lodge: "There's plenty of steam. The men put their heads on the ground. Their mouths are covered with something so they can breathe. The guys inside holler, and the man on the outside raises one side of the lodge to give them air. When they yell 'Put it down,' he puts it down. Then they pour some more water on the rocks."[55]

Sage, a medicinal and ritual herb, was an essential part of every sweat lodge ritual. Fred Bigman explained its use:

They use sage in the sweat lodge. They just take a bunch of this sage and hit it all over their bod[y]—arms, shoulders, back. That's the way them old Indians bathed. Used the sage like a washrag. Sage would be dry to start with, but your body would be wet from steam, and sage would get damp. Use this bunch of sage like you would use something to scratch on your back. Sage is better for this than other kind of weeds. . . . It's better 'cause it's good smelling.[56]

After an hour or more, when those who were sick had sweated out the sickness and the others had been weakened by the steam, the ritual was over. Rose Chaletsin advised: "Sweating this way is good for rheumatism. If you are sick, you sweat it out. Use it to help people. When they get through, they put buffalo robes on and run to the creek. The body be red, and they dive into the water. They get dizzy when they come out and fall all over and around. You got to stand it. Some of them can't stand it. Just a medicine man, they say, do these things."[57]

After describing the ritual's effect on the participants, Susagossa warned of disastrous consequences for anyone who bothered the abandoned willow frame:

They stay about an hour, and then they go around on the south side. They used to sit on buffalo hides, now they just use old quilts or something like that. They sit there to put their dry clothes on. When I see them they look like meat that has just been dipped in hot water—all gray and all. The woman comes along and takes away the quilts and canvas, but the frame of willows is left standing till it just falls down. They say if you bother the sticks you might get paralyzed.[58]

In summary, the Apache universe was conceptualized as a trilevel structure. On one level was the cosmos, the inhabited part, that became an orderly functioning universe as a work of the semidivine gods, Coyote—the culture hero—and his animal companions. The cosmos's origins were explained in a series of sacred myths that, once told, were considered absolute truths. The lower level was within the earth and within waters where reptiles, the water monster, moles, armadillos, and similar others could be found but that had no semblance of a Christian hell. The upper level of the universe, the uninhabited part, was the sky where the birds flew and the celestial spirits lived—the moon, the sun, the stars, and the gods: Great Spirit, Man-Up-There, Blue-White Man. The fact that the sky was eternal, of infinite height, and, for the most part, inaccessible to humankind was critically important in inspiring transcendent experiences.

Apaches communicated with the celestial spirits and nature spirits primarily on an ad hoc basis. Sometimes they directed prayer to a particular spirit or god, but at other times they prayed to an amorphous being or simply the sky. The celestial spirits were captured in symbols—the lunar, solar, and stellar designs on shields and tepees and the ubiquitous circle. The sacredness of the circle was enhanced by the inclusion of fire and tobacco that prepared Apaches for communicating with the supernatural and making critically important tribal decisions. Water was an important sacred element constantly sought for spiritual regeneration and therapeutic renewal. By showing respect for the sacred elements, sacred space, celestial spirits, and nature spirits, Apaches found harmony with their surroundings.

The supernatural in Apache everyday lives was incredibly pervasive, but the easily summoned Coyote with his often absurd antics helped everyone keep in touch with reality. Coyote was an ever-ready reminder to use one's own wits when possible and not depend exclusively on help from the supernatural.

Prayer on Top of the Earth

Medicine Bundles

The four tribal medicine bundles, addressed as *sitsoyan*, an Apache term for "four grandfathers," or *nὸ.bikágšé·Ái·*, a generic term meaning "prayer on top of the earth,"[1] served as the physical locus of tribal supernatural power. The term *soyan*, which regularly translates as grandfather, although strictly speaking it refers to either grandparent or grandchild,[2] added to *sit*, the number four, becomes "four grandfathers." With either term, the four medicine bundles can properly be viewed as the equivalent of the Kiowas' "ten grandmothers," or ten medicine bundles.[3] As objects of highest veneration, the bundles were visible symbols of transcendent power that could be invoked for assistance and protection when needed. In times of individual or tribal crises, the bundles were particularly important because they were believed to hold the power of good fortune. Apaches prayed to them for good health, safety on the warpath, good luck on the hunt, protection from the elements, and diverse kinds of material benefits. To increase the chances of a positive outcome, individuals would make a vow to undergo some difficult endeavor for the bundle or bring a gift to it.

In an emergency, prayers to the bundle were made in absentia. Susagossa told a story about her grandfather and a friend being pursued by a pack of white men's dogs. The men stopped running to pray to the power of the medicine bundle back home. The friend said, "We pray, make dogs go in a different way. I'm gonna make a vow. When we get back, I will put up a big tepee and give it to you [the bundle's power], and you use it for your medicine bag." Miraculously, the dogs went a different direction, and the two men were spared.[4]

The sacred bundles were in the custody of families from which one adult person was designated the "bundle-owner." Bundle-owners, by virtue of possessing such hallowed objects, were the most important persons in the tribe. They had prominent roles in ceremonies, functioned as the principal authorities and bearers of tribal traditions, and were the chief arbiters of disputes. Their advice was routinely sought by others on a variety of matters, and their judgments, once pronounced, were seldom, if ever, contravened.[5]

The ownership and transfer of ownership of a medicine bundle were regarded seriously. A bundle-owner took great care to bequeath the bundle to someone, preferably in the family, who had experienced a vision quest or had some supernatural experience so the bundle's potency and special powers would remain intact and be in the custody of someone who could effectively administer them. Some preference was found for passing medicine bundles to succeeding generations through the male line, but a family member who had not had a supernatural experience usually declined the responsibility of a bundle, in which circumstance the bundle would likely pass to someone from a closely related family.

Obtaining help and power from the bundles depended a great deal on observing the rules. Many rules surrounded the bundles, and if they were disregarded, bad luck could result. But most rules had a purpose, explained Joe Blackbear. Some ensured respect by prohibiting irreverent or unconventional behavior near the bundle—for example, no stirring anything with a knife, no whistling, and no playing hand games. A rule requiring that the bundle always be approached clockwise repeated a commonly followed procedure in all rituals. The rule requiring that a portion of any cooked meat in the bundle's presence be given to the bundle-owner not only showed gratitude but also provided payment to the bundle-owner for permitting access to the bundle. Another prohibiting the presence of pregnant women served mainly to safeguard mother and child from potent and unpredictable powers. Some rules, such as those stipulating that the bundle be touched only with the left hand and carried only under the left arm, did not have obvious rationales. Many rules were arbitrarily applied, often not pertaining to all participants all of the time and sometimes only to the family that possessed the sacred bundles.[6]

When the first thunder of the spring rains was heard, each medicine bundle was opened by the bundle-owner in a specially erected tepee, and the bundle's old cover was replaced with a new one of buffalo calf hide. According to Susagossa: "They save the old cover until the creek gets high and throw it into the water. They can't burn the old cover."[7]

Each of three bundles—Baby Medicine, or Rock Child Bundle;[8] and two named Water Medicine (which originally were one)—was passed around in the individual tepees so everyone present could touch it and cover it with a large piece of cloth to be assured of having a long life and happiness. The peace pipe followed, and green roots were placed on the central fire to create smoke, which everyone inhaled to ensure good health. As keeper of the bundle's story, the bundle-owner told it to all encamped, often embellishing and expanding the story to last all night. A feast was held and, when finished, everyone left, and the bundle-owner became available for individual requests.

Fred Bigman stressed the great care with which the cloth was handled:

You keep it on there four days. Take it off, fourth day. Anytime. I took one off this morning, and when you take it off just rub it on yourself four times, make motions toward ground, Mother Earth. Fold it. Put it up. Or you can make use of it someways. . . . Never throw it out or burn it. Just get 'em together . . . just tie it up and take it and tie it to a tree somewhere and let it rot. Not destroy or throw away or be laying around anywhere. Don't burn it.[9]

Throughout the year the bundle was available in the owner's tepee to persons on an individual basis, and it was approached with the same reverence, expectations, gifts, and vows. Its presence empowered the owner's tepee with a sacredness that could not be violated, and anyone in need of a refuge went to the bundle-owner's tepee where he or she was safe from harm.

With the passage of time, several of the stories faded from Apache memories, and bundle-owners with supernatural knowledge and power were in short supply. When a bundle was passed to someone without supernatural powers, the new owner refrained from opening it. According to Joe Blackbear, the last remembrance anyone had of a bundle being opened in public was by Apache John about 1925. Apache John was believed to have been the last owner who possessed the knowledge and power to open a medicine bundle and the last person to experience a vision quest.[10]

The Water Medicine Bundle was closely linked to sickness, and according to Alfred Chalepah, after it was opened at the sound of the first thunder in the spring, its owner told the Devil's Lake myth in an all-night ceremony. When finished, he took from the bag a piece of buckskin showing painted marks and added another mark to indicate that the story had been told again.[11]

As the Apaches became more scattered in the late nineteenth century, the original Water Medicine Bundle was split so everyone could have easier access to a bundle's powers. The four quartz rocks in the bundle were divided so two newly fashioned Water Medicine Bundles held two quartz rocks each.[12] Both bundles were believed to be particularly efficacious in treating illnesses, although one more than the other, and both were credited with numerous good works, such as swaying the legal system in an Apache's favor or changing the weather.

One version of the Devil's Lake myth recorded by McAllister in the 1930s and published in 1965, two versions recorded by Bittle in 1956 and 1959, and one by Brant in 1949 are similar structurally, differing only in minor detail. The basic premise in each was that diseases could be cured with the Water Medicine Bundle that derived power from the mythical lake. In McAllister's published version only smallpox was excluded from the diseases cured. In Bittle's version narrated by Ray Blackbear, four diseases—measles, smallpox, cancer, and tuberculosis—were designated incurable.[13]

Apaches believed white people had deliberately brought the incurable diseases that struck frequently and claimed many lives. Susagossa harbored a suspicion that white people's food was responsible:

> When white people came they give us new kind of food, and a lot of people get sick and die because we don't understand their food, and the worst thing they gave us was milk. Before, I eat meat and I'm healthy. My grandma, she don't like those days when white people come. Say the white people make us eat all these bad things, kill all our buffalo, keep us tied up all the time, can't move around. We all get sick and die. They don't have these sicknesses in the old days—just smallpox and chills and fever. But here lately they get TB, stomach trouble, liver trouble, kidney trouble. In the old days we don't fry nothing, just barbecue meat or dry it. Nowadays we eat like rabbits—have to eat all those vegetables.[14]

The Devil's Lake myth is a cultural variant of Orpheus, the classic Greek myth, in which Orpheus descended to the Land of the Dead in pursuit of his dead wife. He was allowed to take her back to earth providing he did not look back at her, but he failed and lost her forever and lost his own life as well. The Apache myth differs from the Orpheus myth mainly in being a vision quest (memorate) of Running-to-Meet-the-Enemy, who sought power from the mythical lake rather than the retrieval of a ghost wife.

The Apache Orphic hero sat by Devil's Lake four successive uneventful nights, followed by five nights of frightening visions. He sat stoically as all tests to discourage him failed. Even the ferocious water reptile failed to stir him. Having been put to the test and shown exemplary courage and fortitude, he was ready to proceed. The spirit-chief appeared and instructed him to throw four stones in succession into the lake. Running-to-Meet-the-Enemy did so, the waters parted, he stepped into the lake, the waters closed in on him, and a lodge appeared, which he entered.

Having arrived at the Land of the Dead, Running-to-Meet-the-Enemy's name changed to Running-Under-the-Water. He unknowingly broke a serious taboo when he declined to sit by four diseased men. As punishment, he was given medicine power to cure everything except the men's diseases—measles, smallpox, cancer, and tuberculosis. He was allowed to return to his camp until some future time when he would be called back. He made a medicine bundle and told his people to always ask for a blessing from the water when anyone was sick. He performed many miracles. He provided food for his people when they were starving and cured them during an epidemic. But one day a flock of geese circled overhead four times, which was a call for him to return to the lake. He went back into the lake. He never died, and he never returned. To memorialize him the Apaches picked up bits of debris along the shore of the lake and made the Water Medicine Bundle out of them.[15]

Among North American Indians the Orpheus myth was most common among hunting-and-gathering societies that were located in a band stretching from the eastern Great Lakes to the Northwest Coast, the same route the European westward expansion initially took. The myth was adopted by Indians in California, the Plateau, the Great Basin, the Northwest Coast, the northern Plains, and the Northeast. Brumbaugh argues that this pattern of distribution of the Orpheus myth reflected the worsening existential circumstances of American Indians after the European invasion when European diseases were introduced. He believes that because of these societies' relatively low populations and small sociopolitical units, they were unable to absorb epidemic stresses, and the adoption of the Orpheus myth helped them understand the rapid spread of decimating disease over which they had no control.[16]

According to Sam Klinekole, Apache elders often discussed parallels between the Devil's Lake myth and stories from the Bible, pointing out that as Jesus fed a multitude from a few fish and loaves of bread, so did Running-Under-the-Water produce a great quantity of food for his people. Jesus walked on the waters; Running-Under-the-Water went through them; and in both stories, waters parted.[17]

The Devil's Lake story was only to be told when it could properly be followed by prayer. Apache Ben Chaletsin, who, through an interpreter, told Brant one shortened version of it in 1949, assured his listeners: "It is not against the rules to tell this story. It should be told down over the generations. But you are supposed to pray at the end, and I am going to do that now." Apache Ben then prayed to Running-Under-the-Water and asked that people remember him and ask his blessing as they drank water. He said that now that he had told the story of the Water Medicine Bundle again, he hoped he would be forgiven if he had not been accurate in any way.[18]

The Baby Medicine Bundle, about the size of one's hand, was the smallest of the four bundles. It, too, had a buffalo calf hide cover but was always kept covered with a scarf.[19]

According to Fred Bigman, a special rule pertaining only to the Baby Medicine Bundle required that any visitor who slept in the same tepee or room with the bundle should place a symbolic bow and four arrows on his or her pillow for the night:

So anybody is sleeping in your room, you make four arrows, just from
common stick, you know, make bow. Just like little bow, it be small and
put about four arrows in it. Just any kind, matchstick or anything.
Whoever it be put it on his pillow. That's the rule that medicine has.
Like you be in there yourself, you sleep in that room with that medicine.
You put that bow and arrow under your pillow all night.[20]

Specifically prohibited in Baby Medicine's presence, Bigman emphasized, was the use of any kind of ball—a baseball, softball, basketball, or marble. The beating of a drum inside or on the west side of the tepee or house was also forbidden.[21]

At times, people who were truly desperate would visit all four medicine bundles, using the required procedures, and pray to invoke all the spirit powers in their behalf.

In 1961 Rose Chaletsin articulated a changing attitude of some Apaches toward the medicine bundles: "The people have stopped believing in the medicine bundles long time ago. After the old people died out, they [the others] just don't care for anything."[22]

According to Bittle, the bundle rituals became more secret as Christianization progressed so that eventually the stories required for opening the bundles had virtually been forgotten, and the proper inheritance of the bundles had become more difficult to accomplish because of a lack of interest, a conflict with the Native American Church, and the dying off of persons with ceremonial prerogatives.[23] Another factor undoubtedly was people's fear of the bundles. Often, persons who were next in line to have custody of a bundle wanted nothing to do with it for fear possession would bring bad luck.

Today, the four medicine bundles are one. In the period between 1925 and 1964 when no Medicine Bundle ritual was performed, three that were kept in the custody of various bundle-owners' families eventually could not be located. There was a general knowledge of who had them, but because of the bundles' unknown and unused powers, no one wanted to know too much about them. Poor Owl Bundle, the remaining one, after being opened in 1964 by a small group of families, is once again being given ritual care. Today it is opened in a regularly scheduled sacred ceremony.

For the handful of Apaches who participate in the revived Medicine Bundle ritual, the medicine bundle embodies the supernatural. Although the bundles may have lost their sacred meaning for some members of the tribe, they are respected by all, for they are important symbols of times past when Apaches enjoyed economic, religious, and political freedom. In Alonzo Chalepah's words, "The medicine bundles are solid and powerful indicators of the religious identity of the tribe."[24]

Birds and Spirits

Feathers

Birds, because of their flight, were especially important as supernatural symbols, and this importance was reflected in the ubiquitous use of feathers in rituals, in doctoring, and on the warpath.[1] Specific symbolic values were linked to a distinguishing characteristic or characteristics of particular birds, and Apaches believed that by association or possession they could be empowered with like characteristics. If certain bird feathers endowed them with extraordinary power, they could better defeat enemies, conquer illness, or be successful in the hunt.

Not everyone was entitled to wear or carry these visible symbols of power, but individuals who exhibited exceptional bravery, skill, leadership ability, or doctoring competence could possess fetishes, clothing, and regalia made of highly prized feathers or animal parts thought not only to impart supernatural power but also to convey honor and prestige. In Ray Blackbear's words, "If you really have the power, some of your friends will say, 'You have a right to wear that.' If his abilities are beyond the average man, he wears these to signify that he has that power, endurance, can do without water for two days or go without food for four days. Those things have to do with war times, with what they have to endure. Indians always had that. They could turn us loose in the mountains and I could endure it."[2]

The ritual use of bird feathers was central to Apache religious life. Particularly coveted were feathers of birds that possessed qualities of exceptional strength and endurance or displayed beautiful plumage. In general, utilitarian and flamboyant feathers from large birds were in greater demand than those from smaller birds. Feathers from birds that had anomalous characteristics, such as nocturnal owls and carrion-eating buzzards, however, were taboo. Rose Chaletsin explained the distinction between good and bad feathers:

> The Indians they raised with feathers, and they love it. They used all kinds of feathers, eagle, scissor-tail, water birds, parrot, pheasant, and others . . . any kind of feathers used for dressing up, just so it look pretty. Any kind of feathers from good birds were used for a fan. There's lots of good birds, not those little birds but those big birds, magpie—not no chicken hawk, buzzard, and owl.[3]

Ray Blackbear added: "The best feathers are taken in the fall. From May through August the birds begin to shed their feathers. In the fall you don't find a blemish on those feathers. Feathers in June or July look old."[4]

Eagle

The eagle, or ʔí-tšààh in Apache, Susagossa believed, was "the best bird in the world." Ray Blackbear especially admired it because it was a "clean bird that never ate foul meat."[5]

Morphologically, the eagle was ideally equipped to be the most powerful raptor of all birds. Its strong, curved talons to pierce, grasp, and kill; its large hooked beak for tearing flesh; and its proportionately long wings with which to glide and soar aloft many hours at a time, higher than any other living thing, gave it an extraordinary advantage over small animals and other birds on the ground. Once it sighted prey, it would plunge from the sky with lightning speed and impale it.

Eagles were highly prized not only for their exceptional physical capabilities but also because finding and killing them required a great deal of skill and bravery. Susagossa stressed that although occasionally eagles could be trapped by snares hidden under freshly killed small animals, most were difficult to catch because of the inaccessibility of their nests. Eagles built their nests at considerable heights—on cliffs, on rock ledges, or in tall trees where only the boldest climbers would go. To complicate the task further, the most opportune time to catch them was a few hours after dark while they were in a deep sleep.[6]

Never eaten, these powerful birds were killed for their feathers only. Rose Chaletsin described the carcass as particularly offensive: "It [the eagle is] like a person, it smells just like a person when it's dead."[7]

Eagle feathers were essential for the highest honors, the most sacred rituals, and difficult curing. The prized feathers from the tail were reserved for war bonnets and could only be worn by a war chief. According to Ray Blackbear, the wearing of the eagle war bonnet meant

> they couldn't be defeated. There are twelve feathers on the eagle's tail; some people go so far as to make war bonnets only out of the two center feathers. If you get enough center feathers for a bonnet, that means there's twelve or so eagles involved; you're a skilled man.
>
> Just the chiefs could use those tails on the bonnets. There's thirty or so altogether in a tailed bonnet, and that means fifteen eagles for the tail. It will take about twenty eagles altogether for the whole bonnet. You got seven months to hunt for the eagles. One bonnet represents about two years of hunting.[8]

Because of the supernatural aura surrounding the eagle, its feathers were required for distinctive ritual paraphernalia—the chief's peyote fan, the Manatidie Dancing Society staffs, and special doctoring tools.

A frequently used part of the eagle was the wing bone from which a whistle was fashioned. A whistle hole was cut approximately one inch from the end of the bone, and a stick was inserted to push out the marrow, after which it was "fixed with chewing gum." Rose Chaletsin remembered the whistle sounding "just like a bird that was used in the dances, the war dances. They used it at the peyote meetings at midnight and morning. If a woman is still in the house, she hears that whistle and comes with the water."[9]

Generally, eagle feathers "brought good luck and were used for everything." Specifically, Susagossa and Rose Chaletsin believed, eagle feathers transferred the special characteristics of the eagle to the wearer. On the warpath an eagle feather might be put on the horse's tail so the horse could go fast like an eagle. Or the eagle's down feathers were worn by those who wanted to move "light and easy," like down in the air. The beauty of the feathers was especially appreciated: "The bald eagle has good feathers—white as snow."[10]

Hawk and Falcon

The hawk and the falcon, like the eagle, also fed largely on other vertebrates. Rare birds that killed their own prey, these raptors were highly regarded for their cunning and endurance. Once prey was sighted, whether on the ground or in the sky, their attack was swift and fearless.

Many different kinds of hawks and falcons inhabited the Apache environment, but sighted most frequently were the swift hawk, or prairie falcon; the sparrow hawk, or kestrel, also a falcon; the red-shouldered hawk and the red-tailed hawk, both of which were sometimes called "chicken hawks"; the sharp-shinned hawk, known as the blue darter; and the black hawk. All were diurnal birds of prey except the nocturnal black hawk, and all were equipped with hooked beaks, curved talons, and acute vision, but their habitat and diet varied considerably.

The prairie falcon was called swift hawk, or "bird kills two at a time" in Apache. It was distinguishable from its close relative, the peregrine falcon, by different black markings and a paler color. Fiercely predatory, it fed on different kinds of birds, squirrels, rodents, and insects.

Morphologically, it was the most streamlined of the hawks. It had a bullet-shaped body with long, pointed wings and a long tail, which equipped it for swift flight. Swifter than the peregrine falcon at higher altitudes, it was judged to be capable of attaining speeds of 100–150 miles per hour in a vertical dive and of overtaking many birds that could escape it in ordinary straight flight. The swift hawk was particularly agile and skilled at killing prey and was known to seize prey from other predators in midair.[11] Apaches especially admired swift hawks because, in Ray Blackbear's estimation, "they're cunning, they're skilled, they're smart."[12] Swift hawk feathers were "supposed to have a unique power" and were used for fans and doctoring, especially those from the forked part of the tail, which were thought to impart cunning and were judged particularly efficacious in curing rituals.[13]

Other hawk feathers valued for curing came from the sharp-shinned hawk that lived both in the timber and on the prairie. A woodland hawk, which Apaches called "blue darter," had a rusty-barred breast and a distinctive black-striped bluish tail of twelve feathers. Ray Blackbear described its special use in doctoring: "They [Apaches] doctor with the tail. They put some perfume on it—cedar or something—and fan you with it and knock the bad spirits off you. They claim it's pretty effective."[14]

Although some Apaches did not care for feathers from "chicken hawks," the red-shouldered hawk and the red-tailed hawk, because their tail feathers were reputed to be "too rough" and "unclean," others judged the feathers to be pretty and appropriate for fans.[15] Feathers of "chicken hawks" were sometimes used, although not enthusiastically, even though the birds were raptorial and particularly adept at soaring—two commonly admired characteristics.

70

A Buteo-like hawk that hunts amphibians from perches along streams is the black hawk, variously referred to as bull bat, night hawk, thunderbird, and rainbird. Although a nocturnal bird, which Apaches found anomalous, the black hawk had special capabilities that transcended its negative nocturnal habits. Most notable, as the rainbird and the thunderbird, was its ability to make thunder, which Fred Bigman described as "a funny noise when it was going to rain," and lightning, "the great big old bird opening and shutting its eyes."[16] Ray Blackbear declared that the black hawk was too clumsy to have power and that the reason it was called "bull bat" was that "at the creation he was appointed to be thunder and lightning. He struck so many things that they took it away from him. He still has that notion, but he doesn't have the power."[17]

Some regarded the black hawk as a source of medicine power, a belief Susagossa conveyed in her account of a woman who acquired thunderbird power while mourning the death of her son. The woman, following the Apache mourning custom, cut her hair and slashed parts of her body:

> There was a big storm, and it was raining, and she was just walking and crying. And she said to the lightning, "If you want me, take me. I lost my boy. I'm ready to go."
> They say the lightning is a big bird with a long bill. And the lightning kept coming at her, trying to scare her.
> She kept saying, "Take me if you want to. I don't care."
> Finally this thunderbird . . . say, "All right, if I can't scare you, you can become great doctor. You can use my electricity to cure with."
> He said, "Your son be all right. Don't worry."
> Made her mind easy. She became big electricity doctor, and she could doctor people that were struck by lightning.[18]

Scissor-tailed Flycatcher and Woodpecker

Other birds with highly coveted feathers for doctoring were the beautiful scissor-tailed flycatcher and the woodpecker. The scissor-tailed flycatcher, a pale, pearly gray bird with sides and wing linings of salmon pink, made a striking appearance. According to Ray Blackbear and Fred Bigman, the long, streaming tail feathers were reserved for sacred purposes and were particularly prized for use in peyote fans, in which fifty or sixty flycatcher feathers were often used per fan. When the feathers "turn pink, they sure pretty. They turn in the fall. People get them . . . out there in the Wichitas . . . in mesquite trees. These feathers made only for one purpose, just for religious way, ceremony way. Past midnight at peyote meeting, use feathers, everybody gets their fans out."[19]

71

Not everyone had the skill to make a peyote fan because the tail feathers had to be bunched together in a special way before being wrapped with buckskin. Ray Blackbear detailed the process: "They bead the handle, put fringes on the buckskin . . . [and] they tie the feathers like they are on the bird originally. The way those feathers spread out, that shows how skillful they are. . . . Some men go as far as when they kill a bird, they can throw a feather out and they can put that feather right back where it came from just by looking at it."[20]

Other feathers strictly limited to doctoring came from two different woodpeckers, the yellow-shafted and red-shafted flickers. The Apaches called them "yellow hammers" and "red hammers" because of the hammerlike sound of their pecking bills but also referred to them as "yellow wing" and "red wing."

Yellow hammers were identified as flickers by flashing white rumps and a striking display of yellow feathers when in flight. Both sexes had a wide black crescent across the chest and a red nape patch; the male had black "whiskers." Particularly prized, Ray emphasized, were the yellow feathers with black tips:

> Apaches sure like those yellow hammer feathers. They come in two
> kinds of feathers—male and female. Their tail feathers are different.
> Male ones are notched at the ends and kind of reddish looking, and the
> female ones are [whole] and got little yellowish look. But now they
> don't allow us to shoot these or those scissor-tails. Their feathers are 5
> inches long and sharp on the end. They are yellow with black tips. They
> are sturdy and stiff.[21]

The fascination Apaches held for this bird's coloring and intelligence is revealed in the following story, narrated by Ray Blackbear, that tells how Yellow Hammer got the black color on his tail. The story also teaches Coyote the folly of trying to cross the boundary into the bird kingdom:

COYOTE VISITS YELLOW HAMMER: THE BUNGLING HOST

> Coyote was going along. Yellow Hammer had a camp, and he met
> Coyote and asked him to visit him there. Coyote went along with
> Yellow Hammer. Then Yellow Hammer said, "Come on in, Coyote, and
> visit with us." Coyote went inside.
> Then Yellow Hammer said, "Since you came to visit me, I'll treat you
> good and give you a nice dinner."
> He said to his wife, "Take that piece of dried buffalo hide outside and
> scrape it good. Take the scrapings that come off of it and bring them
> back inside to me."
> His wife did this and collected a whole pile of scrapings. Yellow
> Hammer turned these into dried meat.

Yellow Hammer said to Coyote, "Here, eat this meat." Coyote was watching very carefully. Then Yellow Hammer took a feather out of himself and stuck it up his nose. He said some words, and tallow came out of his nose, ran along the feather, and dripped on the meat.

Then Yellow Hammer said, "Here, eat this meat."

Coyote ate a lot of it. While he was eating, Coyote was looking at Yellow Hammer's children. They kept raising their wings up and then putting them down. Under their wings Coyote noticed a little red spot. "Hey," said Coyote. "Your children are on fire."

"No," said Yellow Hammer. "That's just their color."

A little later Coyote said again, "Hey, your children are on fire."

But Yellow Hammer answered, "No, that's just their color."

Coyote just kept saying this. Before he left, Coyote invited Yellow Hammer to visit him at his home.

When Coyote got home he told his wife and his children about the visit to Yellow Hammer. He told them about what had happened. Then he told his kids, "Before Yellow Hammer comes, you put some grass and some coals under your arms, and then do what I tell you."

When Yellow Hammer came to dinner, Coyote said, "I'm glad to have you. We'll find something good to eat."

Coyote told his wife to scrape a buffalo hide. Then Coyote put a stick up his nose and tried to drip tallow over the meat. But all that came out was blood. Coyote gave himself a nosebleed. Then Coyote told his kids to blow on the coals under their arms. The little Coyotes did this. But it didn't make a red spot at all. Instead, the little children all caught fire. The whole tent caught fire and began to burn down.

Yellow Hammer flew out through the smoke hole, but just as he flew out he got his tail singed. And that is why the Yellow Hammer still has a little black spot on his tail, even today.[22]

Red hammers differed from yellow hammers only in coloring. The red hammer had red wing and tail linings but no red patch on the back of the neck, and the male had red "whiskers" instead of black ones. Red hammer feathers were highly valued for ceremonial purposes but were rarely used because of their scarcity. Tail feathers from other woodpeckers had multiple uses and were used in peyote fans, on dance costumes, and on hunting paraphernalia.

Magpie, Roadrunner, and Pheasant

Other birds with feathers valued for ritual use, specifically for fans in the peyote ritual, were the magpie, a black-and-white land bird; the roadrunner, a large streaked cuckoo that often traveled on the ground; and the pheasant, a large, beautiful grouselike bird. All of these birds were uniquely colored and relatively rare.[23] The magpie, with its long, iridescent greenish-black tail, was considerably more abundant on the northern Plains where the Apaches had once located than in their present Oklahoma location. Consequently, most magpie feathers were transported from the north. Particularly scarce were the white-tipped tail feathers of the roadrunner, which may have contributed to the premium placed on their use in doctoring.

The pheasant, a bird that shed and renewed its long, sweeping tail feathers annually, was relatively more abundant. Feathers from the male, compared with those from the female, were spectacularly colored and highly prized for decorative and ritual use. A mystique emanated from pheasant feathers. As Rose Chaletsin recalled, "Sometimes the men would sit on their horse and fan themselves with the feathers. Maybe they would just sit there under a tree looking for another woman."[24]

Owl

Apaches mentally categorized birds and animals according to specific characteristics they deemed proper, and when something deviated from the accepted norm or had characteristics of two categories, it was anomalous and unacceptable for use. Anomalies formed the basis of many Apache taboos and were found throughout the animal and bird kingdoms. For example, birds of prey and scavengers could not be eaten—eagles, buzzards, owls, crows, bears, wolves, and coyotes. Animals or birds that were awake at night were clouded with superstition and taboos—for example, bats, owls, coyotes, and moles; and any birds or animals that were revolting to look at, smell, or touch, namely snakes, skunks, and owls, were considered true abominations.

Yet among the anomalous birds and animals, some were viewed ambiguously because of unique positive characteristics, such as owls, which were considered a source of wisdom or instruction. The owl, called isí·čì, an Apache word meaning "skull," was, according to Rose Chaletsin, one of the most feared of all animals and birds.[25] It had a large flattened face, large eyes that were open at night, enormous external ear openings, and "horns" (ear tufts common to some species of owls), which have engendered the names "devil" and "devil's bird." Possessing acute and discriminating hearing, the owl was adept at locating prey at night and could dart from concealment to swiftly render victims helpless. The fact that, unlike other birds, the owl was nocturnal was considered anomalous. This characteristic, added to its overall scary appearance, formed the basis for many owl taboos.

The presence of an owl was an ill omen and was regarded as a certain warning of impending disaster, in particular the death of a relative or friend. It also was credited with causing a variety of other misfortunes and was to be avoided if possible.

Yet although greatly feared, the owl was valued as a source of wisdom and a willing helper in such matters as assisting in locating missing relatives or horses and warning of approaching enemies. Those who could decipher the owl hoot "code" were summoned when there was a need to tap into this special knowledge. Ray Blackbear characterized the owl specialists as persons who "wore [owl] feathers, supposed to bring them good luck, and [were] immune from sickness and poison and death."[26]

Several accounts of the owl's uncanny abilities were told in sequential order by Rose Chaletsin and Susagossa. In the first account, Chaletsin declared:

> They're just like radar. They find out things. This Apache man learn
> that. The owl said, "The enemies gonna come at daybreak." He gave
> this man the smoke. He smoke and make a sweat tent. He took a gourd
> and made some signs. Then he sang some songs. Finally, the owl comes,
> and all the people surround the tent. There was sage in there, too. He
> was facing to the ground on this sage. This owl then brings the news. He
> say, "You all better move camp. The enemies coming." He tell them
> where to go. He points out a place to them. He say, "You better move as
> quick as daybreak." The medicine man understood what the owl was
> saying. Then he came out and told the news.[27]

In Susagossa's owl story, which follows, Owl helped find the lost horses:

> There was a man who understand owl talk. One day some horses were
> lost. There was one white one in the bunch. This man had a tepee. He
> got a bunch of men in there—no fire, nothing. He tell them to cover
> their heads.
> Man holler, "Owl!"
> They hear owl on top of tepee around smoke hole, hear him scratch-
> ing around up there, hear him come in, take a deep breath, and rest.
> The man say, "We gonna give you smoke. You smoke and tell us
> where the horses are."
> Owl hoot four times, then say, "Horses are way over there at mountain
> foot."
> Owl lead them to foot of mountain. He fly a little way and wait in
> tree for them to catch up. They found the horses—they were all
> hobbled. There was one white horse with them.[28]

Whether owl news was good or bad appeared to depend a great deal on a person's state of mind, as Rose Chaletsin explained:

> If a real owl comes down when they are dancing, it brings the bad news
> or the good news, either way. Some hear it and some don't. When a
> person hear it, if he's got a good heart and a good mind, he'll talk to it.
> He might say, "Well, he's bringing good news." But if he's got a bad

mind, first thing he thinks the other way. It's just a bird. I wouldn't be afraid of it. But it really scares you. You know it's one bird that's bad. People who got weak minds or nervous, it gets them.[29]

Susagossa warned that an owl with witching powers was capable of inflicting a paralytic stroke on anyone: "The owl scare you and witch you. That's why some . . . are crippled. They have stroke. Louise's boy was OK when he was little, but he seen an owl in the garage after his daddy died, and it twist his arm and eye and leg. They took him to Indian doctor and white doctor. They fix his eye and leg but couldn't do nothing for this arm he got twisted."[30]

Rose Chaletsin reiterated this fear, stating that Apaches were "afraid to be out at night and hear it. They think it got bad spirit and witch you. They say sometime he throw at you with some kind of root. If it hit you, it paralyze you."[31]

Owls could be repelled by a variety of means—loud noises, smoke from the burning of grease and rags, and placing one's shoes wrong side out in front of the tepee. All owls were feared, including the barn owl and the screech owl, but the white owl, with its yellow eyes, declared Susagossa, was the "worst of all."[32] Owls were never eaten and owl feathers never used except by the Tlintidie, the Contraries Dancing Society.[33]

Buzzard and Crow

The vulture, or "buzzard," was considered a true abomination. Although it possessed many of the admired physical characteristics of the eagle, it lacked the important strong talons needed for killing live prey and so subsisted on the bodies of dead creatures, eaten fresh or in various stages of decomposition. Apaches, according to Rose Chaletsin, called them čìdĭč ìs, a word meaning "raw chapped head" or "eats rotten things."[34]

In the "Fire Boy and Water Boy" story in Chapter 3, Buzzard acquired a bald head as punishment for his disgusting habit of eating rotten victims. Ray Blackbear called the buzzard "a condemned bird" because it was uncouth and revolting to look at. Furthermore, Susagossa added, "When he sees humans, he always pukes."[35]

Everyone was also repulsed by another carrion-eater, the gregarious crow. Rose Chaletsin warned, "You don't go off, or a big bird with long claws may grab you and peck on your eyes and on your throat and feed you to her little ones, so we afraid of crows."[36] Crow's transformation to carrion-eater is discussed in Chapter 6.

But crows, stated Ray Blackbear, were given some respect because they "ate fresh meat, and they early bird—always out hustling." Also, their feathers were valued for repelling owls.[37]

76

A Coyote story, narrated by Ray Blackbear, explains why Crow's color is black. In the very beginning, when Coyote was making bylaws for the universe, White Crow wondered if his color was all right. Coyote answered, "No!" and threw a rock in the pond to determine what color Crow should be. Coyote declared that if the rock sank, Crow had to be black. The rock sank.[38]

Crane, Egret, and Goose

Two other birds Apaches avoided were the crane and the egret, both, in Rose Chaletsin's estimation, white birds with "bad spirits." An all-over white animal or bird was often equated with a ghost. Ray Blackbear described the scary ghost effect of the crane: "The crane was bad. At nighttime they scare you. Person that sees that gets sick. It stands there like a man—you get a stroke like with owl. Apaches don't use them for anything—just like buzzard."[39]

The egret also looked like a ghost, Susagossa believed: "When you see the egret way off, look like man with white sheet. When you go after them they keep walking backward. They keep going and you get lost. They got bad spirit."[40]

The white goose was perceived more favorably, both feared and admired. The fear stemmed from its mythological association with one of the sacred medicine bundles. Ray Blackbear explained, "People are afraid of this bird. . . . They carry superstition with them from Devil's Lake area. They seem to carry some power about man that went back into the lake alive."[41]

The power associated with the goose was medicine power, and the medicine man, Piyeh, who lived in the late nineteenth century, had goose power. In the 1940s Joe Blackbear gave this account of how Piyeh acquired and used goose power:

> Piyeh said he was fasting, up on top of the hill. The geese came and spoke to him. They gave him the medicine and told him how to care for it. The geese said that they always lived in water and never got sick from it. They said they were giving him the medicine to cure sickness in which the belly was all swelled up with water.
>
> Piyeh began his goose power doctoring ritual with the singing of a special goose song. He then opened his medicine bundle, pulled out a goose bill, and punctured the patient's belly and legs to drain away the infection. His goose medicine cured the sickness.[42]

Many admired the goose because, Ray Blackbear believed:

> It had to travel from Canada to the Gulf of Mexico. They [the Apaches] think of it with endurance or power. They eat them but don't use the feathers. Apaches always had a special relationship with geese. Whenever the Indians saw the geese, they would sing one word over and over, and the geese would make a V formation even if they were flying in

some other formation. Then the Indians would change the tune a little bit and say the same word, and the geese would turn and circle four times. This meant that their prayer had been answered. Someone in the camp would always get credit for saying this and for making the geese circle that way. But nowaday all that power is gone. I tried that last week, but it didn't work at all.[43]

Geese, if appropriately petitioned, were also believed to be capable of causing rain to fall, as they do in Chapter 9 as a result of a rain dance ceremony conducted by the medicine man Dävéko. He synchronized the dance ceremony with the flight of the geese. After the fourth day of the rain dance, the rains came.

Whippoorwill and Meadowlark

Another bird possessing a taboo characteristic, that of being nocturnal, but which was regarded favorably was the whippoorwill, or "medicine woman bird," as the Apaches called it. The whippoorwill, which had the distinctive habit of singing "vespers" with clocklike regularity every evening, was enshrouded with mystique. Harking back to his childhood, Fred Bigman remembered "its beautiful song, sure sound good. You listen to that bird at night, and you sleep tight. They put you to sleep, they say."[44]

Ray Blackbear added that an opposite interpretation was made when an imitation of the whippoorwill's song was believed to drive one's horses away.[45]

The whippoorwill's punctual, appealing song may have had something to do with the very old belief, which Rose Chaletsin articulated, that whippoorwill feathers were an aphrodisiac: "Way back, one thousand years or more, medicine man use this on a woman. Then when a man want a woman, he get that medicine."[46]

The yellow-breasted western meadowlark, identifiable by its beautiful flute-like, gurgling, and double-noted song, was esteemed, according to Ray Blackbear, for its ability to "whistle out words in Apache, especially in fall. That's an old bird—been here as long as Apaches."[47] So clear-throated was the meadowlark, stated Joe Blackbear, that a mother "took the head and rubbed it on a baby's lips to make the baby talk plainly when it began to talk."[48]

Prairie Chicken, Quail, and Turkey

Of the various fowllike wild birds that were part of Apache diets, the most important were the prairie chicken—although sparse in number—quail, and turkey. The prairie chicken, a native grouse, had the most distinctive behavior of the three, which probably explains why its feathers were in demand for curing. During mating season the males congregated on hereditary dancing grounds to strut, dance, and wage battles to establish dominance. The ritual in which they inflated their colorful neck pouches and expelled the air with a characteristic "boom" created a spectacle.

The Apaches felt endearment for the quail, a small bird with little feathers that, according to Rose Chaletsin, were used mainly on small arrows.[49] The quail's special status was established with its role in this story, which Joe Blackbear narrated:

COYOTE AND QUAIL

One day a long time ago, Coyote went somewhere to look for something to eat. He went down along the creek and met Quail. Coyote said to Quail, "Brother, where are you going?"

Quail replied, "Well, I'm going out West to look for something to eat."

Coyote said, "Me too. I'm looking for something to eat. I'm just going down to the creek. I want something that has meat on it. That's what I'm looking for."

Then Coyote said, "Brother, what's your name? I've known you a long time, but I don't know your name."

Quail answered, "No, I haven't any name."

But Coyote said, "Well, everybody's got a name. You're lying to me. Even I've got a name. I don't cheat people, but that's what they call me. When I was a boy they gave me the name 'Cheat People.' They just call me that. Actually, I don't believe you because I think you've got a name."

And that time Quail answered back, "Well, I'm a small bird, but I don't know how the people got this idea, but they call me Scare People."

And Coyote said, "You got a bad name."

"Yeah," said Quail, "I don't scare anybody, but they just call me that."

Then Coyote pushed Quail's head. "Sure, you got a bad name," he said, "and I want you to scare me now."

But Quail said, "No, I didn't scare any people. They just call me that."

Pretty soon Quail said, "Well, I'm going up the creek to look for something to eat. You go along, too." So Quail started up the creek, and Coyote started down the creek. Quail looked back and saw that Coyote had gone over a little hill, and Quail flew right ahead of him, and he lay down there in the grass, close to a high bank where the road passed it. He lay there real quietly in the grass. And then Coyote came along, and he was singing some song. All at once Coyote started to holler and was making fun of Quail. He walked along and didn't notice Quail. Well, all at once Quail flew up at Coyote, and Coyote got so scared that he jumped and fell down in the creek. He laid there for quite a while, like he was dead.

Quail said, "Coyote. So you know it now. That's why they called me 'Scare People.' Now you found that out."

And Coyote said, "Yeah, sure enough, you'd better go away 'cause as soon as I come to myself, I'm sure going to kill you."

And that Quail, he just went on laughing and laughing.[50]

The turkey was one of the most utilitarian of the wild birds. Its many uses, which Rose Chaletsin and Susagossa enumerated, included a food source; feathers for brooms, fans, arrows, and headdresses; and bones for children's rattles and other toys. White turkey feathers were highly valued because they could pass as eagle feathers if their tips were dyed black.[51]

The turkey had never been perceived as a medicine bird, but it was a popular character in the folklore. In one tale Ray Blackbear told, Turkey overcame incredible odds and killed two eagles with his stiff shoulder feathers.[52] Another of Ray Blackbear's stories about Turkey, which follows, is called a charter myth because it explained the origin of a tribal custom, the Apache practice of self-mutilation in response to the death of a relative:

TURKEY ESCAPES FROM COYOTE

Coyote was going along. He saw Turkey in the woods, but Coyote knew that he couldn't catch him by trying to outrun him, so Coyote pretended that he hadn't seen him at all. Coyote came near, and Turkey froze.

Then Coyote said, "That looks a little like a turkey over there, but I think it's just a burned stump." He said this loud enough for Turkey to hear him.

Turkey said, "Huh, Coyote thinks I'm just a burned stump."

Coyote moved a little closer and said, "That looks a little like a turkey over there, but I think it's just a burned stump."

Again Turkey said, "Huh, he thinks I'm a burned stump."

Three times this happened, and each time Coyote got a little closer to Turkey. Finally, he got so near that he could grab him, and he did.

"I've got you now," said Coyote.

Turkey answered, "Yes, you've got me now."

Coyote said, "I could eat you right here, but I don't want to. I want to have you fixed in a special way and eat you then."

Coyote let Turkey go for a second. Then he said, "You go home to my camp and tell my wife that I sent you. Tell her to kill you, pluck you, and fix you up nice and then to cook you."

"All right," said Turkey, and he went over to Coyote's camp.

But he said to Coyote's wife, "Coyote sent me here. He said to tell you to kill your youngest child and fix him up nice. Then you should cook him real good."

Coyote's wife was angry and said, "Oh, that crazy man. What is he going to do next?"

But she obeyed her husband as she was supposed to, and she killed her youngest child, fixed him up, and cooked him. Coyote came home that evening and saw the cooked meat and ate it. He ate his own child.

Then Coyote said, "Where is the baby?"

Coyote's wife said, "You're eating him."

She told him what had happened and what Turkey had told her. Coyote got angry and said, "Why didn't I eat Turkey while I had him in the woods?"

Coyote ran out of the camp and rushed into a patch of briars. He let the briars cut him all up to punish himself. When he did this, he set an example for the Indians. Now, when a loved one dies the Indians cut themselves with knives and sometimes chop off their fingers, just so they can hurt themselves. It makes them feel better.[53]

The true indicator of the turkey as kindred was its role in at least one version of the hand game story. In the final episode of the hand game, after the animals and humans had successfully separated from the monsters, Turkey placed the hand game sticks in his boots. The sticks became small bones, hence the origination of Turkey's "extra" leg bones.[54]

Dove and Hummingbird

Two birds with no economic or supernatural role but that were part of the Apache kindred were the dove and the hummingbird. Because the dove always had a mate, explained Rose Chaletsin, "like a man and woman can't part and are always together," it symbolized faithfulness.[55] The hummingbird had an Apache name Ray Blackbear translated as "flies through the rock. That's how fast he is. He's fast enough to fly through rock. They're the only bird that I know that can fly backward."[56]

Other birds of negligible supernatural importance were the swallow, robin, and blue jay. Sometimes their colorful feathers were used decoratively, but the birds were considered too small to eat.

Embedded in Apache culture was an affinity for birds that was rooted in ancient time when birds could speak the human language. Many birds were admired, especially the larger ones with beautiful plumage that were relatively rare. Those that exhibited strength, cunning, endurance, and intelligence were highly prized because the bird's positive characteristics were believed to be transferable to the possessor of its feathers. When Apaches adorned themselves with important feathers and congregated for major ceremonies and minor rituals, the embellishment and symbolization transported supplicants to a sacred realm.

Animals
and Spirits

Spirit Orchestration

Prior to the mid-nineteenth century, the abundance and diversity of wild animals inhabiting the Great Plains and its environs for the most part assured the Apaches of a relatively carefree existence. Although many animals were feared and avoided, others on which the tribe depended most for survival were in plentiful supply. To actively pursue and lure some animals while avoiding others, in a world where "some animals have more power than we do," required prudent supernatural orchestration.[1] Apaches endeavored to accomplish this by scrupulously observing taboos, performing required rituals, and, above all, treating the animals with respect. In return, the beneficial animals offered their bodies and valuable powers, and the anomalous animals and their harmful spirits rendered themselves innocuous. Together, Apaches believed, they and the animals could cure disease, share in abundance, and preserve the Indian way of life.

Buffalo

This relationship was most strongly marked with the buffalo, the prey that furnished most of the Apaches' food, shelter, clothing, and tools. Numbering in the multiple millions on the Plains, at least from the mid-sixteenth century,[2] the buffalo was never far from Apache wanderings, even during winter months when its distribution was erratic and its numbers varied. After 1850, however, when droves of white men crossing Indian territory began wholesale decimation of buffalo herds, prolonged periods of buffalo scarcity became increasingly frequent, and the entire tribe faced starvation.

Exactly when and how Apaches first encountered the buffalo is uncertain, but according to folklore, tricky Coyote, disguised as a puppy, found and retrieved the buffalo from Crow's possession. Selfish Crow, who lived in a tepee (a human abode) and spoke the human language, hid all of the buffalo for his own use. Coyote spied Crow retrieving buffalo meat from a concealed opening under his fireplace, so when Crow and his wife left the tepee, Coyote entered and freed the buffalo. In the middle of the escape Crow returned and began throwing rocks in an effort to stem the tide, but Coyote took cover under one of the fleeing buffalo and saved himself. Crow lost his human status because of greediness (a personal failing), and Coyote condemned him to a life of living in the brush and eating carrion (both living crow characteristics).[3]

Apaches prudently utilized the seasonal supply of buffalo, which virtually ensured an abundant food supply. After a successful kill, members of the tribe moved quickly and thoroughly to use every part of the animal. The veins were often opened, and blood was drawn from them and ingested on the spot. The udders of the cows were slashed and the milk sucked out. Entrails and other organs were eaten raw. The warm liver and kidney in particular were coveted as delicacies believed to impart the strength of the buffalo, and the tripe was an important digestive aid. Ray Blackbear explained the benefits: "That one with leaves in it [tripe], Indians wash every part of it clean. They eat that raw. The taste or ingredients or whatever you call it helps your digestive system the same way as liver or kidney. . . . Because it's inside the animal, if it is taken raw it'll go to your insides, and they'll correspond the same way, and you're naturally going to gain health."[4]

A medicine man, if present, was certain to exercise his prerogative to consume the first portion of raw parts, after which other persons at the kill joined in. Depending on the plentifulness of the tribe's food supply, a portion of buffalo was cooked for immediate consumption, and the remainder was dried and stored in rawhide bags for future use. Meat was the mainstay of the diet and was eaten throughout the year either dry, boiled, or mixed with fat and berries as pemmican.

The exalted importance of pemmican, or pounded meat, to the Apaches is communicated in a Coyote story with pounded meat in the central role. Ray Blackbear's story tells how anthropomorphic Wildcat and Coyote trick and get tricked:

COYOTE AND THE BALL OF POUNDED MEAT

This is a story about pounded meat. The old-time Indians used to get tallow, and they would mix it with pounded meat and make it into a ball. They usually carried the tallow around in sheets, in a parfleche, and they would take it out, pound it up fine, and mix it with meat and something sweet to make this ball out of it. The little kids ate this kind of thing like a snack.

This meat ball was rolling along one day. Coyote came along, and Coyote said to the ball, "Hey, where are you going?"

Meatball answered, "Oh, I'm going out East. I'm going down this way."

Coyote said, "Well, I'm glad to see you. But before you go I'd like to take a little nibble out of you. I want to get my hands greasy so I can rub my arrows with the grease."

"Go ahead," said Meatball, "take a little bite."

So Coyote took a little bite. Then Meatball started to roll off again. Coyote said, "Wait. You'll probably run into more Coyote-Men like me. There are a lot of them out there where you're going."

Meatball said, "Oh, thanks for the tip."

Coyote took off and went out ahead of Meatball. Finally, Meatball came along again. Coyote said, "Hello, I'm glad to see you. Where are you going?"

Meatball said, "Oh, I'm going out East."

Coyote said, "Before you go, let me take a little bite of you. I want to grease my arrows."

Meatball said, "Go ahead. Take a good bite." So Coyote did. Then Meatball went on his way, and again Coyote ran out ahead of him. They met again.

Coyote said, "Hello. Let me take a bite out of you so I can grease my arrows."

Meatball was beginning to get kind of suspicious about this, but he said, "All right, go ahead. Take a big bite."

So Coyote took a great big bite out of Meatball. Then Coyote ran off again.

Meatball was still pretty suspicious. He wondered if Coyote was telling the truth. He argued with himself about this. But then he went on his way again. Pretty soon he met Coyote again. Coyote said, "Well, hello there. How about letting me take a bite out of you so that I can grease my arrows?"

But Coyote had such a full stomach by this time that he was getting tired. He yawned, and Meatball saw that little pieces of meat were sticking to his teeth. Meatball said, "Well, I'm going to fix him."

So Meatball went off a little way and called back, "You're the same Coyote-Guy. You're not following me any more."

But Coyote said, "I'm going to get you and eat you entirely up."

Coyote chased as fast as he could, and Meatball rolled as fast as he could. Finally, Meatball came to a little pond and jumped in. Coyote couldn't follow him. So Coyote built a fire right there and piled rocks in the fire. When they were hot, he threw them in the pond. Soon the water got hot, and Meatball began to melt. The tallow floated to the top, and Coyote started to taste it. He said, "Boy, that's good. It tastes like soup, but it's too hot to eat now. I'm going to take a rest first."

So Coyote lay down and went to sleep. Wildcat came up there and saw what had happened. He picked up the grease with his big spongy paws and ate all of the grease off the top of the pond. He just left the water. Then he took off but left greasy paw marks.

Coyote woke up and said, "Oh, that was a good rest. Now I can have some soup." But he saw that there was nothing left. "What happened here?" he said. "Someone has double crossed me." Coyote went around and saw the tracks of Wildcat. He said, "I'll fix him."

So Coyote went off to look for Wildcat. When he found him, Wildcat was asleep. So Coyote pulled out Wildcat's ears, pressed his face into a little ball, stretched out his body and his legs. When Wildcat woke up, he went home. But his children were afraid of him and said, "You aren't our daddy."

Then Wildcat knew what had happened, and he went out to find Coyote. When he found him, Coyote was asleep. So Wildcat pulled on Coyote's nose, pushed his body up short, pulled out his legs, and put a bushy tail on him. And that's how both Wildcat and Coyote got to look like they do today.[5]

Buffalo hide, bones, hooves, horns, and sinew had myriad practical uses. As clothing, buffalo hide was particularly valued for use in protective robes and boots in the winter. As shelter, the hides were sewn together to make tepees. The bones were used for tools, the dewclaws for rattles, the horns for racks to hold things, and the sinew for sewing, rope making, and strings on bows.

The herding instinct of the buffalo made an indelible imprint on Apache minds and inspired the annual Buffalo Dance in which men in ceremonial dress sought to imitate the movements of the buffalo. The dance was originally performed in the summer in conjunction with the Scalp Dance or another ceremony, but with time it grew in popularity and now is danced year-round. According to Ray Blackbear:

> They call it the Buffalo Dance because they grouped like buffalo. They imitated buffalo. They get in a herd and dance around the drum. They dress up for the Buffalo Dance. It's the same as for the other dances. They wear the best they got. This is more of a man's dance. The warriors all dance, shoot their guns and holler. . . . The Buffalo Dance is mostly like a War Dance. It's a special dance for various men of combat and their relatives.[6]

The buffalo, which is difficult to kill, symbolized endurance. Choice buffalo, the yearlings and two-year-olds, demonstrated a stamina that even the ablest men in the tribe with the fastest horses had difficulty matching. Apaches, explained Ray Blackbear, believed buffalo body parts could transmit endurance: "They believe the buffalo has a tremendous living power, similar to a Brahma. They can endure a whole lot. They're hard to kill. That buffalo got that endurance, and the Indians believe that by taking part of that [buffalo body parts], that they get some of that power—that they will possess that power to a certain extent. You admire someone who has that power."[7]

Buffalo fur, horns, hooves, and the tail, perceived as conveyors of sacred power, were used ceremonially to increase the effectiveness of buffalo curing; and the buffalo eye in particular had empirical efficacy in healing old sores that had not responded to other treatments. Rose Chaletsin detailed the procedure:

> They busted the eyeball, just like glass. In the middle there is a black spot, the pupil. . . . They take it out. . . . They use the rest of the eye, the clear part, they bust it and clean it. They spread it out flat with a stick and put it in the sun and let it dry, just like meat. When it's dry they turn it over. It gets real thin. They get rawhide and pound and crumble the eyes on it. They pound it fine as they can pound it. They use it for old sores—the ones that won't heal. They mix it with a little fat that has been warmed and put it on the sores. Some people use it for children when they got sores. They never ate the eyes.[8]

Buffalo curing power was deemed formidable and could only be acquired in a vision quest. Medicine men with buffalo power held some of the most privileged positions in the tribe because they possessed the most powerful medicine. Susagossa described the transfer of buffalo power:

> The buffalo is a medicine man. . . . Indian medicine man use it [buffalo power] to doctor with. They go out on prairie all alone seven or eight

days without drinking water or eating. Buffalo pity them and show them what to do. They don't drink water or eat or sleep. They learn something. They think about something, and that's the way they get the power. They suffer for it. Buffalo know what they want and comes up and breathes in their face. Then they got power. When they give this medicine, they give him ride back to his home.[9]

Some Apaches, including Susagossa, believed buffalo medicine was powerful enough to protect warriors from bullets: "The buffalo say, 'I gonna give you this medicine, this power, this knowledge.' You could put this medicine on boys if goin' to the warpath. If boys go to warpath and be in a big fight [and] bullets coming all around. If bullet come and hit him, it just turn flat and fall off."[10]

Prudent hunters took care to mollify the spirits of a freshly killed buffalo to keep the animal from using its medicine power for witching. Especially important, Joe Blackbear warned, was not walking in front of the animal for fear of being inflicted with a hemorrhage. If witched by a buffalo, the victim could only be cured by a medicine man with buffalo power.[11]

The awe-inspiring rare white buffalo was perceived as the ultimate possessor of power. Judged always to be the leader of the herd, it was never to be killed.

In Apache the bull buffalo is called à·há, which literally translates as "big butt" but also has an opposite meaning, "minus the butt." Ray Blackbear explained: "You know, he's got big shoulders and then he tapers down. [The name is] like the Tlintidie,[12] men who do things in reverse. In this case somebody turned it [the buffalo name] around."[13]

Reverse naming was a practice prescribed by the Tlintidie, or Contraries Dancing Society, for the oldest and bravest men in the tribe. Likewise, reverse naming of the buffalo was an added marker of its special status.

Warnings against excessive human familiarity with powerful animals, in particular the buffalo and the bear, were embedded in Apache folklore. Birds, animals, and humans that crossed or attempted to cross each other's boundary lines did so at their peril, a message reiterated in various stories of forbidden sexual practices, including bestiality. In every account of bestiality, either the animal or the human met a tragic end, and often the tragedy was compounded by a series of other deaths or disasters. The earlier Pleiades myth about a Bear-Girl, descended from human parents, and a Man-Bear illustrates the retribution that could be exacted when rules were disregarded. Not only was the Man-Bear killed, but the Bear-Girl, after being transformed into a total bear, killed everyone in her camp—including her parents—with the exception of one sister.

The following story, which Ray Blackbear narrated, has a similar message about a foolish woman who unwittingly found herself with a buffalo husband. The story ends with the death of the buffalo:

WOMAN WHO ADMIRED THE BONE

Women admire a lot of things, like bracelets and horses, anything that catches their eye. Away back, when the earth was still soft and soggy, a woman went out to get water one day. She came from a big camp. She saw a bone sticking out of the ground; it was kind of shiny. It was a buffalo bone. She admired it very much and said, "Sure is pretty. If it were a man I'd marry it. That's how much it appeals to me."

The next morning she went again to the spring, and a young man was standing there. He was dressed up good. She blushed. The man said, "Remember what you said yesterday about that bone."

The woman said, "Yes."

The man said, "Well, that was me. Here I am."

So the woman didn't hesitate, and they went off together. The woman just left her kettle there at the spring.

On the fourth night, they came to where the man belonged. There was a big herd of buffalo. He got into the middle of the herd and took her with him. She was sorry that she had admired that bone and cried every day. The buffalo milled around. She cried and wanted to get away.

Then she heard a voice, and it said, "What is the reason you cry every night?"

The woman said, "I made a mistake when I admired a piece of bone. It turned into a man and then turned into a buffalo. He's real mean. He kills yearlings that come around me."

This voice was a mole. Mole said, "I'll help you." So Mole dug a tunnel past the buffalo and dug it real long. He dug under the woman. She fell into the hole and crawled through the hole. When Buffalo came back, he missed her. He ran around and got mad. He killed a lot of other buffaloes. Then he found the hole and dug at it with his horns. He followed her.

She got pretty far away. Then Mole said, "Now, you can go afoot." The woman started running. Buffalo got her scent, though, and took out after her. She saw him.

Soon she came to an elm tree. Elm Tree said, "What's the matter? Why are you crying?"

The woman said, "That buffalo, my husband, is going to kill me."

But Elm Tree said, "It's not that bad. Climb up here, and I'll help you."

The woman climbed up. Buffalo came along and hit that tree and began to tear off the bark with his horns. His horns had turned into iron. Little by little, he tore at the tree and whittled the bark away. It began to totter.

The woman said, "What are you going to do now?"

Elm Tree said, "Let him wear himself out."

So Buffalo hit the last time, and the tree suddenly grew together again and caught his horns there. Then Elm Tree said, "Now get down. Don't be afraid of him."

All this time that buffalo had some kind of magic, a power, that made him like iron. He had told the woman earlier that he could only be killed at the soft spot above the clavicle. So the woman remembered this and killed him there.

Then Elm Tree said, "Don't ever admire anything like that again."

Things that people admire don't always turn out the way they expect.[14]

Two similar stories of bestiality in which a woman crossed the human/ animal boundary and married an animal or a reptile also ended in disaster. In one, the woman who married a stallion was killed by her human husband. In the other story, the snake a widow married was killed by children in the camp.[15]

Horse

Another hoofed animal, the domesticated horse, had an economic importance equal to that of the buffalo, not as a major food source but as a superior means of mobility. Before the horse, when men hunted on foot, animal foods were scarce and extremely difficult to procure. But with the acquisition of the horse, food and trading items became more plentiful and accessible, and Apaches were able to dramatically increase their quality of life.

Two narratives in the folklore, related later in this chapter, tell how Apaches obtained horses. One, which is part of the "Fire Boy and Water Boy" story, is a transformation story that relates how the culture heroes changed into moles to capture a wild horse and replace the horse's evil eye, which had been killing people, with a good eye. From that point forward, the horse became gentle and useful. In the second story Bear, as a possessor of medicine, guided Apaches to horses.[16]

Apaches mentally linked the horse with storms, the violent form of celestial waters, and they believed the horse possessed the power to dissipate a storm or at least keep it at bay. Susagossa spoke of the enormous power of the horse:

This Kiowa woman told me about a storm. She said if there was a storm coming, just talk to it. 'Cause they think the storm belong to the Indian. There was a horse over there and they say, "What we gonna do with this horse? Seems like every time the horse breathes, sparks come from his nose."

And one man say, "Well, I'll make him breathe harder." And he blew at the horse, and the horse just got stronger. And the horse went up in the air and his mane just was standing up.

They said to the horse in the air, "Well, when you see us Indian people, just pity us. Don't blow away our tepees."

That's why some Indians think when they see a storm cloud they see a horse. . . . And they just talk to it, and it goes on by.[17]

Gray and white horses in particular were believed to be imbued with power over storms and therefore were not eaten on the rare occasions when horses were consumed. Rose Chaletsin pointed out that in later times the taboo on eating a white horse was disregarded:

On a pretty day like this, if some horses are running around, some people say the horses are making a sign. There will be a big snow, bad weather. But in summertime it means lightning and thunder. One thing, the Apaches don't eat white or gray horses. It's a sign about the storms. That's why they don't eat them. Now we eat the white horse but not the gray horse, even now. You see, the black and the white horse are the ones that jump at each other before a storm."[18]

According to the oral history of the Cheyennes, Apaches got horse power from sacred Bear Butte in the Black Hills.[19] Horse power was used to cure sick horses or persons who had been witched by a horse. Any person who mistreated a horse could expect to be witched. And then, Datose maintained, only the services of a medicine man could help: "They say if a horse kick you or run over you, they might witch you. That's what Indians believe. That's what my grandpa tell me. . . . A horse could witch you if you make it mad. That's why you have to get a doctor to doctor you."[20]

The importance of the horse was conveyed by a strict decorum Apaches followed in decorating it. Handprints were placed on the neck, and crescents, circles, and crosses in outline or filled with dots were drawn on the body. Although of no particular significance, the colors were determined by the color of the horse. White was used on dark-colored horses, yellow and red on light gray and white horses, green on light horses, and black sparingly on black horses. The most important stipulation pertained to the selection of the person who applied the design. Given the importance and potential danger to the horse and its rider in a war party, the design could be painted only by a veteran who exercised great care, as an elder explained: "You design a horse for a new warrior so that he will come back unscratched. If you survive, then you're qualified to paint horses. . . . Only brave men can paint horses. If a man is asked to design a horse for another man, he's got to oblige. It's considered a great honor."[21]

Deer, Pronghorn Antelope, Elk, and Moose

Other hoofed animals—the deer, the pronghorn antelope, and the elk—had relatively minor religious significance, but they provided an important part of Apache diets and material needs. The hides were used extensively for clothing, with the heavier elk hides preferred for moccasins, leggings, and drum covers; and teeth, particularly those of the elk, were choice decorations for clothing. Rattles made of hooves from all ungulates Apaches ate, with the exception of the horse, were frequently hung over the tepee door for good luck, and rattles of dew claws were used to decorate women's leggings.

The pronghorn antelope, one of the swiftest and most numerous of the mammals on the Plains, together with the deer and elk, was admired for its fleetness of foot, an important attribute for Apaches.[22] Pronghorn antelope horns and antlers, symbolizing new life by their yearly renewal, sometimes decorated the sides of the peyote drum, and the leg bone of the deer was considered the best material for making the sacred Apache pipes.

Moose, Ray Blackbear declared, were animals "they didn't mess with. It's kind of a weird-looking animal—kind of superstitious."[23]

Bear

The bear was perceived as anomalous because it hunted at night and possessed human characteristics. Although four-footed, it frequently stood and walked upright on two legs like humans and ate the same kinds of food humans ate. Apaches would not eat bear meat or use bear hide, as Susagossa pointed out, because "bears were certain things that carry superstitions."[24] Apaches especially did not like to smell them. The only parts of a bear considered safe or desirable for use were the claws, which, strung together, made necklaces.

Bears had "bad spirits," that is, they possessed medicine that could harm humans and were greatly feared as man-eaters. In Susagossa's opinion: "They smart, they shrewd. Tricky like deer. Old story goes that up in north they attack and eat humans. One good reason they [Apaches] don't mess with them."[25]

Stewart Klinekole reiterated that fear: "[The bear was] one thing they rejected. It's some kind of medicine animal, the bear. Bear has good fur, but they afraid of the bear. They afraid of something that wild."[26]

Significantly, the compound destruction visited on an entire village in the Pleiades myth, related in Chapter 3, as punishment for sexually crossing the human/bear boundary evoked a more consequential retribution than the death of a single buffalo in the tale "Woman Who Admired the Bone" for sexually violating the human/buffalo boundary.

The great fear people had of the bear is conveyed in the next story, narrated by Ray Blackbear, in which Bear wreaked wholesale destruction on a camp after hiding his heart to render his body impervious to arrows:

COYOTE KILLS THE BEAR WITH THE JUMPING HEART

Coyote was going along one day in a thick woods. He was going toward a big camp. On his way he saw a bear over in a thicket. Bear was going to this camp, too. Coyote watched and saw Bear take out his heart and hide it in the bushes. Then Coyote went along toward the camp. When he got there he told the people, "If something comes and threatens you, come and wake me up. I'm going to go in this tepee and go to sleep."

Soon the Bear came into this camp. The people were very frightened and began running about and screaming. Bear tore up tepees and destroyed everything that he could find. The people were shooting arrows at him, and many of them hit him, but they couldn't kill him because Bear had left his heart in the bushes in that woods. Someone thought of Coyote and went over to the lodge and said, "Wake up, brother. Bear is running around the camp and tearing up the tepees. We can't do anything with him. We can't kill him."

Coyote said, "All right. You go outside the tepee and announce to the people that Coyote is awake and is coming out."

"All right," said the man, and he went outside the tepee and called, "Coyote is awake and is coming out."

The man went back inside the tepee and said, "Hurry up, Coyote, this is getting very serious."

Coyote said, "Go back outside and tell the people that Coyote is coming toward the door of the tepee."

The man went outside and called, "Coyote is coming toward the door of the tepee."

All of the people said in chorus, "Coyote is coming toward the door of the people."

Then the man went back into the tepee and said, "Hurry, Coyote."

Coyote said, "Tell the people that Coyote has one foot outside the tepee."

So the man went outside again and called, "Coyote has one foot outside the tepee," and the people repeated, "Coyote has one foot outside the tepee."

The man returned to Coyote, and Coyote said, "Tell the people Coyote has both feet outside the tepee." The man called this out, and all of the people repeated it.

Then Coyote said, "Tell the people Coyote has his whole body outside the tepee." The man told the people this, and they all repeated it in chorus.

Then Coyote said, "Tell the people Coyote has begun to run."

"Coyote has begun to run," cried the man, and the people responded, "Coyote has begun to run."

But Coyote began to run in the direction away from Bear. On his way, he picked up a lance and ran to where he had seen Bear hide his heart. He threw his spear at the heart, but the heart jumped to one side. Bear, who was still in the camp, began to catch on to what was happening, so he left the camp and went running to the woods. Bear saw Coyote and knew what he was doing. "Jump, heart. Jump away from him," cried Bear.

The heart jumped, but Coyote kept trying to hit it with his lance. Bear got very near Coyote, and just as he did, Coyote hit the heart, and Bear fell dead at Coyote's feet.

All of the people ran over to the Coyote, calling out to him.

Coyote said, "Go to the chief's tepee and get me his best painted buffalo robe." The people did this and brought the robe to Coyote.

Then Coyote said, "Carry me back to the chief's tepee and put me in the place of honor." The people carried Coyote back to the chief's lodge and put him in the place of honor.

Then Coyote said, "Bring me the best food you have so that I can eat." And the people did this.

Coyote said again, "Bring me the daughter of the chief to marry," and the people did. Coyote married the chief's daughter.

Finally, Coyote said, "Bring me the chief's horses and all of his possessions and make me the chief."

But the people said, "That is too much, Coyote," and they refused. They ran him out of the camp, and Coyote just barely got away.[27]

Even though the bear had a bad spirit, the good news was that its spirit could be smoked away. In Susagossa's words: "If they killed a bear, they would go over there and smoke them with a medicine. I don't know if it was a root medicine or a leaf medicine. And they would smoke away the bad spirit that was in their system working away."[28]

For those who knew how to properly communicate with the bear, the bear could be quite helpful, as Joe Blackbear relates in the next story:

BEAR STORY

One time an Apache man was hunting. It was cold and snowing. He was up in the mountains. He saw a big hole, and he thought he would go in there. He went in, and it was dark. On the other side he saw light coming in. He saw two small bears.

Soon he heard growling outside. A big She-Bear came in. The man grabbed the little bears and held them on his lap. Pretty soon the She-Bear lay down and watched the man. Then the He-Bear came in. It spoke to the man in Apache. It said, "Let the little ones go."

Mother Bear began to nurse them. Father Bear asked her if she had spoken to the man. She said, "No."

He told the man, "It's too cold outside to go home. I will take you home when the snow stops." He took some dried meat out from beneath a hide and gave it to the man. Then the man went to sleep.

The next day the sun was shining outside. Bear said he would take the man home. He told the man to ride on his back. Bear took him to his camp. It was warm riding on the bear's back. Bear told the man, "Whenever you go on the warpath, come to me and I will tell you where to find horses. When you kill a buffalo, bring me the guts."

After a while the people were going on the warpath. This man told them, "We will stop and see my father over there."

When they got there, he called Bear. Bear came out. The man asked Bear where the best place was to get horses. Bear told him, "Not far off there are some people getting ready to move. Go up into the mountains, and tomorrow you will see a camp. You can get lots of horses, and no one will get hurt."

The people traveled on all day long. By afternoon of the next day they got into the mountains and saw a camp. At sundown they went toward the camp. They waited by the creek until morning. At daylight they attacked the camp while the people were asleep, and the people there fled into the mountains. Then the man and his people took the horses from the camp and drove them back home.

The bear is a kind of medicine animal. This man knew how to talk to the bear, and the bear helped him. They understood each other.[29]

Wildcat and Mountain Lion

Apaches were frightened by the bobcat, or wildcat, and the mountain lion, two nocturnal felids that not only preyed on other wild animals but also attacked people. The menace of the mountain lion was compounded by the fact that it preyed on domestic animals, particularly young colts and calves. Apaches would not eat lion meat or use its hides. They believed the hides transmitted ferocity to children, impelling them to bite.

The bobcat had a more exalted status than the mountain lion. Although Apaches were afraid of the bobcat, they admired its "good looks" and thought it was "pretty," even though its shape—the acquisition of which was narrated in the "Pounded Meat" story—was inflicted and was meant to be a reproof. Bobcat meat and hides were generally avoided, but in very early times, when other hides were not plentiful and commercial blankets had not yet reached the Apaches, hides of animals with dubious status were utilized, most commonly for bags and children's coats.

Coyote, Wolf, and Fox

Another group of anomalous animals included the wild canids—the coyote, wolf, and fox. All were nocturnal or seminocturnal predators that fed mainly on rodents, rabbits, poultry, and, to a lesser extent, large hoofed animals that were weak, newborn, or domesticated. The wild canids routinely gorged when food was available, leaving almost nothing behind, and they readily ate carrion. Apaches scrupulously avoided their meat and hides.

Some species, specifically the wolf and coyote, were natural reservoirs for disease-causing parasites. Most feared was the rabies virus that attacked the human nervous system. The prevalence of endemic rabies in these populations meant that a single wolf or coyote was a predator of unknown quality. Mrs. Bigman described the fear: "They kept the doors closed at night. They were afraid a wolf might drink standing water on the prairie and it would give him hydrophobia [rabies]. If you got bit, you might as well give up because you will go crazy and die."[30]

For the same reasons, Susagossa feared coyotes: "When they [the coyotes] get like mad dog, they try to kill them before they bite dogs. My grandmother told me that one came in tepee one time, but they were all under cover. He started trying to bite his tail. That is why people are afraid of them."[31]

The unforgettable sound of a coyote or a wolf howling at night was considered a sure sign of either bad luck or bad weather. Ray Blackbear warned: "When a coyote howls they say that it is a sign of bad news or maybe a change in the weather, maybe a storm coming or something, mostly the weather. If something does happen, it is supposed to happen within four days of hearing them howl."[32]

The coyote, known for its incredible swiftness, could overtake the buffalo and pronghorn antelope in a chase.[33] A highly intelligent animal, it was known to be wild and dangerous. In Fred Bigman's words: "He always had a bag of tricks. You couldn't trust a coyote. He might attack you or even bring you bad luck. People afraid of them. They were mean."[34]

Rose Chaletsin elaborated: "Coyote afraid, but at the same time he sure can steal chicken. He on both sides—like when somebody will talk to you good, but at same time they don't mean it."[35]

Although the coyote and Coyote the trickster shared "a bag of tricks," they did not share the same name in Apache. In the Apache language Coyote the trickster was called dá·ʐé à and the coyote ʐá·ʐà-γàà. Coyote was almost always portrayed as a mythical being restricted by human boundaries as other humans were. His differentiation from the mythical animals that turned into real animals, however, was not always clear in the oral literature. Today's Apaches are convinced, according to Alfred Chalepah, that Coyote and coyote are the same and that Coyote was never conceptualized as a human.[36]

The wolf, which possessed analogous negative characteristics, was detested even more than the coyote because it was more powerful, more gregarious, and a menace to domestic livestock. The wolf not only was labeled mean and dangerous but, Rose Chaletsin maintained: "It's more ferocious than coyote, and you don't fool around with it. They [Apaches] just kill it."[37]

The fox, a crafty animal like the coyote, was regarded ambiguously. Some Apaches were afraid to use fox hide, although in earlier times they used it in a variety of ways, most notably attached to the whip of the "bull" in the Manatidie Dance. Rose Chaletsin recalled that Apaches also used fox to "make shield, hunting bag, and other things. They used [fox] hides for dancing. . . . Used to put it on some kind of stick to dance with. Way back, but not now, though."[38]

Dog

The domesticated canid, the dog, the main mode of Apache transportation before the horse, was valued but feared for its reputed clairvoyance. Its howl, declared Susagossa, was a warning of death: "In old days they didn't like to hear dogs howling. They say it means death's coming. Somebody going to get hurt in their family."[39] So portentous was the dog's message that it was often beaten and sometimes killed, but as Joe Blackbear emphasized, "They would not let him hang around the camp and howl."[40]

The dog, Susagossa believed, could understand the Apache language and knew who was Apache and who was not. She told a story of a dog warning a family about approaching enemies, and in a heroic gesture the dog sent the family ahead to safety while it stayed behind to bark and warn others.[41]

Weasel, Otter, and Beaver

The weasel and the otter, both mustelids with powerful scent glands, and the beaver were never eaten, but their fur was highly valued for commercial, supernatural, and practical use.

General use of the short-tailed weasel's hide was relatively minor, but its white tail had supernatural significance. Four white tails were placed on each side of a war bonnet, which Datose believed bestowed adaptability—an important attribute for a Plains warrior.[42] The origin of the nocturnal weasel's symbolism probably dates from a time when Apaches were located in a northern provenance where the weasel's coat turned completely white with colder

96

weather, in which case it was an ermine.[43] The weasel was admired not only for its ability to change color but also for being a fierce predator. White, the absence of color, inspired both fear and respect.

Pelts from the river otter and beaver were of exceptional quality, especially valued for their suppleness and durability. In nineteenth-century America they were frequently used as a standard medium of exchange between Indians and non-Indians.[44]

Both the otter and the beaver had supernatural significance, Ray Blackbear believed, "because it takes skill and patience to get an otter or beaver, just like the feathers of an eagle. Some [Apaches] use parts of beaver or otter. This signifies they possess some portions of that animal's power."[45]

Otter hide, considered a source of good luck, was used in men's braids and, according to Rose Chaletsin, was particularly favored by young girls to "dance with and dress up with."[46] Coincidentally, the folklore has a story about Otter capturing all the pretty girls with his beautiful flute music.[47] Otter's most important use, however, was ceremonial. The four staffs that served as the symbolic focus of the Blackfeet Dancing Society were wrapped with otter hide. So critical was the hide for this purpose that without it the dance had to be deferred until it or a suitable substitute could be found.

The beaver, an aquatic rodent, was greatly admired for being industrious and skillful. Although its power could be transmitted through its pelts, it was the musk gland that was widely used for this purpose.[48] Apaches extracted liquid castoreum, which is utilized by present-day commercial perfumers, from the beaver's musk glands and assigned it a nebulous use as medicine. Beaver musk was mainly valued for being "good smelling," an attribute that, coupled with its fatty consistency, made it a substance of choice to mix with red clay to be used as facial paint.

In the following story, which is common to other Apachean tribes, Coyote tricked Beaver, who in turn outsmarted Coyote. Beaver's diligence paid off, and Coyote's punishment was that he had to avoid water forever except to get a drink. The story, narrated by Ray Blackbear, reflects the Apaches' high regard for the beaver:

COYOTE CARRIES BEAVER FAR FROM WATER:
BEAVER SURROUNDS COYOTE WITH WATER

Coyote was going along. He saw a beaver lying on the bank of a river sunning himself. Beaver was asleep. Coyote picked him up and carried him away from the river. He took him 3 or 4 miles away and then put him down. Then Coyote said, "Hey, brother, wake up. Look where you are."

Beaver woke up and looked around and then said, "Brother Coyote, take me back to the river."

Coyote answered, "I haven't got time to take you back. I'm pretty busy." Then Coyote went on his way.

Beaver walked and walked toward the river, then he rolled awhile, then he crawled, and finally, he got back. Beaver said, "Some day I'm going to catch that Coyote."

One day Coyote was sitting on the bank of the river fishing. After a while he fell asleep. Beaver saw him lying there and began to make a dam. He dammed the creek up near where Coyote was sleeping, and pretty soon the water flowed all around Coyote. It formed an island where Coyote was sleeping. Beaver made a great big lake there.

Then Beaver kicked Coyote and said, "Wake up, brother, and see where you are."

Coyote woke up and saw where he was and then said to Beaver, "Brother, I can't swim. Help me out, and take me off this island."

But Beaver said, "No, I can't. I haven't got time. I'm pretty busy." Then Beaver went off.

Coyote jumped into the water and swam a little way, then he got tired. He got his mouth full of water. He tried again and again, and finally he was able to reach land. He almost drowned, though.

That is why even today a coyote will never go near water except to get a drink. A coyote will never sleep near water.[49]

Skunk, Badger, Raccoon, Opossum, and Porcupine

By virtue of being both nocturnal and carnivorous and possessing powerful scent glands, the skunk, also a mustelid, was an absolute abomination. Quick to spray foul-smelling secretions from anal glands, the animal was detested most for its repelling method of killing chickens—described by Fred Bigman as "getting the heads off and sucking the blood."[50]

The tail of the skunk commanded both fear and respect and, according to Joe Blackbear, was attached as a warning to the tail of the Apache horse that goes on a raid.[51] The skunk's tail was also considered a handsome choice for a dancer's garter because its whiteness was "pretty when they dance." Skunk's black and white markings were attributable to his being on the losing side in one version of the hand game. His black hair was clipped from head to tail, and when it grew back it was white.

In general, the skunk was held in low esteem along with the badger, another mustelid. One memorable story Alonzo Chalepah told is about an angry husband killing his two unfaithful wives and cutting strips of flesh from their backs that turned into a skunk and a badger.[52]

Another nocturnal animal with prominent markings—a black mask and a tail ringed with black bands—was the raccoon, considered a source of powerful medicine. A roasted raccoon liver was one of four ingredients of "red medicine" used to treat stomach troubles, diarrhea, and a sore mouth.[53] Apaches believed liver was a source of strength, and because strength was the distinguishing characteristic of the raccoon, the raccoon liver was regarded as particularly powerful. The raccoon's agility, cunning, intelligence, and fighting ability were other desirable traits that could be transferred by means of its liver. The raccoon was utilitarian because not only was its meat in demand as food, but its skin was used for bags—arrow bags in particular—and frequently it was kept as a pet.

One of the most peculiar animals in the Apache world was the nocturnal opossum, the only marsupial on the North American continent. First, among its curious characteristics was that of being implacental, meaning that twelve days after conception its immature young, which were then about the size of bees, made their way to the abdominal pouch to nurse. Second, the male possessed a forked penis, presumably to correspond to the double uterus of the female. Third, the opossum had a peculiar hairless prehensile tail that, according to one story in the folklore narrated by Rose Chaletsin, was acquired as a consequence of naively putting its tail in a frozen pond.[54] Finally, it had the distinctive ability to "play possum," keeping absolutely still and feigning death, an actual temporary paralysis.[55]

Apaches did not like the opossum, which had a reputation for "eating people," sometimes sick people. Datose had heard "about possum eating people. That's why," she explained, "some people don't like possum. If people die with some kind of sickness, they [the opossums] would get sick if they ate them."[56]

The porcupine, with an armor of spikes to discourage predators, was feared. But on a utilitarian level, its quills were highly valued for use as decoration, mainly by other tribes. Ray Blackbear explained, "They shoot those quills. That's why Apache afraid of them. The northern people use them. They make roach [a headpiece made of porcupine fur]. They dye them different colors. Old-timers used quills for needles—like beads."[57]

The sharp porcupine quills frightened small animals, even larger animals. In Ray Blackbear's Coyote story, which follows, Buffalo loses his life for being generous to Porcupine, and Coyote loses his life for making a dumb decision:

COYOTE TRICKS PORCUPINE: PORCUPINE TRICKS COYOTE

Porcupine was traveling along, and he came to a river. He lived on the other side of that river and had crossed it several days before. But now it was swollen and running bank full. He couldn't get across, so he sat down and cried. Some buffalo were crossing the river, and one of them came over to Porcupine.

Buffalo said, "What's the matter? Why are you crying?"

Porcupine said, "I can't get back to my home. That's why I'm crying."

Buffalo said, "Well then, climb on my back and I'll carry you across."

"No," said Porcupine, "I might fall off or get washed off."

Then Buffalo said, "Well then, hang on to my tail."

But Porcupine said, "No, I might go under the water and drown."

Finally, Buffalo said, "Well then, crawl into my anus and ride inside."

Porcupine crawled into the Buffalo's anus and moved up and sat right by Buffalo's heart. Buffalo walked across the river with Porcupine inside of him. When he reached the other side, Porcupine stuck Buffalo with one of his quills, and Buffalo died. Then Porcupine came out. Coyote was watching all of this.

Porcupine began to butcher Buffalo, and Coyote came into view where Porcupine could see him. Coyote was limping, like he'd hurt his foot. Porcupine said, "Oh, here is Coyote. He's up to something."

Coyote said, "Hello, brother. What are you doing?"

Porcupine answered, "I'm going to butcher this buffalo."

Coyote said, "You sure got a nice buffalo."

But Porcupine replied, "Don't ask for any of it. I can't spare anything, not even a drop of its blood."

Then Coyote said, "I'll tell you what. We'll have a contest. Both of us will try to jump over the buffalo, and the one that does will win the carcass."

Porcupine looked at Coyote again and looked at his limp. "All right," said Porcupine.

Then Porcupine tried to jump over the buffalo. But he could only jump to the middle and then he would roll back down again. He tried three times. Finally, Coyote took his turn and jumped clear over the buffalo and won the carcass.

Then Porcupine said, "Brother there, could you spare me a little of the meat?"

But Coyote said, "No, I can't even spare the manure. I'm going to take the blood and everything."

Coyote got Buffalo all butchered and then laid out the kidney, the liver, and all of the good parts. He just laid them out there on the ground. Coyote said, "Now, you leave these things alone. Go on your way."

Porcupine pretended to go away, but he just went over the hill, and he turned around and sneaked back. Coyote had gone home to tell his family what he had done and how he had won a buffalo. He sang a song for his family and said, "The one that dances ahead of all the rest will get the kidneys." All of Coyote's family went dancing back toward Buffalo.

But during this time, Porcupine had pulled all of the meat up into a tree and had climbed up there with it. Coyote came back and couldn't find any of his meat. He knew what had happened, and he said, "I'll find that Porcupine."

One of Coyote's children saw the reflection of the meat in the river. It was hanging in a tree right over the river. He said, "Hey, father, see that meat down there."

Coyote said, "Yeah, I'm going to get it." So Coyote jumped into the river. He jumped two or three times, but he couldn't get the meat. He couldn't stay down there at the bottom. So he said, "You tie some rocks to me and then throw them into the stream. I'll follow them down to the bottom, and then I'll get that meat." So they tied rocks to Coyote and he jumped in. But he didn't come up again. He just drowned.

One of Coyote's children, a little runt Coyote, saw Porcupine sitting up in the tree. He called out to Porcupine, "Hey, my dad drowned trying to get that meat."

Porcupine looked down at him and said, "If you want some of this meat, lie down with all of your brothers and sisters and cover yourselves up with a blanket. But you have to lie down in a straight row." The Coyotes did this, and Porcupine said, "Now I'll feed you some meat."

Porcupine took the buffalo ribs and sharpened them. He didn't take them apart but just sharpened the whole row of them. This runt Coyote was looking out through a hole in the blanket, though, and saw what Porcupine was doing. Soon Porcupine dropped those ribs and killed all of the little Coyotes except the runt. He got out from under the blanket in time.

Porcupine came down from the tree and said to the runt, "Now I'll feed you all the food you can eat." So he fed this runt Coyote, and he ate all that he could eat. He just stuffed himself.

Then Porcupine said, "From now on you're always going to stuff yourself with food whenever you get a chance. After that, you'll always have to lie down and sleep."

And that's the way coyotes are now. They always eat as much as they can, then they always sleep right after that.[58]

Rabbit, Squirrel, and Prairie Dog

The cottontail rabbit, jackrabbit, red squirrel, and prairie dog—all small animals available in different seasons and in varying numbers—had no special supernatural significance, except perhaps the rabbit. All were included in the Apache diet, and their hides were often used for small items such as baby moccasins, gloves, and caps.

The rabbit was one of the most prolific animals in the environment, the female often pregnant while raising a new litter. The cottontail, with a gestation period of only twenty-eight days, could produce four to five litters annually, and the black-tailed jackrabbit, actually a hare, with a gestation period of forty-one to forty-seven days, could produce three to four litters.[59] As the most visible symbol of fertility, the rabbit's name, appropriately, was given to the Rabbit Dancing Society, discussed in Chapter 9, in which sexual indoctrination for children of all ages was accomplished directly and indirectly.

Prairie dogs were most easily hunted after a heavy rain when water collected in large puddles near their towns. The men constructed ditches from the puddles to the holes so water would flood the holes and force the evacuation of the prairie dogs, as well as their stored nuts, which were highly prized. When the animals surfaced, they were grabbed by the neck and quickly dispatched.

Mole, Armadillo, and Rodent

The mole, a prodigious burrower, was regarded ambiguously, feared because it was an underground animal that avoided the sun but admired because it could accomplish important tasks hidden from view. In the folklore, Mole helped rescue a woman from her Buffalo husband, and in the "Fire Boy and Water Boy" story, Mole helped the culture heroes capture the horse. But the negative side of the mole was that it possessed witching medicine. Rose Chaletsin harbored a suspicion that "the fresh dirt that mole piles up will give you sores and red face. Lips, cheeks, and face get sores. Some say a mole can witch you. That's why Indians don't use it for nothing. They got little eyes. They look dangerous. If children play with them, you got to wash them off."[60]

Datose confided: "It has got some medicine. People scared to touch it when it's out. They [moles] don't want the sun to see them. If it does, they die."[61]

Another abominable animal associated with dirt was the armadillo, "found in that soft dirt on graves." The armadillo, encased in overlapping, sharp-edged bony plates, was a powerful digger that commonly burrowed beneath carcasses to seek and feed on maggots. The widely held belief that "they go around fresh graves and eat the body" actually happened, not where Apaches live but in South America where giant armadillos have been known to uncover fresh graves to feed on corpses.[62]

Rodents on the Plains were plentiful, and they were credited with originating the "giveaway," the ritual sharing that is an important part of Apache group ceremonies. According to Rose Chaletsin: "They live in old buffalo skull, and they steal from each other. Sometimes they have a dance and give away nuts and all the other things they can gather. They run to nest and bring back everything and give away. That's why Indians have giveaway today."[63]

In the following story narrated by Ray Blackbear, mice living in a skull teach Coyote the folly of ignoring advice:

COYOTE MEETS THE MICE: EATS SWEET POTATOES

Coyote was going along. He saw a buffalo skull lying there in front of him, and he heard noises coming out of the skull. He peeked into the hole in the back of the skull and saw a group of mice inside, playing the hand game. Coyote just had to see what was going on, so he knocked on the skull. He said, "Hey."

The mice heard him knocking, and they said, "Wait. Listen."

Coyote knocked again and said, "Hey, mice."

The mice recognized his voice and said, "Listen. It's Coyote."

Coyote said, "I'll build a fire for you. Let me in."

So the mice let Coyote in. As soon as Coyote was inside, he built a fire for the mice. But as usual, Coyote had to go too far. He asked the mice for a pretty necklace that one of the mice was wearing. Coyote said, "I'll be a good fireman if you give me that necklace."

They gave him the necklace, but one mouse warned him, "Don't ever eat sweet potatoes while you're wearing this necklace."

Coyote said he wouldn't, and then he went out. Coyote said, "Well, I got better sense than to eat sweet potatoes while I'm wearing this necklace." He began to pile up wood for the fire inside. He piled and piled, and finally, he piled it so high that it covered the skull over completely. Then Coyote left the mice and went walking down the creek.

He came to a bend in the creek and saw a whole lot of wild sweet potatoes growing there. They looked very good. He picked one up and took a bite out of it. Then he spit it out quick. "I'm not supposed to eat sweet potatoes while I'm wearing this necklace," he said. He walked a little farther on and then did the same thing again. Over and over he did this, took a bite out of a sweet potato and then spit it out.

Soon he said, "Oh, I don't believe anything bad will happen to me." So he collected a lot of sweet potatoes and ate them all. Soon he got full. Then he started going along toward home. When he was about halfway home, his stomach filled up with gas. Coyote had to let out a little air, and when he did he kind of flew up into the air away. He went along farther and then let out a little more air. This time, he went into the air a little farther. When this happened again, he flew clear into the

103

air, did a couple of somersaults, and hit the ground pretty hard. This went on and on. But each time he passed gas he grabbed at a tree. And each time he passed gas he flew up a little and pulled the tree right out by the roots. So he went, passing gas and pulling trees.

When he got home Coyote said to his wife, "There's something wrong with me," and he told her what was happening. "Let's move camp and get out of this place," he said. "Put my mother-in-law on my back, and put the metate on top of her. That will hold me down, and I won't have to grab at trees."

So his wife put his mother-in-law on his back and put the metate on top of her. "Hurry up," said Coyote. Well, the next time he passed gas, Coyote, the mother-in-law, and the metate flew up in the air. They came down real hard, and the metate, which came down last, hit his mother-in-law on the head and killed her.

Coyote ran to the creek and flew in the air again. When he came to, he remembered the necklace and what the mice had told him. So he took off the necklace and threw it down. Then he was okay, and he didn't pass gas anymore. Coyote killed his mother-in-law for nothing. He could have just taken the necklace off.[64]

Bat

The one creature in the animal realm with distinctive characteristics of a bird was the bat. The only mammal capable of true flight, the bat had fur like a mammal and flew like a bird. It had wings like a bird but fur rather than feathers, and supporting its wings were forelimbs that resembled tiny feet, giving the illusion that it was four-footed, like the animals. A real abomination, the bat was not only nocturnal and ugly, it had a bad reputation for sucking blood out of people. Ray Blackbear believed the "[Apaches were] superstitious about them because they resembled the devil, like owl. They come out at night. They come up to you like fly, stay close, and get blood out of you. [They're] same family as vampires." Datose regarded bats as harmless but warned, "If you fool with it, it will bite you."[65]

Turtle and Horned Toad

The turtle played an important role in the folklore, helping to bring fire and daylight to the Apaches. The only reptile consumed, it had "the most delicate food on the Plains" and was systematically hunted.[66] The terrestrial box turtle was much more common than the various aquatic varieties, but the latter were preferred for food.

Rose Chaletsin remembered seeing bones of the prairie turtle strung together and worn on children's clothes to repel snakes.[67]

The heart of the snapping turtle was important medically for its ability to cure short breath, as Chaletsin explained: "It was boiled, dried, and crumbled for medicine. The snapping turtle heart, they use it. . . . It just for anybody. They use it on horse if it got short breath and make it long-winded. You got short wind, they doctor you four times. When they doctor you four times, you okay."[68]

Rose Chaletsin believed "the horned toad was good-hearted but was mean just like a snake." But according to Joe Blackbear: "Children were told to rub their hands on the horned toad and then rub their body. It would make them healthy and smart."[69]

Snake, Mountain Boomer, and Alligator

Of all the reptiles, the snake was considered the most abominable. Not only did it have witching powers, but it did not seem to fit in any specific category. It could crawl on the ground, it could climb trees, and it could swim in water. Joe Blackbear believed Apaches "feared snake the worst. They would not touch any part of a snake, not even the skeleton. We don't eat them or use skin. Anything out of snake they afraid of. When you try to kill it, they might spray some kind of gray stuff on you. That will paralyze you. That's how they witch you."[70]

Gifted persons, however, were able to hypnotize snakes into submission, and others could repel them by burning trash or spitting in the snake-infested area.

Another reptile Apaches feared was the "mountain boomer," the chameleon or tree lizard. Ray Blackbear described them as "two or three times as big as a lizard. They're greenish, turquoise, pink, and yellow—all in one. They witch you."[71]

Susagossa declared that she was "real afraid of them. You look at them. They look like some witch Indian man. They just stare at you. Before you move they gone. People kind of suspicious. They some kind of bad medicine. They might witch you some way. Some people afraid of them."[72]

Apaches, especially Rose Chaletsin, expressed a pervading fear of "water dogs, or snakes with legs that sucked your blood and gave you bad sickness."[73] Although the alligator is nonexistent in the present-day Apache environment, it was common in south Texas and northern Mexico where Apaches formerly made forays. Several versions of a story were told about alligators stealing neglected babies, a lesson, no doubt, to remind parents of their parental responsibilities. One version, which Tennyson Berry told, follows:

THE ALLIGATORS STEAL A BABY: THEY GIVE IT BACK TO ITS PARENTS

A bunch of people were camping one time along the bank of a river. When night came a baby began crying for his mother. But his mother kept right on sleeping.

In a very deep part of the water some alligators lived. This was their home. A female alligator crawled out of the water toward the camp. She crawled over to the baby who was crying. She got the baby and took it into the deep water.

In the morning, some men told the mother and the father about what had happened during the night.

The father said, "I'm going in the water, but you stay here. If I don't come back in four days, then you go and move away."

Then the man went into the very deep water and sank clear down to the bottom. Finally, he came to a little bank at the bottom and went over this bank. Beyond it there was no water, and over there an alligator man and his wife had the baby with them. The baby's father went over to the alligators.

The alligator told his wife, "I told you, everything loves its children. But there is danger for children." [Apparently this refers to the lack of attention the child received when crying.]

"But since you came," he said to the man, "I'll give this baby back to you. Now take these four stones, and throw one into the water."

The father did this, and the water parted.

The alligators said, "You go that way, that is the way to your camp, and you can get home."

The man took his baby home to the camp. He brought it back to their camp. The baby's mother saw her again. She was given her baby back again. This is the way this story happened sometime—a long time ago.[74]

The next alligator story, also narrated by Tennyson Berry, serves as a dire warning to persons who ignore the rules and cross the human/animal boundary:

THE MAN WHO BECAME AN ALLIGATOR

A long time ago, two men went out on the warpath. After many days had passed, they got hungry. Somewhere they came to a big lake. "Let's drink," said one of the men, so they both took a drink from this lake.

There, at the edge of the water, they found two eggs. Now one man said, "My friend, let's eat these eggs."

But the other man said, "No, I don't want to eat those."

"Come on," said the other. "Hurry, I don't want to wait. Let's eat them." He didn't want to wait for the first man, so he ate them.

After quite a while he said, "My friend, wait for me. I'm going to take a swim." He wouldn't listen to an argument, so he went into the water and dove in several times. When he came out he looked different. He had turned into an alligator.

The other man said, "See, look at you. That's the reason I told you not to eat those eggs. Now you have turned into an alligator. You go off by yourself now."

Alligator said, "You go back to the camp and tell my mother and my father that I'm staying here."

The man went back to the camp, and he told the alligator's mother and father and the other people. Then he brought them back. He took them this way, and after several nights they arrived at the water.

"Hey, my friend," he cried, "come out of the water."

Then the water parted, and Alligator appeared. He swam toward them. He came out of the water. His father and mother and the others saw him, and they talked with him and gave him things to eat. He ate what they gave him. That's the way his father and mother and the others saw him and knew about him.

But Alligator said, "I'm going to stay right here. You come see me again sometime."

That's the end. These people went away. They went home. That's the way the story goes. The man ate those eggs and became an alligator.[75]

In summary, the Apaches classified animals into categories so they would know which ones could be eaten and which ones could not. Those avoided were anomalous. They were either nocturnal (wolf, coyote), weird-looking (moose), odoriferous (skunk), reptilian (snake, mountain boomer), or scavengers (fox, wolf); or they exhibited a bird or a human characteristic (bat, bear). The hides or body parts of anomalous animals were generally not utilized, and those from animals classified as true abominations were never used.

Analogical thought that characterizes native religion guided decisions about which animal hides or body parts could be used for supernatural purposes, for example: (1) the buffalo's raw liver and kidney because they imparted the buffalo's strength to the person who consumed them; (2) the ermine's white tails placed on a war bonnet because they transmitted the adaptability of the ermine to the warrior; and (3) a roasted raccoon liver, an important ingredient in powerful "red medicine" for stomach troubles, diarrhea, and a sore mouth, because it transmitted the strength, agility, and intelligence of the raccoon to the patient. In the final analysis, the system worked well because it provided a blueprint for everyday decisions that were based on experience.

People and Spirits

Kin and Death

Ghosts and evil spirits caused excessive fears in everyday Apache lives. No one knew when to expect these ghosts and evil spirits to appear, but if someone in the family had shown disrespect for an affinal relative, a menstruating woman had appeared at a curing ceremony, or a pregnant woman had failed to observe a certain taboo, there was the increased possibility that a revenging ghost would appear sometime in the future. Ironically, the ghost of a close relative engendered the most fear. The small size of the tribe, and the close cooperation required of family members for all tribal endeavors, furnished innumerable chances for animosities, jealousies, and dislikes to develop that had to be repressed. These grudges and guilt feelings, Opler and Bittle observed, often festered for a lifetime and were not openly expressed.[1]

Basic to gaining insight into Apaches' pervasive fear of ghosts and evil spirits is an acquaintance with the extraordinary importance of kinship relations to Apaches and the ramifications of those relationships.

Kinship Structure

Few in number, generally endogamous, and with a strong sense of unity, Apaches could be likened to one vast family in which every member was related in some way to every other member. As one woman surmised, "I guess I'm kin to just about everybody."[2]

The perception of being kin to almost everyone was integral to the all-encompassing kinship system that embraced fictive relatives as well as persons related by blood and marriage. Fictive relatives, who might be newcomers, persons left alone by death or abandonment, and female and child captives, were customarily adopted by various extended families and thereafter considered kin. The bonding of extensive kinship was important on the Plains because it ensured that no one had to try to survive alone. It also provided a ready resource of persons who could be called upon for help in the hunt, raiding parties, ceremonial preparations, the tanning of hides, child care, and various other tribal endeavors.

The most vital function of the kinship system was its role in the ordering of society. By reckoning closely the specific relatedness of one individual to another, it classified all persons into socially recognized kin categories, each with a particular code of prescribed behavior. The code of specific responsibilities and attitudes of one category of kin toward another, implicit in the kinship terminology, minimized conflict and gave substance and order to Apache lives.

The kinship code also formed the underpinning of Apache understanding and expectations of supernatural justice. Adherence to the kinship rules ensured equilibrium in one's life, whereas disregard for them, whether conscious or unconscious, was believed certain to produce dire consequences. So ingrained was this belief that when things went awry, the explanation was often sought in some forgotten affront, real or imagined, and if nothing of that nature could be recalled, the victim would seek help from the medicine man, who could provide a diagnosis and perform ritual purification to rectify the adversity.

The most important Apache social groups were extended families, or *kustcae* in Apache, consisting of any number of biological kin and social nonkin. The extended families were spread across a large encampment in clusters of tepees that included the tepee of the primary conjugal family of parents and children; sometimes tepees of grandparents, parents' siblings, other relatives, and friends; and often tepees of married daughters and their husbands and children because matrilocal residence (husbands moving to the wife's parents' camp) was somewhat more common than the reverse, although there was no hard-and-fast rule.

Apache lodge in Pacer's camp on the Kiowa, Apache, and Comanche Reservation. Mt. Scott in distance. Photo, William S. Soulé, Bureau of American Ethnology. Courtesy, Smithsonian Institution (neg. no. 2580-c).

Groups of kustcae formed *gonkas,* or local bands that camped together for mutual protection. The Apaches, because of their small size, were especially vulnerable to the hegemony of larger tribes surrounding them on the Plains. Customarily, the camps of the gonkas ranged over an area of 1 or 2 square miles in the proximity of a friendly tribe, most frequently the Kiowas but earlier the Cheyennes and Arapahos as well. But Kiowas and Apaches never "camped together . . . no. They each have their own camp. We don't always like them, sometimes lots of fussing. But they always go around together."[3] Apaches had three, possibly four gonkas, each of which owned a medicine bundle.

Lacking any formal organization or chiefs with mandated authority, the Apaches were a highly fluid group with constantly changing alignments. Generally, they made decisions within the context of the family, but when extrafamilial advice was needed they turned to a leader, a person who commanded respect, was perceived to be generous and wise, and could act as a spokesperson for the group. The leader was consulted solely as an adviser or mentor, however, and families who disagreed with his advice could disregard it if they wished. The last four leaders to be recognized as chiefs, although serving in perfunctory roles, possessed above-average abilities and were highly respected by others. The earliest Apache chief anyone could remember was Blackhawk who, during the turbulent years after Medicine Lodge, went to Washington in 1872 as a delegate offering peace from the Apaches. Pacer, also an Apache chief during those difficult years, was an important leader who advocated peace and urged Thomas Battey, a Quaker teacher from the nearby Wichita Reservation, to come to the Kiowa, Apache, and Comanche Reservation to start a school. With the farsighted leadership of Kickingbird, a Kiowa, the school finally opened in February 1875 on the Ft. Sill post. Blackhawk and Pacer were appointed to serve on the board of education. Pacer died later that year. Whiteman was a chief during the 1890s, and Apache John was the last chief and a powerful medicine man. He died in 1925.[4]

How did Apaches know what was acceptable and proper? Over time, by custom they had developed an unwritten but elaborate code of varying degrees of formality, congeniality, and intimacy expected to be observed between any two relatives, whether consanguineous, affinal, or fictive. The small size of the tribe and its high degree of interrelatedness not only complicated proper behavior patterns but made them more discernible. When what was proper was perceived to have been ignored or abused, the Apaches fully expected the spirits to inject themselves into human affairs and reward or bypass those who behaved properly and punish those who did not.

So intense was this belief in the inevitability of supernatural justice that it affected almost every aspect of a person's life from the moment of birth. As a person approached death, he or she and all relatives and friends became increasingly fearful, for at death all old scores were settled. Heightening the fear were the unknown grudges and hostilities people might have harbored for decades but never expressed. The fear was particularly unsettling because the possible retribution was of an unknown quality and quantity.

To gain insight into the Apache understanding of the role of supernatural justice in interpersonal relationships, it will be instructive to first examine kinship terminology, which by its structure dictated ideal family behavior, responsibilities, and duties; and second, to recount stories of actual kinship behavior that corresponded to or clashed with the ideal. Although a gradual widening of the gap between ideal and actual behavior could be expected as the aboriginal Apache culture began to disintegrate during the reservation period of the late nineteenth century, as late as the 1960s some Apaches still adhered to the ideal code.

Blackhawk, Apache chief who was a peace delegate to Washington, wearing a peace medal that has a picture of President Jackson on one side and clasped hands representing friendship on the other side. Photo, William Soulé, 1867–1874, Bureau of American Ethnology. Courtesy, Smithsonian Institution (neg. no. 2580-e-2).

Pacer, Apache chief who was a strong advocate of peace and education. He was one of the first Apaches to have a Christian burial. Photo, Alexander Gardner, 1872, Bureau of American Ethnology. Courtesy, Smithsonian Institution (neg. no. 2582-b).

Kinship Terminology

On the Plains, where a premium was placed on cooperation among relatives of the same generation, or "brothers," the Apaches' kinship system emphasized horizontal classification along generational levels rather than vertical classification along lineage lines. As a general rule, distance distinctions between relatives of the same generation were minimized, and those between generations were more apparent.[5]

Following McAllister's analysis, four points were distinctive to the Apache kinship system: (1) It was strictly bilateral; an individual belonged equally to father's kin and mother's kin. (2) Considerable lumping of relatives occurred at all generational levels. All kin in a person's own generation, including all cousins on both parents' sides, were called "brother" or "sister," with an added "elder" or "younger" to distinguish relative age. In the parental generation, mother, mother's sisters, father's brothers' wives, and mother's female cousins were called "mother"; and father, father's brothers, mother's sisters' husbands, and father's male cousins were called "father." A different term was reserved for mother's brother and father's sister's husband and yet another for father's sister and mother's brother's wife. (3) A male had three categories of kin in the first descending generation, but a female had four. A man called his son and his brother's son "son," his daughter and his brother's daughter "daughter," but his sister's children—both male and female—were referred to by a single separate term. A woman similarly called her daughter and the daughter of a sister "daughter," her son and the son of a sister "son," but, divergently, referred to her brother's female children by another term and his male children by yet another term. (4) All grandchildren and grandparents used self-reciprocal terminology, with no sex distinction. They called each other by the same term.[6]

Lumping lineal and collateral relatives under the same term was an advantage because doing so increased the number of people upon whom an individual could rely. The term *brother,* which was given to brothers, male cousins, and brothers-in-law and extended to any number of fictive kin, designated a fairly sizable group of individuals who could be expected to protect, defend, assist, and share with each other. Similarly, the term *mother,* which was given to an individual's mother, aunts, and mother's female cousins, automatically included women who functioned as surrogate mothers.

The range of kinship extended far and wide so that everyone in the tribe was related in several ways to several others. Those not related biologically were either affines (related by marriage) or fictive kin. Newcomers to the group, most often female captives since male captives were usually killed, were automatically fitted into the kinship system. Captive women usually became Apache wives, and captive children became part of an Apache family and over time came to be regarded as Apache.

Kinship Avoidances and Obligations

Integral to the kinship system was a prescribed code of conduct that dictated the proper behavior of every person toward every other person. These prescribed behaviors ranged on a wide scale from a very formal relationship of respect and avoidance to an informal one of congeniality and joking. The most informal and closest relationship was among siblings, cousins, and friends of the same sex, who addressed each other as brother or sister. The relationship of brothers became more intense with maturity as men came to depend greatly on each other in warfare and hunting. In the Dancing Societies each man paired with a friend, or brother, with an understood obligation to share all possessions and help each other. Sharing with brothers included sharing wives. As one old man explained:

> If the unmarried brother comes to visit, the married one tells him to sit down by his wife. Maybe he will say, "Brother, I'm going way down there. I come back tomorrow; you sleep with my wife tonight." It is all right for a brother to sleep with his brother's wife. If a wife dies, you can get another woman, but if a brother dies, you won't see him anymore. Then he will say, "Brother, if I die, don't you leave our wife."[7]

The informal relationship of sisters was arguably as intimate. The practice of sororal polygyny, when present, was a much desired form of marriage because the sisters usually got along well with each other. The wives lived in separate but nearby tepees and shared household and camp duties with each other as well as with other "sisters."

Marriage to sisters most frequently occurred after death with the practice of the sororate (marriage of a man to his deceased wife's sister). The levirate (marriage of a man to his brother's widow) occurred but was relatively rare. Both customs ensured that no Apache had to live alone.

Respect relationships were the most burdensome. In their extreme form, they required total avoidance by members of the elementary family and parents-in-law who commonly saw each other daily.

Rose Chaletsin recalled the difficulties of observing the prescribed avoidance behavior between relatives by marriage. A mother-in-law and a son-in-law avoided each other, as did a father-in-law and a daughter-in-law. Whereas in the Apache kinship system daughters and nieces were called daughters and sons and nephews were called sons, the same avoidance was required between an uncle and his nephew's wife and between an aunt and her niece's husband.

Apache mothers are afraid of their sons-in-law. . . . He [my son-in-law]
won't talk to me or touch me or talk rough. In the old days if a son-in-
law comes to the tepee, the old lady has to beat it out, and an old man's
the same way with his son's wife. And if it's his nephew's wife, it's the
same way and woman doesn't talk to niece's husband. Give you bad luck. I
don't know why. If my son-in-law walks in, I just have to throw my blanket
over my face and beat it out or he have to hurry out. Nowadays you got
to do something for your son-in-law before you can talk to him—fix
him moccasins, give him a horse, fix him some clothes or something. If
your daughter died, it would still be same way—never dies out.[8]

The same avoidance, added Rose Chaletsin, was observed between siblings of the opposite sex:

Brother and sister just like mother-in-law and son-in-law. Your brother
won't come up to you and talk [to] you in the face. He won't use any
kind of bad talk to you, just use good words. When you're in [the] house
by yourself, if your brother's coming you have to go in the other room
and he won't stay in there. He will go out. My brother lives with me,
and he won't come in when I'm there alone. When we are all eating at
the table, he won't talk to me and I won't talk to him. My daughter has
to interpret for me.[9]

Marriage

At the core of the extended family was the important conjugal family of
mother, father, and children. The formation of the family, which began with
marriage, was considered a very serious matter and was dictated by strict
notions of proper conduct. The ideal marriage was arranged when the couple
was very young and required approval from the young woman's brother. If all
agreed, the boy's family was expected to give substantial gifts to the young
woman's family and the couple. The young woman's opinion was not considered, and she commonly accepted her fate with resignation: "The girl has to
go. Her brother makes her. If she like it or not, she goes. She be crying,
wants to be back to her parents. It was the relatives who decided."[10]

Another woman remembered the frustration she felt over having no say
in the matter:

I was married like that. My brother gave me away with a horse and
saddle. . . . I don't know nothing about it. I was fourteen. I didn't know
nothing about him. I never talked to him before. I didn't know what's
marriage. I was still playing with the children. When my sister came after
me I cried, but they said, "No, no, you got to go." Later I ran back to
mother, but they came after me and took me back. They said, "You're
married."[11]

Not all marriages were arranged. Sometimes a young man with a roman-tic interest would offer to work for the prospective bride's brother. If the brother accepted, he was obligated to give his sister to the young man in marriage if asked. Again, the young woman had no choice. Sometimes mar-riage occurred without prearrangements if the couple made their romantic interests in each other known to their parents. Occasionally a couple eloped, in which case marriage was considered a fait accompli. The girl's family usu-ally accepted the fact but sometimes exacted retribution by confiscating all the boy's parents' belongings. In extreme cases, the girl's brother or brothers punished their sister mercilessly: "Two brothers might shoot the girl with bow and arrows. Just make a target out of her. Might even kill her. This can be done when a girl runs off. Some brothers beat the girl since she has insulted the family."[12]

Once married, the couple were expected to show respect and reserve toward each other, although there was considerable deviation from this ideal.

Pollution

Apache men and women were regarded as totally different, and rules gov-erned the circumstances under which the two were to be kept separate from each other. Women's procreative powers were greatly feared as a source of pollution, and when women menstruated or were pregnant, special care had to be taken to neutralize or avoid pollution from them.

Apache girls were not isolated during menstruation, as was the custom among many other tribes with whom they had contact; nor did they partici-pate in elaborate puberty ceremonies. But a menstruating Apache woman was considered particularly dangerous in the vicinity of sacred rituals. She could not attend a curing, peyote ritual, or Medicine Bundle ritual for fear she would pollute the medicine.

During pregnancy, women were also enveloped by many rules and avoid-ances. The pregnant Apache woman was supposed to exercise and, Susagossa cautioned, "not get lazy so the baby would be born the head way." She was expected to increase her intake of food—of meat in particular but not meat from the leg of a cow because it clung to the leg bone and could result in a difficult delivery. She should avoid fat because "the baby has white stuff all over it and it makes the birth dry"[13] and avoid eating pounded meat forced into the intestine of a cow because it could cause the child to be born with the umbilical cord wrapped around its neck. She should eat heart and tongue, but only after cutting off the tips. While holding the heart, according to Ray Blackbear, "she say this word, which means she feed the whole world by throwing out the top of the heart. She pray to the ground, up in the air, and say, 'Give me good luck.'" Removing the tip of the tongue had a more specific aim of preventing the child from being tongue-tied or slobbering.[14]

The pregnant woman was advised to avoid certain animals for fear their undesirable attributes might transfer to her child. Susagossa listed other rules. The woman was not supposed to look "at ugly things, an ugly dog or ugly horse or something like that," or the baby would be born ugly. She was not to fix her gaze upon a rabbit for fear her child might be born with a harelip, nor was she to look at a snake for fear she would bear a timid child.[15]

After delivery, the placenta was taken away from the camp and buried. The umbilical cord was encased in a small beaded bag and placed on the cradle board until the child began to walk, after which it was attached to the child's garments.

Occasionally, children were born with major seeing or hearing defects. The cause was quickly traced to some evil influence on the mother: "Sometimes they think the mother must be out someplace at night [where the evil contacts are]. When the baby is born, they get a special doctor for that kind of people. [They] keep on doctoring till they cure the child or give up. He [the doctor] will make smoke out of burnt cedar and use that to smoke the child. A child that is born that way, that can't be cured, they feel sorry for it."[16]

If birthmarks were discovered on a newborn child, Apaches attributed the cause to some event predating the birth. Ray Blackbear recalled that one mother, who bore a daughter with a large purple birthmark on her forehead, attributed the cause to her having daily seen the child's father who always wore a black handkerchief across his forehead.[17]

An Apache woman had rules not only for pregnancies and menstrual cycles but for gender demeanor and sexual behavior as well, and she had two main avenues for learning these rules. The most direct way was to observe the behavior of others and listen to their advice. The indirect way was to learn vicariously through tribal folklore, which abounded with interesting perspectives on women's roles. For example, a woman was warned repeatedly not to be unfaithful because if she were, she could expect some dire fate. She might lose her life or be turned into some disgusting animal. If in her unfaithfulness she dared to cross the animal/human boundary and take an animal as a husband or lover, she could experience a variety of terrifying consequences. In real life, a husband was entitled to cut off the nose of an unfaithful wife or even kill her, but no Apache had ever heard of this happening because the wife had always been able to take refuge in a bundle-owner's tepee where no one could touch her.

Importantly, one of the few stories about a man's aberrant sexual behavior, defined as oversexed, ended in his forced satiety, not death or transformation to some bizarre creature.

A woman's status in the folklore was clearly inferior to a man's. She was depicted as one who obeyed orders from her husband "as she was supposed to do," even when she was told to obey an outrageous command like roast her own child. The folklore message throughout was that women were to be entirely subservient. Keeping in mind that the folklore only provided a map for ideal behavior, actual behavior may have fallen short. In the Coyote stories especially, the portrayal of a dumb, acquiescing woman who clearly did not exist in real life always brought smiles or laughter to audiences.

Ghosts and Evil Spirits

An overriding fear of the deceased, particularly deceased relatives, was conspicuous in Apache lives. Apaches believed that at the moment of a person's death a čį·yé, or ghost, was released that could cause serious harm to the living. Although the ghost emanated from the corpse, once freed, it lost its individual identity and became part of a general ghost community. Ray Blackbear explained:

> [It] isn't present when a person is alive, just after his death. There is no one ghost for the whole body. . . . It's more like some kind of vital part that you have in all parts of your body, and it goes away when that part is destroyed. . . . The ghost is just everywhere. It's a general idea. I guess maybe you would say it's general "deadness." But each person doesn't have his very own.[18]

Some believed the čį·yé, or "spook," returned as an owl or a whirlwind, whereas others, according to Tennyson Berry, "imagine they can 'feel' the presence of the čį·yé. If a deceased person had a grudge against another, the čį·yé might come back and cause sickness in this person."[19]

The intensity of fear the ghost produced was directly proportional to the amount of imagined bà´é·h, or evil spirit, associated with the ghost. The bà´é·h was present before and after death, but the ghost only came into existence after death. Ray Blackbear explained that "after death took place, the čį·yé is contacted by the bà´é·h and pulled out of the body. . . . After life, the čį·yé and the bà´é·h travel about together."[20]

The bà´é·h was a complicated concept that in general meant evil but encompassed antisocial behavior as well. Ray Blackbear elaborated:

> It's devilish. When you do something that you would think was impossible, like maybe standing on that ledge out there and jumping off onto the ground, and you didn't get killed, then somebody might say, "He's a

devil, he's magical." Or maybe a bunch of cars might run over somebody, and he would come out all right, then you would say the same
thing. The bà´é·h never dies. It's just a word that means a person is
clever, something about him that is beyond our comprehension. . . .
Each person doesn't have his own bà´é·h. It's just an idea about
something.[21]

If a čį·yé were benign, it was alone. If potentially dangerous, the bà´é·h
had joined with it. When the čį·yé appeared as a whirlwind or owl, it was up
to the observer to decide how dangerous it was. Ray Blackbear explained: "In
the old days there was a belief that one could see spirits of the dead. Appeared in the form of a whirlwind. Can't see them well. But at night one
could see sparks of light preceding the wind. This would be the čį·yé in
spirit. If it is a good spirit, it may just bring a message. If it comes back with
the bà´é·h, it may paralyze one."[22]

As mentioned earlier, the living had the most to fear from the ghosts of
persons who might have accumulated a lifetime of unexpressed hostilities,
likely members of the extended family. According to Ray Blackbear:

> It bothers mostly the members of the family if one member of the
> family believes in the čį·yé. I think that the more closely related you
> are to the dead person, the more the ghost may bother you. . . . The
> ghost of babies won't hurt you. They don't have any bà´é·h at all.
> People believe that there is a lot of love between a mother and a baby,
> and the čį·yé will be with the mother afterward if the baby dies. But it
> can't hurt anyone.[23]

The amount of bà´é·h one accumulated during a lifetime was directly
proportional to the amount of hostility a person had developed toward others and the amount of mischievous behavior in which he or she engaged. A
person who had an evil spirit associated with hostility did not necessarily
have an evil spirit associated with antisocial behavior, but he or she could
have. The person who engaged in devilish behavior was observed by all, and
this kind of evil spirit was of a known quantity. Contrarily, the evil spirit
stemming from hostility was of an unknown quantity because in Apache
society, every effort was made to repress hostility. Although an individual
was born without any evil spirit and may not have accumulated any in an
entire lifetime, there was always a slight suspicion that some bà´é·h had been
concealed. Only the ghosts of the very young, because "they were innocent,"
and of the very old, because they were weak and benign, were not feared—
the exceptions being the ghosts of doctors or known witches.[24]

Apaches also did not feel threatened by poltergeists, or ghosts who minded
their own business, as Datose explained:

I tell you what grandpa said. They was camping out down by the river, a bunch of them. [It] was summertime. They sat around outside, smoking and telling stories. They heard a noise. Pretty soon they heard tepee poles making noise and people talking, but they couldn't understand the talk. It was up in the air. One of them said, "Well, they're Night-Movers. Dead people been dead long time still using tepee. They moving somewhere." Then they heard dogs barking up in the air. They say, "That must be a road up there and those people moving. It was dead people, and they was moving someplace."[25]

Because ghosts brought illness and death, an elaborate system of avoidance made certain they were not unduly aroused or summoned. The best protection against ghosts, Susagossa believed, was cedar smoke: "Take old dry cedar, put it in fire and make smoke, put your hands on it, smell four times. Put it all over your body." Ray Blackbear's recommendation was to "take some cedar ashes and put them on your [fore]head in the form of a cross. This will keep you from being bothered by čį·yé."[26]

Susagossa also recommended cedar smoke for the person who dreamed about the dead: "Indians don't like to dream about dead people. Sometimes they dream about dead persons. They say it means bad luck or death to the person that dreams about the dead person. If they dream like that, they burn cedar, put smoke all over themselves to keep from having bad luck."[27]

Another prophylactic, recommended by Datose, was to "get an old tub or something and put some old rags and some trash in it, and you burn some animal grease with it. They [the ghosts] can't stand that smoke. It scare them, and they will go away."[28]

Datose related an incident about her husband scaring away a ghost:

We went to bed in the wagon. . . . I seen something, I hear something walking as fast as it could. It was a man . . . an Indian man. He might be somebody who was dead. The man came toward us. Just before he got to the well, he disappear. . . . [My] old man say, "Old woman, take kids in house." My husband going to fix that ghost. He put bones in can with rags. I watched, and it never came back. The ghost was afraid of it [the can with the bones].[29]

Children were particularly vulnerable to ghosts, Joe Blackbear believed, because "ghosts always go where a child has been playing. They go there at night, where the child's tracks are and where he has been talking. I always rub out the tracks that Jumbo makes when we go down to the creek together."[30]

Ray Blackbear advised, "If you have to lay a baby down, like in the house or in the old days in a tepee, and have to go out for a while, you should put a stick across his cradle, on his chest. This keeps ghosts and evil away."[31]

Children also had to be protected from owls and whirlwinds. According to Joe Blackbear: "They believed that if you lived an evil life you turned into an owl or a whirlwind after death. That is why Apaches don't like whirlwinds. . . . When a whirlwind comes up, you cover up the children with a blanket."[32]

Apaches were particularly fearful of the owl, called čį̀·yé, ghost, or bà´é·h, evil spirit. Datose articulated her graphic impression of the owl: "I seen the owl, that's bà´é·h. He's kinda bad looking. He's got eye, that big yellow eye. He's funny bird."[33]

The particular horror the owl inflicted, explained Tennyson Berry, was facial paralysis: "They claim owls are mean. They can twist your eyes, mouth, and body. The owl was supposed to be a dead person that had turned into a bird."[34]

One way to be safe from harm was to kill the owl, as Susagossa's husband did in the incident she described: "One time we were camping, and there was a big owl in a tall tree. I tell my husband, 'That owl bothering us. He seem like he breaking sticks to throw on us.' My husband shot him in the wing. He die. We turn him over, and he had buckskin earrings. Must been some old Indian. My daddy make fire and burn it up."[35]

Owls could also be repelled with crow feathers, as Datose believed, because "bà´é·h's scared of crows. [If] the owl is somewhere around, the crows get to him. Put him blind, then let him go. That's how come they afraid of crows. That's how come when they [Apaches] get feathers, [they] tie them on the bedstead. Yes, that's how they keep the owls away."[36]

Those who were fearful of ghosts avoided being out alone at night. Susagossa explained, "Some Indians are afraid of the night. Some people say that's when ghosts and bad spirits is running around." Above all, it was important to stay away from the cemetery. Fred Bigman expressed fear of sleeping in a cemetery as his mother had because he was afraid the spirits would scare him and give him a stroke—a facial paralysis commonly termed "ghost sickness" or "ghost did it."[37]

Although no clearly defined difference existed between ghost sickness and witching sickness, discussed in Chapter 8, in general the presenting symptom of ghost sickness was facial paralysis, whereas the presenting symptoms of witching were more diverse. In addition to facial paralysis, witching sickness might involve paralysis of the arms, legs, or both, or an object or substance intrusion into the torso.

Some Apaches, however, blurred the distinction by using the word *witched* to refer to the horror of "ghost did it," the affliction caused by an imaginary person, as Datose recalled:

When there be funeral here, their ghosts might come around here. They might whistle at you, and that make them twist you. I got brother-in-law. He down here in church one time by hisself, and he see woman walking on fence. When we see him, his mouth all twisted where that woman witch him. He say there wasn't no wind blowin' anywhere, but that woman, she look like she walking in strong breeze with her sleeves flappin'. I tol' him that must be whirlwind he see, but he say, "No, I seen that woman with my own eyes. She had red dress on, and I see her real plain." The brother-in-law was unwitched by Indian doctor. He all right now.[38]

The people most vulnerable to ghost sickness were those who expected to be victims. Curiously, sometimes a person had to be informed by others that he or she had a twisted face. In Datose's words: "People say that bà´é·h twist your mouth, eye. If it make some sound at you and you turn to look, it witch you. Sometimes a person don't know they were twist. Someone else always see your mouth twisted and your eye."[39]

Death and Burial

Warnings of impending death in the camp came from the appearance of an owl or a whirlwind, both of which were believed to be ghosts of dead relatives, or from the howl of a dog. When a relative died, an Apache commonly recalled having seen an owl in the recent past, although sometimes as far back as two or three years. The whirlwind was more likely to predict imminence. If a dog howled and a person subsequently died, the dog was killed—"otherwise it will howl again and be asking for more people to die."[40]

After the medicine man had exhausted all lifesaving cures for a critically ill patient to no avail, it was customary for the dying person to give away his or her most prized possessions to persons he believed could best care for them. To do so meant the possessions, which might include a medicine bag and one or several horses, would not be buried with him or destroyed. Great prudence was particularly important when giving away a medicine bag to ensure that the recipient would learn the cures and administer them properly. A gift of ponies to a brother was regarded as an exceptional honor. The horses' manes and tails were cut, and they were never ridden again except into battle.[41]

As death neared, relatives caring for the dying person burned mountain cedar and sage to keep the ghosts at bay. Ray Blackbear explained: "They thought that the spirits of the dead would come after his [the dying person's] spirit. Living people were afraid of these spirits, and they would burn mountain cedar to prevent the spirits from taking him."[42] Even the ghost, whose only task was to lead the new ghost to the afterworld, was considered a threat, since it was interpreted as an attempt to extinguish the life of the living.[43]

As soon as the person died, Susagossa explained, relatives began wailing to let people know that "somebody died. They let them know by crying. They [the others] know somebody was sick, and when hear them crying [they] find out somebody is dead. People go over there and cry with the kinsfolk—kinsfolk and nonkinsfolk cry. They cry loud."[44]

Mourning escalated as close relatives—particularly the women—continued to wail; cut their hair or let it fall loose; tore off their best clothes; lacerated their bodies, splattering blood all over; and sometimes cut off a finger joint. According to Bittle, the intensity of mourning, which was a function of genuine grief, "was also an effort to placate the ghost of the dead, assuring that its survivors regarded it highly and expected similar regard in return."[45]

Although the immediate family was responsible for preparing the body for burial, a distant relative was usually prevailed upon to prepare and dispose of the corpse as quickly as possible. Rose Chaletsin described what was involved in selecting someone to prepare the body: "The relations wouldn't handle the body. But if some of those other people come and handle the body, then next time you can do that for them, help them."[46]

Persons who had previously prepared a corpse for burial were likely to be asked again. Chaletsin, who was asked frequently, specified her role in the preparation: "I handled dead people. I washed them, cleaned them up, combed their hair, painted their face [with red paint and white clay] . . . dress them up in their best clothes, their best moccasins, take all the bedding out and put on clean sheets, put good stuff on the beds, and lay them on the bed."[47]

The body was then wrapped in a blanket, buffalo robe, or piece of canvas; tied with a rope; and transported for burial as quickly as possible. Susagossa emphasized the haste: "As soon as you get it ready, you put the body away. Those days they had some tepee poles. Put the body on it and take it away. . . . They tie the poles to a horse [to make a travois]. If the person died at night they keep the body all night, and first thing in the morning they take it away."[48]

The closest relatives were not expected to attend the burial. In Rose Chaletsin's words, "If my husband die, they wouldn't let me go over there to see him buried. You think too much of him or her if you go over there and see them buried."[49]

The lack of proper tools dictated that the body be buried in a rock crevice where it could be mounded over with other rocks because, according

Group of Apache children, 1901. Phillips Collection. Courtesy, Western History Collections, University of Oklahoma Libraries.

to Datose, "when they have to bury somebody in old days, they don't have nothing to dig with, so they look for washed-out place where it's deep. They cover that body they put in there with big rocks to keep out everything. Those rocks on top, they so heavy nothing can get in there."[50]

When weather did not permit, according to Rose Chaletsin, the body would be buried in the ground inside the tepee where a shallow hole sufficed: "If it's a real cold, bad day, snowing, they just bury the person right there in the tepee. They dig in there, in their own tepee, and take all the stuff off what they got in there and move it out and dig a grave in there and bury them. And then [they] just leave that tepee there, let it rot down. The family moves somewhere else."[51]

Apaches were aware of scaffold burials found elsewhere on the Plains, and there was some evidence that they sometimes employed them for warriors who had been killed some distance from camp. The overwhelming majority of Apaches, however, were interred in the usual manner described here.[52] Pacer, the very able leader and chief who died in 1875, was given a Christian burial at the request and consent of his people. He was the first Apache to have such a burial.[53]

125

Remaining possessions of the deceased were promptly disposed of so the living would not have to be unduly reminded of the dead. Customarily, these possessions were buried with the owner, burned, or thrown in the river, and the tepee was sometimes burned or abandoned. Rose Chaletsin explained the custom: "If a man dies, they leave everything what he's got, they just throw it in the grave. And what stuff in there, sometimes they burn the tepee down. They just put it on the side and burn it up."[54]

Susagossa stressed the importance of discarding material belongings of the deceased: "When a person dies, we have to throw their things away. My father died, [and] when a high water came we threw his things away in the water. We don't want to see them any more. We threw his medicines away that we don't know nothing about, but what we know and can use, we keep it."[55]

Some people boldly went to the dwelling of the deceased and took belongings they wanted, such as a favorite pipe or a parfleche. Wallace Redbone bemoaned the inevitability of the practice: "That's the way they used to do in the old days. The old men would come and take the things that belonged to the deceased. There wasn't anything that the relatives could do about it."[56] This practice has continued into the present time, although many perceive it as greedy, even brazen. People not closely related to the deceased believed they were justified in taking what possessions they wanted because they had less to fear from contamination than close relatives did.

Horses belonging to the deceased were either killed or abandoned, explained Rose Chaletsin, because of the painful association:

> When a person with two or three horses died, they'd move away from that place, they'd give one man authority to get rid of the horses. Some man might just kill the old ones. If a man died his wife didn't want to keep anything of his around, she didn't want to fool with it. Sometimes they didn't kill horses, but they'd take them out somewhere and leave the horse in the mountains. The horse might just die if a man didn't want to kill them. Men hate to kill or abandon a horse. But if he takes it back to the camp, the widow might see it and cry.[57]

Given the value of horses, weaponry, and household goods, Bittle doubted the Apaches were prone to the wholesale destruction of property and may have kept more of it than has been reported.[58] Certainly, in more contemporary times the old practice has abated.

After returning to camp, the mourners fumigated the tepee, or house, as detailed by Ray Blackbear:

> They used to use cedar and sage. They would take hot ashes and put cedar or sage on them and then walk through the whole house, smoking each one of the rooms. That was supposed to keep the čį·yé away. It also

is said to bring good luck and protection. Some people used a certain kind of grass. . . . They also took roots called "medicine-fat." . . . They smoke the whole house and the tepee. If you have touched the body, then you wash yourself clean. If you have cut your arms or your hands in mourning, you don't wash for a couple of days. This is just out of respect for the dead.[59]

The period of mourning lasted an average of one to three months, except for those who had lost a member of the immediate family, in which case mourning might last as long as one year. During that time mourners, especially female relatives, took great care to show respect by their dress, as Blackbear described: "The women dress differently from usual when a son or a husband or another relative dies. They wear any old kind of hide. They cut it at the neck and let it hang down [like a poncho]. Instead of wearing buckskin dresses, they keep the poncho on for so many days. . . . They dressed like that when the men were killed."[60]

The other practice that showed respect but also ensured that the ghost would not return was never speaking the name of the deceased because "it hurts your head and it hurt your heart." Ray Blackbear stressed the importance of name avoidance:

You never call dead people's names. If you accidentally do, their relatives would cry, this would cause them to mourn again. You can change some parts of the name after the death of a person and then use it again. You avoid even those words in the language that are like the parts of the names of the dead, for example, yellow would be avoided in all contexts for a while after the death of someone with yellow in their name. You just avoid the name of the dead around relatives and close friends. To use them, you show ignorance and bad manners. It's kind of an insult, people just think you don't know anything.[61]

Since the period immediately following the burial was the most risky in terms of ghost contamination, Blackbear emphasized how important it was for all relatives to continue protecting themselves by "burning mountain cedar every night before they went to sleep."[62]

Afterlife

Apache beliefs about an afterlife centered on the concept of the dà·γá·´, the animating principle, or soul, every person had. The dà·γá·´ was considered part of the personal nature of the individual during his lifetime, and in Ray Blackbear's words, "If you are really sick, they say that your dà·γá·´ is fading; it's slipping."[63] If the person's condition improved, the dà·γá·´ again gained strength and reentered the body.

It is difficult to ferret out the concept of an Apache afterlife, even though some older respondents referred to a place after death where, Ray Blackbear believed:

all the dà·γá·´ of people will be reunited. The dà·γá·´ is in contact with the living relatives, but it doesn't harm them at all. They know it's around because they can feel it. When one person dies, his dà·γá·´ makes a path to the hereafter, and his relatives follow it when they die. . . . The dà·γá·´ of all people, whether they were good or bad, go to the same heaven. Bad people are good after they die. They never harm people again. The blind and crippled people become well and whole.[64]

Some Apaches who participated in the Ghost Dance claimed they had been to heaven and seen all of their relatives, but others denied having any knowledge of a heaven or an afterlife.[65]

Although inconsistencies were expressed about the concept of a heaven, the opposite was true of a hell or an underworld. Apaches expressed no confusion about the existence of an underworld. Typical was Datose's comment: "I don't think there's no hell. There's just one way, heaven, that's where we go, I think. . . . Some white man say that now there was hell. If they was, when a person dying they get scared, but they don't."[66]

Actually, the notion that people, no matter how evil, could be doomed to eternal misery was anathema in the Apache belief system. Although Apaches believed a person's life could justifiably be taken if his or her offense were horrendous enough, they also presumed that rehabilitation was a matter of course for that person, as well as for anyone else who had committed misdeeds. Punishment was reserved for the years of living and ceased upon death.

Any complete reconstruction of aboriginal beliefs about an afterlife, as well as of a Supreme Being, is impossible given the Apaches' early exposure to Christianity. The contradictory philosophical opinions of Apaches interviewed are probably a true reflection of the same contradictions that exist in the population at large.

Doctoring

Sickness and Disease

In the Apache world, where a person's well-being indicated harmony with the universe, serious illness and disease were regarded as evidence of supernatural imbalance. Ailments perceived to have a purely physiological basis were routinely doctored with an assortment of herbal medicines and special procedures to effect a cure or at least relieve the symptoms of distress. Other, more serious disorders required treatment of the whole person with potent medicines and intervention by the supernatural. The probable cause of these sicknesses was believed to be some taboo transgression on the part of the stricken or witching by another individual. But even when no obvious cause could be found, the perception was that the body had been invaded by malevolent supernatural forces, and curative methods were required to appease or release those forces. Cures frequently employed included scarification, cupping, and the ingestion or application of medicines administered by the medicine man or woman with supernatural contacts. Even "white man's diseases"—cancer, tuberculosis, smallpox, and measles, discussed in Chapter

4—that could not be cured by traditional methods because the original visionary, Running-Under-the-Water, offended the healing spirits—were often treated in the same manner.

All families had medicine bags (not to be confused with the tribal medicine bundles, which, as collective fetishes, were objects of worship) that contained doctoring paraphernalia and medicines. The bag, or pouch, was customarily in the possession of an older family member who used its contents primarily to treat minor illnesses of close relatives. Although most medicines were kept enclosed in a skin pouch, not all were. Gertie Chalepah kept her medicines tied in the four corners of a tea towel.[1]

The family bags generally contained herbal medicines; animal and insect parts in a dried, pulverized form; and other miscellaneous items believed to have empirical or cabalistic medicinal value. Medicines categorized as general panaceas, as well as specifics for certain ailments, were included in every family's inventory and routinely administered to family members—although sometimes to outsiders—without aid from the supernatural. Knowledge of these medicines was gained from experimentation, inheritance, and sometimes but not necessarily from dreams or visions.[2] Datose explained that her father doctored but was not a medicine man: "He [her father] had medicine. He's not no big doctor, but he fixed medicines for fever, pneumonia, and stuff like that. He didn't make a vision quest."[3]

Potent medicines and doctoring paraphernalia that had specialized uses were selectively kept and administered by "specialists," or medicine men and women, to individuals with serious or puzzling illnesses. Knowledge of these medicines and special curing procedures was acquired primarily through supernatural revelation. Although the boundary between the ordinary Apache and the specialist was not sharply defined, in general the specialist had access to more powerful spirits and medicines. One medicine man, Piyeh, for example, had goose power, buffalo power, and dog power;[4] and another, Dävéko, got his power from the snake, owl, and turtle.[5] The specialist's proficiency in treating the whole person, mind and body, made his supernatural contacts indispensable for treating critically ill or witched patients.

Medicine Men and Medicine Women

Medicine men and medicine women, as possessors of specialized doctoring skills and supernatural powers, were accorded great prestige and respect by others in the tribe. They were mystically gifted persons who, in individual endeavors, had acquired supernatural power through visions or dreams. Although this power was commonly granted in spontaneous dreams, the most potent powers were reserved for individuals who submitted themselves to vision quests in nature. Visionaries who acquired confidential curing powers became full-fledged "big doctors" and functioned in the tribe as skillful intermediaries between the living and spiritual worlds.

To undergo a vision quest, the supplicant traveled to a sacred place in the mountains or on the prairie and devoted himself or herself to a period of no sleep, fasting, and prayers to induce a vision. Although the vision was expected to come by the fourth day, sometimes it took seven or eight days. When the spirit power finally appeared and communicated with the supplicant, it offered its protection, granted the power to cure, and taught its songs and rituals. None of the persons who had experienced a vision quest were living when the first oral history was recorded in 1934, but several accounts of the visionary experience were circulating among older Apaches still living in the mid-twentieth century. Rose Chaletsin gave her account:

> If a man wants to be medicine man, he go way out into the prairie, all by himself. He starve himself. Don't drink no water. Stay six or seven days. They dream, and by the dream they know what kind of medicine. Just a brave man can do it. They lie out in the weeds. Them days, these men, they have to be smart. Not scared. Them men was kind to their people. Have good, sound minds. [Out on the prairie] they used sage pillows, lie all naked. No robes, neither. No hides to cover 'em.
>
> [The power] is just like a shadow. They know what it is. But if they brave, it goes over them, just like a wind is ahead. Sometimes like a big rain coming toward you, and you start to pray, and it goes over you. So many nights you do this, and you learn your medicine.
>
> These medicine men, they would come back and bring their story. Each one got a different one. If you would dream about something out there, you could take it for your medicine. I don't know what they pray to. They always got a peace pipe with them. They pray with it. They imagine things, they dream, they see certain weeds. They think about sickness. That's why they call them medicine men. When he sees things in his sleep, like a snake or a buffalo or wildcat or leopard, he finds out how they can cure.[6]

During the vision quest, the spirit instructed the visionary about healing paraphernalia and how to assemble a fetish as a visible token of the spirit powers. If the spirit animal was a bear, some part or parts of the bear would be included in the fetish; if a snake, a part of the snake would be essential. The visionary then gathered various items of animal and bird body parts, plants, seeds, rocks, and other required items and placed them in a skin pouch. That individual was then recognized as the owner of a medicine bag with special curing powers.

To acknowledge acceptance of power, the visionary participated in ritual bathing and smoking, as described by Rose Chaletsin:

> He don't come back home and start doctorin'. He don't come in the tent, but he goes in a creek and makes motion to the water. And he dives in seven and seven—fourteen times, and he come out. . . . He does that before he comes into a crowd. They [the people] look at him down there, taking a bath. They say he must be a medicine man. The people may be afraid of him. The women won't look at him. He may be a witch. When he come to the tent, his wife puts cedar on the live coals of the fire. The man goes in and smokes himself with the cedar. . . . The old men come and call on him that night. They listen to him. In the evening, they all smoke. He tells his story, but he can't tell all of it. He keeps some of it secret for himself, how he doctors, that's what he's going to keep secret.[7]

Most specialists were male, but a few women had either inherited curing powers from a relative or acquired them in a vision quest. According to Ray Blackbear, a dying bundle-owner sometimes bequeathed his medicine bag and power to his wife, who "retained some of the power of the husband. They have that right, but they're not full-fledged. People naturally think she has that power since she lived with a medicine man. They will respect her. After he dies, she may try to cure. She may be a little out of place. She wouldn't be like the man, but she has the right."[8]

The few women who had experienced a vision quest and were qualified to doctor on their own merits could not practice their skills until after they had reached menopause. Fred Bigman believed that then "sometimes women got more power than men."[9]

Datose's grandmother was a medicine woman who went on a vision quest and got curing powers from a snake that taught her how to doctor snakebites and six other medical conditions. Datose described her grandmother's vision quest:

> My grandma, she was a doctor. She didn't go far—just down here near Ft. Cobb to Crazy Hill. . . . She stayed there four days and four nights fasting—without any food or any water.
>
> A big snake came to her. He said, "Don't be afraid of me. I'm going to tell you what to do." . . . The snake told her not to cheat anybody, to stay in true way. She got good blessing.
>
> The snake said, "I'll teach anyone who comes to me what I know so they can help anyone that is sick. But when it is time for them to go, I can't do anything."
>
> She had moccasins on. He told her to take them off. When she left he told her to leave one moccasin behind. He tell her what roots and weeds to use.

He said, "Be sure to take smoke when you dig the roots. Blow smoke in the hole and put some back, and they will grow back." . . . She was given seven different medicines for seven different sicknesses—hemorrhage, pneumonia, thrush, broken arms or legs, and several others. Snakebites is what she learned [to doctor]. . . . She's got all kind of snakes drawed on her tepee.[10]

Some medicine men were believed to be "two-spirit people," defined by Blackwood as "persons with social characteristics and behavior patterns of a third gender who have constantly changing and transforming identities in relation to other cultural, political, and economic processes."[11] Jacobs, who stressed the complexity of sexual orientation, suggested that "gender may have little or nothing to do with sexuality, and conversely, sexuality may have little or nothing to do with gender" when defining two-spirit people.[12]

In Apache society few specific references have been found, although clearly two-spirit people existed in earlier times. Alonzo Chalepah remembered hearing stories when he was young about two-spirit people that back before his grandfather's time were subjected to "strong corrections—beatings, whippings, physical torture by . . . could be older brother, cousin, uncle, all the men in the male line, females too, and to my knowledge and understanding they were trying to stop that activity."[13] In Ray Blackbear's opinion, some women married two-spirit people who were medicine men to gain prestige, even though the men were known to be "not straight. Some women like recognition; they marry this medicine man so they can be recognized as an unusual person. . . . It's her job to help him like nurse, and she would have something to do with the fee, too."[14]

The exclusive power of the specialist constrained the transfer of his or her medicine bag to another person upon death, particularly if the medicines were powerful. Fred Bigman recalled:

Old Man Josh's medicine, they just bury him with it, his outfit. They don't keep anything. They just bury it. . . . It ain't fit to keep 'cause you don't know anything about it. You might go ahead . . . that power, that medicine is powerful, they say, and you might do something where you're not supposed to do. . . . When he passed away, they just got all of his medicine and just put it in his box and buried him with it.[15]

But according to Datose, occasionally a medicine bag with special medicines was given away along with instructions on their use: "They say there was a woman who was the first medicine woman. When she got old, she divided up her power among some of the men who could take care of it. You know, when a person is getting old, he gives away his power to those who can use it. It is still strong; it is the medicine that has the power, not the person."[16]

The dress of the specialist was like that of everyone else, except that he or she usually wore amulets and carried a number of curing tools distinctive to the craft—the most important a black handkerchief. This scarf, which was generally worn around the neck, had a cabalistic value and was used in curing and legerdemain. Mainly, it served as an X ray to locate the source of a complaint, and with sleight of hand the doctor could whisk away poison, infection, or pain with it. Susagossa stressed the importance of the handkerchief in her father's curing: "My daddy looked at the spider bite. He looked through his black handkerchief and saw where the pain was. He sucked it out four times and spit in the fire. Then he rubbed the black handkerchief on his chest."[17]

Rose Chaletsin reiterated the importance of the black handkerchief: "The medicine man would dress the same as the others. They would call his name, and everybody would know that he was a medicine man. But not by the way he dressed. But he had to have that black scarf around his neck all of the time. He also wore bones on his wrist, lots of little beads, maybe, or a piece of plain buckskin."[18]

The medicine man Dävéko was particularly skilled in black handkerchief legerdemain. Joe Blackbear recounted some of Dävéko's sleight-of-hand tricks. One time Dävéko covered an empty cup with his black handkerchief, blew on it four times, and produced a cup full of sugar. Another time he produced a stick of candy from a rolled-up piece of paper by covering it with the black handkerchief and blowing on it four times. On yet another occasion, under the cover of a black handkerchief, he changed a white man's Stetson cowboy hat into a skull.[19]

The assortment of bird or animal amulets the specialists wore was associated with the spirit powers. According to Rose Chaletsin:

> When an Apache would see an animal in his dream, he would know
> that he had seen that thing. When the doctor put his mind on that
> animal, he could doctor. He would always wear some part of that
> animal. He might see a bear, and he could make a bear claw necklace or
> put bear ears on his head or a bear hide or bear ears on his wrist. He's the
> one that knows about this bear, that's what they say about this man.
> That's what he saw in his dream.
>   The same if he saw a buffalo. He would try and act like a buffalo. He
> would throw dirt into the air and holler like a buffalo. He might keep
> the skin of that animal in his bed and might tie it to the tepee. He'd
> keep it hanging up.[20]

Fred Bigman harked back to White Beads' buffalo medicine:

> Old Man Josh, Kiowas called him White Beads. He wear white beads all
> the time, that's some of his medicine. He used buffalo medicine to

doctor pneumonia and other sicknesses. The buffalo medicine was the bushy tail of the buffalo tied to a stick and the hooves strung together as a rattle, red hammer feathers, sometimes yellow hammer feathers made into a fan to fan you wherever you're hurting. Got Old Man Apache John to doctor him with buffalo medicine, too. They mixed some kind of herbs, roots with paint, this ground dirt, this red paint. When they get through they paint you.[21]

Medicine men and women also painted themselves. Rose Chaletsin recalled: "The medicine men had red paint on them. They wore it on their cheeks and on their foreheads. Sometimes they just painted it down over their eyes. Sometimes they would paint it all over their face. They said that kept them from getting sunburned. I seen it . . . I saw them paint their bodies."[22]

Although specialists diagnosed and treated disease, they were not obligated to treat everyone, especially if they believed they could not make a patient better. Once the specialist accepted a gift of tobacco from a prospective patient, however, he or she had essentially agreed to take the case and specified the payment expected. In Ray Blackbear's words:

It's prearranged. The doctor outlines what he is going to do when he takes the case. There are different rules. Tobacco is the first thing. Tobacco plays an important part. If I wanted him to take a case, I would offer him a smoke, a cigarette, and he couldn't refuse it. He can't turn down the case after he's smoked it. He can't turn it down, the cigarette or the case. Then he outlines his work—what is to be done.

They [the doctors] took four things as gifts for curing—sometimes a horse, a blanket, part of beaver, or eagle feathers, something they really have to have. The patient's relatives have to go get these things for him. Sometimes they say they want particular feathers. They say, "Give me the center feather of the eagle." Maybe they want a piece of buffalo hide, a black handkerchief. Maybe they will come to eat after they have cured the patient.[23]

According to Susagossa and Datose, however: "If it was a hard case, they had to pay seven things, or if there was no horse with it, fourteen things. That way the sick person gets well."[24]

Before the curing ceremony began, certain precautions were taken so the medicine would be effective. Often, relatives of the patient were asked to refrain from showing anger, fighting, and swearing for a period of four days. The patient might be asked to avoid a certain food until the curing was finished. One safeguard always observed was not allowing a menstruating woman near the curing because to do so weakened the effects of the medicine.

All curing ceremonies began with smoking the pipe. Ray Blackbear described the opening ritual: "They smoke and pray before they start doctoring. They always be facing East—offer smoke to the ground, first to heaven, then north, east, south, and west. Those gestures mean the four winds, that the Great Spirit is consulted."[25] Then crumbled leaves of cedar, sage, or medicine fat were sprinkled on a bed of coals to produce smoke. The resulting fumigants were believed not only to alleviate illnesses caused by bad spirits but also to promote good health in general.

Rose Chaletsin gave specifics of the curing ceremony:

> You have to fix the tepee first, get it in shape. The medicine man brings his feather and everything that he uses to doctor with. He puts cedar in the fire and smokes. He smokes himself, and he smokes a pipe. He uses just plain water. He drinks it and splashes some on the feather. Then he doctors the child with the feather.
>
> After they get through with that, the medicine man mixes his medicine with a little hot water. He puts it in something. He puts it in front of him, he unties his medicine. It's all ground up. . . . He makes a cross with his hands . . . and then takes the medicine at the point where the lines cross and drops it into the cup. Everything dissolves in there. The water turns like tea, or maybe it gets green. He may cook it hard, and it will turn red. He tells the boy to drink that water up. The sick boy drinks it while it's warm. Then the medicine man rubs the residue at the bottom of the cup on the boy, from head to foot, four times. They always doctor four times.[26]

Doctoring Procedures

Bloodletting was one of the most widely practiced techniques in curing and was judged particularly effective for medical problems involving severe pain or infection. Apaches believed superficial cuts allowed "bad blood" to escape the body, thereby alleviating pain or infection, and that the process could be facilitated by sucking through an animal horn placed over the area.

The cutting instrument was commonly fashioned from brown glass, preferably from the bottom of a beer bottle, that was tapped by a knife until small rounded flakes came off. Before commercial glass was widely available, the cutting instrument was flint and, slightly later, a knife. The curer then took a flake Ray Blackbear estimated to be "about the size of a thumbnail and made ten to twelve small incisions over the afflicted area."[27]

Rose Chaletsin described the bloodletting procedure in detail:

> For any kind of sickness they cut the area and let the bad blood out. . . . My daughter cut my head just last week. . . . When she finished, I was all better. I believe in it. . . . Brown glass is better. . . . Beer glass is good, it

isn't poisonous. White glass you have to be careful, got to use the thickest part. Sometimes the white glass, when they cut you it gives an infection. Take a butcher knife and hit it . . . chip it off good and sharp. . . . Brown beer bottles chip a lot better.[28]

The instrument commonly used for cupping was a buffalo or cow horn, 2 to 3 inches long, placed directly over the cuts or area of infection. Then, Ray Blackbear explained:

The curer sucks through the narrow end of the horn. When a strong vacuum is produced inside the horn, pieces of chewed sinew are stuffed into the narrow aperture at the top of the horn to maintain a vacuum. Chewed sinew is much like gum and is very pliable. The horn then fills with blood. A white horn is absolutely preferred since the curer can determine when it is full. . . . When the horn is full, it is carefully removed and inverted to avoid spilling the blood.[29]

Salt, lemon, gunpowder, or ashes were then put on the cuts to protect against infection. "After it was cut," according to Gertie Chalepah, "all that stuff just poured out—blood and pus. Then we put salt and lemon on the cut. Indians always say when you cut, you got to put something strong on it. Old-time Indians used ashes to rub in there."[30]

At times the horn was dispensed with and no disinfectant applied, as Rose Chaletsin related Apache John's treatment of a snakebite:

Apache John . . . took some of the medicine out of the little bag that he carried around his wrist. He told my daughter to go in the house and get some chipped glass. She did and came back, and he took this glass and cut in those two tiny holes. He cut them across and across, like an "H." . . . He put his mouth on the bite and sucked it. He put some of that medicine in his mouth and chewed it up. Then he blew it on the bite four times. Then he took his finger and put the medicine on it and put it on the bite and kind of pushed it in there. That was good medicine. He gave us this medicine. He gave us those sticks, and he showed us what kinds of roots he's got. He called it that wild plum, in the ground. I guess you seen that plant, it's got little cherries like on it. They are red. In the ground there is the root. It's real hard to get; it grows in the mountains.[31]

Cupping and scarification were commonly used to treat headache, breast abscesses, snakebite, rheumatism, and pneumonia. Gertie Chalepah recalled her experience as a patient:

One time I had a bad headache that wouldn't quit. It kept getting worse. So they went to get Bertha Smith—she's an Apache woman—and she cut my head. And when she cut my head, that headache quit. And she used that cow horn on me. She cut all across my forehead. I couldn't feel it, the cutting, but I could hear it, my head was hurting so bad. She use a short horn that's got a hole in it. It's round. Put it on my forehead, big end on my skin, and sucked the blood out. Put chewing gum on the small end of it. Big end was on my forehead. When she got through, I had rings on my forehead where that horn was pressing. Three rings. She just cut my forehead all up. Made lots of little cuts so she could use the horn.[32]

Speaking as a former patient, Datose recommended the treatment highly: "It's good for headache and just aching somewhere. If you aching, maybe you got pneumonia. They suck two or three times with that horn. Get out all bad blood making you ache. . . . When I had pneumonia, that woman suck blood out of my chest. It was bad blood 'cause it was all black."[33]

Rose Chaletsin vividly recalled her mother's treatment:

Once when I was just a little girl my mother had rheumatism. They took her way out in the open. I was there. They had her hold tight to something. They tie her arm in two places. One here [above wrist], another here [above elbow]. The big vein, it get kinda puffed out. Medicine man, he blow something on it four times. Got a knife and little stick. Blood just shoot up. Way up and out.

He [the medicine man] say, "You tell me when you gettin' dizzy. You tell me." That blood kinda red-yellow, bad blood. I got scared. The blood was runnin' all over the ground. He tell my father to untie one the same time that he untie the other one.

He say to my mother, "Now make your arm crooked." Then she keep it that way for a little while. And he say, "Straighten it out. It's all right."

And she got all right. Some of 'em, they got good medicine.[34]

The very skilled medicine men and women were able to extract sickness without scarification or using the cupping horn, and they were likely to be sought for a patient who was critically ill. The curing competence of one such medicine man, Dävéko, was recounted in the 1940s by Joe Blackbear, who had witnessed it as a boy:

My mother's brother, Dayehli, was sick one summer. This was around 1888. My father and mother talked about it. Tennyson Berry's father, Apache Joe, was there. He told my mother, "Dävéko is the man who can cure him."

She told Apache Joe to get Dävéko. She said she would give him beef and blankets to doctor her brother. Apache Joe went for him.

Soon he came back with Dävéko. Dävéko had a medicine bundle with him. My mother told him she heard he could doctor for high fevers. He said to clean things up good inside the tepee. He asked her for a big cup half full of water. He took out his medicine bundle and

removed some of the medicine. He put it in the coals of the fire. He
didn't tell what the medicine was. They never told you that. I watched
him. Smoke came up. He took some buffalo whiskers out of the
medicine bundle. He held them over the smoke of the fire. Then he
drew them across his mouth with a sucking noise. He blew his breath
toward the sick man's lungs, and his breath turned to white clay. It was
just like a trick. Then he put down the buffalo whiskers and sucked
with his mouth on the sick man's chest. He blew into his hand, and it
was a chunk of blood. Then he turned the sick man over and sucked on
his back. Again blood came out when he blew into his hands.

After that he put more of his medicine in the fire, and smoke came up
again. He held the buffalo whiskers over the fire, and then he tapped
them on the sick man's chest and back.

Then Dävéko sat down and said, "Brother, how do you feel now?"
The man stretched out his arm and said his pain was gone, but he still
had the fever.

Dävéko put the cup in front of himself. Then he hit himself on his
sides, by the ribs, with his open hands. A big hailstone came out of his
mouth. He put it into the cup of water. He gave the man the cup of
water after it got cold and told him to drink it up. After he drank it, he
took the hailstone and ate it. Dävéko told him he would return in the
evening and give him the same thing again. He came back again the
next morning and gave him the same thing. The fever went away. The
man got well. I saw it.[35]

Surgery was never performed, although some Apaches had heard stories
of operations "way back" that had been done with a black feather. Ray Blackbear
remembered hearing of an eagle feather used to extract gallstones. Rose
Chaletsin recalled hearing talk of an operation in which a black feather was
used to make the incision, but she believed the story had been made up.[36]

The only medical procedure besides scarification, mentioned earlier, that
could be categorized as surgery was the reported removal of cataracts. Rose
Chaletsin claimed that "in the old days, everyone had good eyes. No eye
trouble. If they did, you take a piece of a glass bottle, examine it good. Then
you cut the little piece of meat in the corner of the eyes. The piece draws
back, and then they cover your eyes. There is a little blood. You don't use
water or nothing in your eyes for a couple of days. That cataract is the little
piece of meat."[37] A blade of prairie grass with very thin and sharp edges,
identified as sideoats grama, was also used as the cutting tool in cataract
operations.[38]

Some Apaches who were not specialists had exclusive rights to certain
cures they had inherited from a medicine man or woman. Ray Blackbear told

about one woman's diphtheria cure that had been passed to her matrilineally from her mother's mother, daughter of Yellow Wolf. The cure, which only she performed, was "to take your forefinger and carefully clean it and rub it with Vicks. Then you put your finger into the person's throat, and you carefully loosen the mucous. This treatment will relieve diphtheria in ten minutes, where penicillin won't help for days. Yellow Wolf had many powers, but he didn't trust anyone with most of these and just died without leaving most of this information for the Apaches."[39]

Medicines

Of the many plants used for ritual and medicinal purposes, the two most important were red cedar and sage, which were found in virtually every ritual context. Both were burned as incense and fumigants and not only were considered beneficial to good health but were also believed to protect the body and surroundings from malevolent forces.

Dried and crushed cedar boughs were burned on ceremonial fires to keep evil spirits at bay. Smoke from cedar was used to fumigate the tepee or house where a death had occurred and to protect relatives who had attended the burial from ghosts' evil deeds. Many families routinely burned cedar because it not only smelled good but also "scares the spook away."[40]

Sage was particularly valued for use in the sweat house ceremony where participants sat on sage and rubbed its crushed leaves on their bodies for physical and spiritual purification. In curing rituals, Ray Blackbear explained that sage was rubbed on aching body parts to reduce soreness and alleviate sickness caused by bad spirits. To relieve headaches, crushed sage was inhaled or a sage ember was tapped on the pained part of the head.[41]

Rose Chaletsin described a third fumigant as

medicine fat that was just like cedar.... It's not fat, it's wood. It's a root—kind of like rotten wood ... they used that when they was sick, you know. They use it on anything. Sometime they use it when they go to bed. They use it on their blankets when they go to bed. They put it on the fire and smoke it when they go to bed. They use it on their fire. It smells good.... It looks greasy, but it's actually not. It looks like it's damp all the time, it's dark. Some are big ones. You scrape it, like they do in peyote meeting when they put the sage in the fire. Scrape off a little and put it in the fire and smell it.[42]

The bush morning glory, called "ghost throw at you," was the one plant Apaches feared. They believed a ghost could cause paralysis by throwing the plant's roots at someone, but contrarily, the plant was used beneficially to treat ghost sickness and alleviate pain from broken bones or other injuries.[43]

Some of the most potent medicines were concoctions of insects, animal parts, clay, and plants. The three most important were yellow medicine, red medicine, and butterfly medicine.

Yellow medicine, also called shingles medicine, had four ingredients—dodder, yellow clay, and the heads of red ants and wasps. The exclusive property of one woman, it was used to treat a variety of skin ailments—swellings, rashes, blisters, sores, shingles, and sore mouth or thrush.[44]

Rose Chaletsin described in detail the preparation of yellow medicine:

> It for bad sores, bad blister. Another kind of sore eating on you like cancer. Just cut around and let it bleed and put powder on it. It really burns. It soaks in and dries. Use it four times. After that you get weeds and boil them and these big red ants and this Indian paint—weeds along any stream—it yellow and cover ground. Let it get dry and crumble it up. You fix it with Indian paint, wasp, and red ant medicine. You grind it fine. When it real dry you use it.[45]

Red medicine, a concoction of four ingredients—roots of puccoon, raccoon liver, brown sugar, and a small aromatic seed called birdseed—was used to treat stomach troubles and diarrhea. Tea made from red medicine was also given to treat measles.[46]

Butterfly medicine was a combination of butterfly parts and two snapping turtle hearts that were dried, crumbled, and tied in a little cloth or buckskin. The medicine, which was "good for heart trouble," was hung around the neck so the patient could smell it periodically. Fred Bigman gave specific instructions on how to mix butterfly medicine:

> Them big butterfly. It ain't really a butterfly, it's something similar to that. And they get it live, you know, and they dry it out. . . . And that heart, the heart of a snapping turtle. You have to take two, two hearts, have to have plenty. They crumble it up with that butterfly. When anybody get sick or anything like that, with heart, you know, they use it that way. You don't give it, you just take a whiff of it now and then, just like that, and they get cured over it. It sure funny how it works. But it's good.[47]

Various animal, bird, or insect parts were used as specifics for certain ailments. Dried and ground rabbit or horse feces was applied to alleviate soreness, crushed flies were used to cure a sty, and a tap on the head with an eagle feather was administered to cool the feverish brain of a pneumonia patient.[48]

Although a comprehensive listing of herbal medicines used by the Apaches in the last century and a half has been irretrievably lost, an inventory taken by Julia Jordan in the late 1950s revealed knowledge of a surprising number of medicinal plants families and specialists used as general treatments for specific disorders. Purple coneflower treated toothache and sore throat pain; mescal roots treated toothache, sore throat pain, arthritis, stomach trouble, and fever. Tea from mulberry roots or blackberry roots was given for intestinal difficulties, and tea from the roots of prairie angle-pod, called "white medicine," was used for respiratory ailments. A paste of red clay and fat was given to relieve itching from rashes, including measles and chicken pox; a decoction from Missouri melon roots served as a purgative and an aid in abortions; and goldenrod was used as a cold and fever medicine. Wild plum roots were used to treat mumps, and the roots of broomcorn were applied to rashes and given in a tea for respiratory congestion. Dotted gayfeather roots treated cuts; a stem of slender parosela burned on the skin was used to relieve the pain of headache, rheumatism, and pneumonia; and the pods of prickly pear cactus were used for poultices that "suck the poison out."[49]

Venereal diseases, perceived to have a variety of causes, from sleeping with an infected or menstruating person to riding a horse to eating raw buffalo or cow, were treated both topically and internally. A paste of powdered dried mushrooms was put on syphilis sores, and a tea made from chinaberry shavings was given to "flush the gonorrhea out." Chinaberry tea was also given to start menstrual flow and induce abortions.[50]

These tribal medicines have generally fallen into disuse and have been almost totally replaced today by Western medicines and peyote, a medicinal and sacred plant that forms the foundation of the pan-Indian Peyote religion, a discussion of which follows in Chapter 10.

Witchcraft

Apaches had a great fear of being witched. Individuals expected the medicine man or woman to cure sickness and disease when the right conditions were met, but they greatly feared those who used supernatural powers for evil purposes and who willfully inflicted damage on others.

Those who had witching power obtained and retained it by the same procedures noted for beneficial power. Datose explained that

> to become a witch, they go somewheres by themselves and they learn some things. . . . They go way out, don't eat, drink. Something will come to them and tell them how to doctor people. . . . They learn everything the same time. How to do good doctoring and how to witch people. If they don't want to witch they don't take it. . . . [Then] he can't cure witching 'cause he never learn that part of it. If the spirit ask him about that part he say, "No, I don't want it. I just want to be doctor, help people, I don't want to witch people." And he don't take it.[51]

The possibility of witching instilled fear in others, but it also had a beneficial function by allowing hostility toward others to be expressed in an institutionalized manner.

Not to be overlooked was the capability it gave the witch doctor for economic gain. Since the common wisdom, although not always followed, was that only the one who did the witching could cure the witched, the doctor was thereby automatically provided with a paying patient—the victim—when he or she witched. Apaches suspected money was an important motive. Susagossa suspected laziness as well: "A witch would witch a child sometimes for the doctor bill if he knows the papa's got money—wealthy. He [the witch] is too lazy to get out and get his own money. He wants the easy money."[52]

Witch doctors were also known to witch their own parents or other relatives. The motive, Susagossa believed, "was just to get more power for medicine. He would kill other people just for meanness, but if he kills his own kinfolks, it gives him more power. To be sure that it worked, a witch would kill someone in his own immediate family."[53]

The particular horror the witch could inflict upon a victim was a paralytic stroke that contorted the face and sometimes arms and legs or an object or substance intrusion that penetrated the victim's torso. Fred Bigman explained that the paralyzed face was identical to that of "ghost sickness," or "ghost did it," but the "being witched" symptoms were more diverse. According to Ray Blackbear: "The paralytic stroke sometimes . . . twists the mouth and eyes. Sometimes the arm will get paralyzed, and they [the victim] can't hold anything."[54]

Witch doctors witched their victims with a variety of things—sticks, whirlwinds, fingernails, bush morning glory, and ashes—any of which could be used either to inflict facial paralysis or invade the victim's torso. Susagossa recalled the witching ordeal:

> There was a man, he was a witch. He always draw a picture of a man on the ground. He used sticks, but he had buckskin tied in a knot in the middle, and he put it in his mouth and then he would work it with his fingers—magician, you know. And that picture, he want to find the heart, and he blow at it. And that man way off got sick, very sick. And the people wanted to get him cured, and they take a smoke over there, and he [the witch doctor] can't refuse it. He set up tepee way off, and they brought the man there and he doctored him. . . . Nobody can go in, and he cured that man. He sucked it out. And they give him lots of things. He didn't tell 'em where it came from. He told them to burn it up. All the people afraid of him—bad medicine man.
>
> They say one witch man could witch with the wind, you know. You can't see the wind. He could witch with the whirlwind, and whenever it

touch anybody they got sick. They say this kind of witches pretty strong. They say witches use their own fingernails, too. They cut it off and use it. They use it like they do the buckskin or the stick. They use their own fingernails because they are afraid someone will find out that they are a witch. Sometimes witches use ashes. They use them the same way they do the fingernails, sticks, and buckskin. Apaches are afraid of ashes, 'fraid they might be bad spirits. A man told me witches would put ashes in their hand and blow it at the person they wanted to witch.

I was very sick, and this old Kiowa lady was a doctor. . . . My nose was bleedin', bleedin', I was so weak. . . . My husband told her, "My wife is sick, and I want you to doctor her. I've got buckskin, white horse, leggins, and things for the doctor bill." . . . At night she started to doctor me. She put me on a bed and sit by me and look at me through a black handkerchief—that way she X-ray me. She look inside me. She say, "You sick right there." She began sucking on me. And she pull out a toenail and she say, "Somebody been witching you." And she say, "There's some gray stuff in there, too." And she suck on me again and spit it into the handkerchief and poured it out on paper. It was ashes.[55]

In most instances of alleged sorcery, the motive of the witch could be narrowed down to some quarrel, jealousy, or thwarted design. Datose related the witching and cure of her uncle:

My uncle [father's brother] was single, and this man got jealous of him. . . . He witched him. [The uncle] got home and he was suffering. That man was camping nearby. Louise's daddy was big doctor. He help anybody and don't witch anybody. He told them that he was going to see that man. He tell him that he have to smoke with them and help that boy. That if he don't, he was going to beat him up. He smoked and put a black handkerchief over my uncle's back and take that thing out with his teeth. He didn't let nobody see it, and he blew it out. Everybody heard it hit the tepee, but we don't know where it go. Maybe in the air or in the ground. The boy say it don't hurt no more but that he was sore where that man bit him when he took it out.[56]

Some medicine men had a reputation for witching women who declined their advances. Susagossa confided: "We all kinda 'fraid of him. I could call him witch doctor. . . . Man no good, he makes women crazy. Too much devil in him. If women turn him down he got something to make her ugly, and she be ashamed to look at people 'cause she so ugly—in her face."[57]

Witches also witched each other. Susagossa explained:

When they know this person is sick, they go over to him. They tell him [the witch] to doctor. . . . Another man came over to him and said, "You been witchin' lots of boys, and if you don't get this boy well, I'm stronger than you are, and I'm gonna see that you're the next one to go. If you don't cure this boy I'm gonna cure him myself, and then I'm gonna witch you." And he cure that boy. They found out that the other man was a witch, too.[58]

All Apaches knew who the witches were. According to Ray Blackbear:

They dress different, maybe wear yellowhammer feather, scissor-tail, parrot, or eagle feather. You could tell a witch just by looking at him. They don't have no special costume. [To cure someone who has been witched] they get a feather and some mountain cedar. They dry the cedar and put it in bag and mash it up, pulverize it like, and make incense out of it. They put it on the fire and let the feather absorb the smell of it. And they wave it over the witched person. They fan him with it. They use eagle feathers, yellowhammer feathers, blue darter feathers, and swift hawk feathers. They have certain things they say. The witching witch has to cure the person he witched. You can't use another witch to cure you. They use two or three different herbs. They chew it up and put it on the feather and waft the odor over to you. It has to do with the sense of smell.[59]

Owls were also believed to be witches. In Datose's words, "My mother used to tell me that a witch could turn into an owl, and if you killed one and found an earring on it, it was a witch."[60]

Both witches and owls made bird sounds and did their evil work after dark. According to Ray Blackbear: "The owl is mostly in the dark, and it has to do with the black arts. It's the same way with witches. Some witches may sing before doing anything, some make a sound like a swift hawk, some use the owl. Owl is the same as witches mostly after dark."[61]

Although the owl and the witch doctor were the primary suspects in witching, under certain circumstances the buffalo, horse, snake, mole, and a whirlwind could witch, too.

Protection from witch sickness was afforded by not going out after dark, carrying sage, avoiding owls and whirlwinds, and, as Susagossa recommended, "praying to the power of the medicine bag. They used to do some praying to the medicine bag to keep the bad spirits away and witches, too. Witches were afraid to witch the person who owned the medicine bag."[62]

What is witch sickness? The answer perhaps lies in the field of psychosomatic medicine, which has demonstrated that mood and personality factors can have a significant effect on one's longevity and over-all general health. A life-sustaining reflex that slows the heart is automatic in some birds and animals but not in humans because the human brain can override the reflex. Evidence indicates that cardiac slowing and sometimes sudden death due to cardiac arrest of a healthy heart may be affected not only by impulses from the integrative levels of the human brain but also by outside impulses of extreme dejection or sudden fright.[63] By implication non-life threatening disorders can also be caused by highly emotional circumstances.

"Witch sickness" and "ghost did it" are organic disorders that perhaps were triggered by extreme fear. Symptoms of the temporary facial paralysis of witch and ghost sickness are identical to those of the neurological disorder Bell's palsy, a viral infection causing inflamation of the seventh cranial nerve. Because Bell's palsy is a disorder that can reverse on its own, it is an ideal disorder for the witch to cure. Symptoms of the longer-lasting witch sickness of a facial paralysis that extends to an arm and a leg on one side of the body replicate symptoms of a stroke caused by a blood clot or ruptured blood vessel in the brain.[64] This was the most difficult witch sickness to cure and many times only a partial cure was effected. In the most common witch sickness, object intrusion, a serious bleeding ulcer or simple indigestion could have explained the pain. It was the easiest to cure because all the medicine man or woman had to do was extract an object from the torso using some legerdemain if necessary.

That the patient could be cured by the medicine man or woman in an elaborate ceremony was well documented, which lends support to a psycho-somatic explanation of witch and ghost sickness. The most likely victims of witching were adults who felt the most vulnerable, and children of parents who feared the witch doctor the most. No doubt some witches used hypnosis as Ray Blackbear believed.[65] In *Sanapia*, David Jones concluded that the most frequent victims of ghost and witch sickness among the Comanches were members of the traditional group, which he believed was the Indian's way of confirming that he was a "real Indian."[66] It is not possible to document the same pattern for Apaches. Some witching occurred between tribes but not between Apaches and the white population. As Susagossa commented, "It's hard to witch a white man 'cause he's not our kind."[67] From her statement we can conclude that witching was a means to assert Apache identity. For the Apaches, as well as the Comanches, the most important consequence of an exorcising ceremony to reverse witching was a coming together as a community in support of the victim and a strengthening of Apache ties to one another in ritual.

Ceremonial Dances

Clustering of Symbols

Ceremonial dances in which participants, led by a leader or chief, evoked supernatural forces by singing and dancing were greatly anticipated in the Apache camp. The periodic coming together of some—and often all—Apaches, combined with prayer to mystical beings or powers, a multiplicity of symbols, the chant of the song, the cadence of the drum, and the rhythmic shuffling of the feet, energized and united participants whether the dances were spontaneous like the War Dance or regular calendrical events. As each person, according to his or her ability, helped prepare special clothing, gathered and decorated ceremonial paraphernalia, prepared food, and practiced songs and dances, a heightened camaraderie could be sensed throughout the camp. Falling within the broad range of ritual, ceremonial dances—appropriately called "cultural performances" by Singer—encapsulated the model for and conceptual aspects of religious life for the believer. Truly sacred events, these rituals focused on a complexity of symbols with unique Apache meanings, symbols that, according to Geertz, "provide a model for the perception, understanding, judgment, and manipulation of the world."[1]

Apaches celebrated a broad spectrum of ceremonial dances. Most notable were those of the Dancing Societies, which were tribal dances for one or the other gender or both, held once a year but more often if the need arose. The Sun Dance of the Kiowas was also an annual affair unless a circumstance such as a shortage of buffalo or an imminent military threat prevented it. The Buffalo Dance was originally held once a year but later was held more often, and the Scalp Dance, War Dance, and rain dance were celebrated when a specific event prompted it.

Dancing Societies

All prominent men and women belonged to one of three, perhaps four, adult Dancing Societies: the Manatidie and the Tlintidie, the men's military societies, or the Izuwe, the old woman's society. All children belonged to the fourth dancing society, the Kasowe, or Rabbit Society. Alfred Chalepah knew of a third men's military society but was reluctant to talk about it because "it wasn't decent."[2] Although the societies were not age graded, they were loosely divided along generational lines. The Rabbits usually recruited from the children, the Manatidie from middle-aged men, and the Tlintidie from old men; but no one had to belong to any one to qualify for another, and often the Manatidie was bypassed. Sometimes the Manatidie also claimed members of the Tlintidie, and some men never belonged to either of the men's groups.

Annual meetings of the societies were held in the spring or summer months, although circumstances prompted other meetings throughout the year. The societies were especially vital in the Apache heyday but began to decline steadily in importance and relevance after the signing of the Medicine Lodge Treaty in 1867. Removal severely fragmented the Apaches' collective sense of ritual purpose, and soon after the first decade of the twentieth century the societies simply ceased to exist. The Manatidie was revived after World War I but died again shortly thereafter. Then, in winter of 1959–1960, through the efforts of Bittle and tribal leaders, the Manatidie was successfully revived, and it remains an important cohesive force for the tribe.[3]

Much of the basic information about the Dancing Societies discussed here comes from McAllister, who worked with the Apaches in 1933–1934. His three oldest informants had belonged to the Manatidie, and although none of the old men living at that time had been members of the Tlintidie, some of them knew others who had. Sources for the Izuwe, the old women's secret society, are nonexistent, and for that society McAllister relied almost entirely on one old man whose mother had belonged.[4] Sources for the Rabbit Society are more abundant because some Apaches still living in the 1950s and 1960s had been members as children and added their recollections to McAllister's description. The Rabbit Society information may be the most reliable.

KASOWE

The Kasowe, or Rabbit Society, to which every Apache boy and girl belonged, was the longest functioning Dancing Society. Parents brought small children to meetings, and as the children grew older they became members simply by beginning to participate.

The Rabbit Dance was an all-day affair that usually took place in the spring when the associated bundle-owner was available. It was held when parents made a pledge when their child was ill or to honor their child. In the case of illness, people strongly believed a ceremony could cure a child. Rose Chaletsin explained, "In old days certain people have party if child not in good health. They didn't have medicine like today. The relations have some kind of ceremony. They call it a Rabbit Dance. Sometime it come out good. The kids, they get well."[5]

Claude Jay concurred: "The Rabbit Dance meant health—victory over sickness."[6]

After the pledge was made, the parents announced the dance, prepared a large dinner, and asked the bundle-owner to officiate. On the appointed day, all of the children gathered in the host's tepee with its sides rolled up so parents and friends sitting on the outside could watch. The bundle-owner, or old man, who sat on the west with the honored child sitting in front of him, began the meeting by placing his hands on the child's shoulders and saying lengthy prayers for the child's health and long life.[7]

When the prayers were finished, the dance began. Two men, acting as assistants, sang and drummed, and an older boy served as the "bull" to make certain every child took part. He carried a whip with which to strike any nonparticipating child and a knife to cut any offending child's hair or clothing.

The children imitated rabbits in the dance, hopping up and down and cupping their hands above their ears to imitate rabbit ears. A considerable amount of rough and boisterous behavior was in order. The children made fun of the old man and poked him with sticks, and the old man jumped up and danced. He wore only a loincloth, which he brushed aside as he danced, and he sang the rabbit song, which contained obscene references to the rabbit's anatomy and behavior—embarrassing the older girls and visitors, who routinely ran away, but not the little ones, who stayed and laughed.[8] The old man's antisocial behavior would never have occurred outside the dance, but the sacredness of the occasion sanctioned his behavior in the dance. By behaving that way around small children who had not yet learned modesty, he was possibly affirming his close relationship with them.

At the end of the dance a prayer was offered, and a meal was served. A large dish of food was passed, and each child in turn took four spoonfuls. When the dish was passed the second time, each one took as much as he or she could eat. The children who ate the most had the right to rough up the rest of the children. The ceremony then broke up in chaos, and all hurried out of the tepee.[9]

McAllister believed the Rabbit Society was important because "it bound the children close together, gave them a feeling of unity and importance. It taught them social discipline by making them conform to rules of the dance and in cooperating with other children, and intimately allied them with the owner of the most important worship bundle,"[10] all of which helped prepare the young men for participation in the military societies most would join in adulthood. The last scheduled Rabbit Dance was held in 1915, according to Brant, but continued sporadically into the 1930s.[11]

MANATIDIE

The Manatidie, or Blackfeet Dancing Society, was one of two adult male Dancing Societies to which many young and middle-aged men belonged. Membership ranged between twenty and fifty, always an even number because members were paired. The bond formed between members of a pair was like that of brothers. The partners sat, fought, and danced together; painted themselves alike; and helped each other when needed. Their families also bonded so brothers and sisters of one became like brothers and sisters to the other and the children of both were as one family.[12]

Although men considered membership an honor, they also believed the commitment was dangerous and burdensome, and they often left the camp when new members were being sought because if asked to join, they could not refuse. Ultimately, though, the most desirable candidates were unable to avoid being tapped and eventually became members.

The origin of the name *Blackfeet* was attributed to two different sources. Some Apaches believed they came from the Black Hills in the north and that the dance came from the Blackfeet tribe. In Rose Chaletsin's words, "The Apache don't know how they got it, but they named it Blackfoot since they had been around the Black Hills. Since we drifted this way we brought that dance from the Blackfoot."[13]

150

Apache Blackfeet dancers. Left to right: Harry Kaudlekaule (whip), Tennyson Berry and Stewart Klinekole (bulls), at Manatidie held July 1961 at Mopope's place between Anadarko and Ft. Cobb, Oklahoma. Photo, Julia A. Jordan.

Ray Blackbear wondered "what kind of people those *mana* [impersonal supernatural powers] were. They spoke Pawnee and the language of some other tribe. This tribe, they had that dance. We adopted it from them, and therefore they named it the Manatidie."[14]

The aboriginal Manatidie had seven officiants: four staff-bearers or chiefs, the "bull," and two *bá'žàyé*. The chiefs' duties consisted of choosing new members, determining the time and place of raiding and war parties (although members never raided, fought, or hunted as a group), sending the bá'žàyé on errands, and deciding the date for a dance. Chiefs were expected to be especially brave in battle—seeking out the most dangerous positions, planting their staffs, and holding their ground. They held their positions for life and passed them and their staffs down the male line. The bull, who carried a whip with the skin of a red fox attached, set all the rules for the dance. The bá'žàyé's duties were essentially menial, although not regarded as such. They found potential members who were hiding, spied on the wives of members at the meetings, started the fire for the meeting, and brought water and tobacco for the members.

One meeting was held each spring when the four staffs were ceremonially rewrapped with new skins. Afterward the members danced through the camp, "shooting blunted arrows into the air and killing any dog that crossed their path."[15] Other meetings were held when needed, usually before a raiding or a war party at a time and place kept secret as long as possible. A Manatidie feast was also given sometimes in fulfillment of a vow or to honor a relative.

The Manatidie had two important tribal responsibilities. The first was to police the buffalo hunt. Because the cooperative hunt yielded greater returns and therefore was preferable to individual hunting, the Apaches, like other Plains tribes, had a police society that exercised strict controls to prevent individuals from prematurely attacking the buffalo. So serious was a violation of the rules that an offender could expect to be whipped, killed, or have his property destroyed. If he accepted his punishment good-naturedly, a dance might be given in his honor.

The second responsibility that was also vital to the entire tribe was to help members who were poor. Food, blankets, and other necessities, although often in small amounts, could always be collected for distribution to those in need.

The four ceremonial staffs that formed the centerpiece of meetings were regarded as sacred. A great premium was placed on the fact that all of the original staffs had been captured in war. Reportedly, one of the curved staffs was captured from the Utes, another from a forgotten tribe—maybe the Blackfeet—and another, Rose Chaletsin thought, "from the Cheyenne or Pawnee or Ponca or Osage by my great-grandfather."[16]

Two staffs were crook-shaped and two were Y-shaped. Each was ceremonially wrapped every spring with new otter skin and buck sinew, after which new eagle, roadrunner, or goose feathers—collected from live birds—were tied at regular intervals on the staff. Rose Chaletsin detailed the involved process:

> They would get four or five of these skins and tan them good. They painted them yellow on the inside. . . . While the drum was going on, one man would cut one strip of otter from head to foot. Then the drum would play again, and they would cut another. . . . When all the otter hides are cut, they sat down and smoke. . . . They would wrap the staffs with otter skin clear to the bottom, then put two eagle feathers tied to white cloth at the end of the crooked staff, two more at the base of the crook, and two more at the point just above where the man would hold

the staff in the dance. When they are through with that, they make an iron point and tie it to the bottom of the staff with buckskin. . . . It takes them about two days to do that. The drum keeps going. They work on the hides in the morning and wrap and sing in the afternoon. When it's all over, they have dance.[17]

During meetings, the four chiefs planted their staffs directly in front of them on a row of buffalo chips, taking care not to allow the sacred staffs to touch the ground. If one was accidentally dropped, the meeting could not continue until a warrior picked up the staff and returned it to its owner while reciting a brave deed.

The ritual of the meetings was similar to that for other Apache rituals. Participants entered through the east door and moved clockwise to places on the north and south sides of the tepee. In the center was the fire, and on the west were the four chiefs with their staffs in front of them. Rose Chaletsin described the ritual:

When the Blackfoot dancers came in . . . they line up on the west side. They smoke the peace pipe. Then after that they pray, and they have the first ceremony. The four staff men march to the north facing south, and they sing the first song. Then when they get through, they sing the second song and march east and face west. The third song, they go around on the south side and face north. For the fourth song they go back to the first part. They stand on the west side and face east. Then they stand there until they quit.[18]

There were many songs, four dance steps, and eight drummers. All dancers went in a clockwise direction except for the bull, who supervised everyone else. When the dances were finished, the participants smoked and started the cycle again. When it was time to stop, the quitting songs were sung, and a feast was held.

Members wore spotted fawn-skin skirts and painted designs on the exposed parts of their bodies. Rose Chaletsin elaborated: "They wore buckskin. They got elk teeth. That's all they got on their buckskin dresses and on the men's leggings."[19]

Hair was worn loose except for the scalp lock to which was attached a piece of buckskin that trailed the ground. The headdresses were of turkey "whiskers," eagle feathers, and a deer tail dyed red. Dressed and painted this way, participants were allowed sexual license.

When a member or relative of a member died, a prescribed manner and period of mourning were observed, which Rose Chaletsin articulated:

When one of the members dies or when one of his relatives dies, one man goes over to the tepee of the survivors. . . . He notifies the relatives that they are going to have the dance sometime way ahead. . . . He talks to them. He asks them if it's all right to dance. He says that they want to have a good time. He tells them not to mourn so much, too much. He says, "I want you to quit mourning. You got a family, you've got something to live for." The man [in mourning] says, "OK, start your dance."[20]

Members brought gifts for the dead person's relatives to the dance. All the members and relatives had one final cry together, and then new clothes were put on the mourner, or mourners, and the old clothes were burned.

In spite of this account of what was traditionally supposed to happen, on one occasion a mother refused to end the mourning period for her son when approached by other Blackfeet members. The matter became so serious that it split the tribe into two factions, and every year since, two separate Blackfeet Dancing Society celebrations have been held.

The revived Blackfeet Dancing Society of 1959–1960, or "new model," so called by some Apaches, blended the old with the new. According to Bittle, it was

a rather remarkable fusion of ethnographic description and modern Apache creativity. When McAllister's account did not tally well with the recollections of the older participants, the versions of the latter usually prevailed. Political expediency in many instances prompted modifications in the ceremony, since the officials of the Society were anxious to maintain the participation of the older members of the tribe, and to give as little reason as possible for factions to develop.[21]

Considering the time lapse and the many changed historical and cultural conditions, the new model was remarkably central to Apache social life. The duties of policing the hunt and planning raids and warfare were no longer viable, but the whole tribe working together was not only a strong cohesive force but also an important means of self-identification and a source of pride.

Many of the changes in the ceremony were necessitated by a changed world. Membership—formerly limited to Apache men, with women only part-time participants—now included Apache women and children and members of other tribes. Some Apaches openly expressed their dislike of the latter because they wanted the dance for themselves. Dress for the occasion, which formerly was simple and traditional, became varied. Some wore elaborate traditional dress, some western clothing, and others a combination of the two. The tepee originally used for the meeting was dispensed with because of the increased size of the crowd, and the entire affair was held on an open field.

In the revived version, the four chiefs were replaced by any four dancers who, at specified times, picked up the staffs and danced with them. The

Apache women giving gifts to their guests, the Comanches. Bates Collection. Courtesy, Archives and Manuscripts Division, Oklahoma Historical Society.

most prestigious participants were the two bulls, who were the two oldest men of the tribe. One bull stationed at the north end of the line of the staffs carried a peyote staff and danced clockwise, taking care never to make a complete circuit of the arena or to dance between the staffs and dancers or drummers. The other bull was located at the south end of the line. Carrying an arrow and a notched war club, he danced counterclockwise, observing the same restrictions.[22]

The bá'žàyé, who acted as janitor, carried a bow in one hand and arrows in the other. In the bend of his elbow he supported a stick that represented a knife previously used in combat. A fox hide, his major symbol of office, was attached to his belt.

Today the revived Manatidie is celebrated every summer and continues for four days. Camping for the event is a multiweek activity, with some families arriving several weeks in advance and remaining several weeks after the festivities are finished.

As in earlier times, charitable giving was an important part of the festivities. Giveaways were periodically integrated throughout the four-day ceremony and began anytime after the opening songs. Some giveaways were spontaneous. For example, a person might drop some money at the feet of one of the dancers and then dance behind the dancer until someone appeared to claim the gift. Other giveaways, called "specials," were planned, and they took two forms. First were those of individuals who wanted to honor a kins-man (usually a recent initiate) by giving gifts to any number of persons. After a special song and dance, the name of the recipient or recipients was called, and the gift was distributed. The other specials were those given for a person or persons in financial need. One of the leaders of the society an-nounced the name or names of the needy and requested that everyone present contribute funds. While a special song was sung, people placed money on a blanket near the drummers. After the song the leader counted the money, announced the amount, and gave it to the needy person. Amazingly, as Bittle pointed out, Apaches, although suffering the endemic poverty of other Indians in western Oklahoma, always managed to collect a sum of fifteen to twenty-five dollars at these specials.[23]

In the giveaway of a Manatidie held July 21, 1963, the most frequently handed-out item was money in varying amounts, usually two to five dollars. Other items that exchanged hands one at a time were 78 pieces of yard goods, 18 shawls, 12 bedspreads, 8 Blackfeet Society shirts, 2 plaid shirts, sashes, 18 shawls, 1 quilt, 8 blankets, 1 peyote blanket, 20 towels, 16 sheets, pillow cases, 2 silver bracelets, 2 earrings, other jewelry, and 2 six-packs.[24]

TLINTIDIE

Membership in the Tlintidie, sometimes called the Horse Society, was reserved for the oldest and bravest men in the tribe. The group was small, usually numbering ten to sixteen. Like members of the Blackfeet Dancing Society, the men bonded as pairs acknowledged duties and obligations to each other as if they were blood brothers.

Meetings were held anytime and lasted one to four days. A religious group, the Tlintidie scheduled a meeting to smoke and pray when the camp was plagued by general illness or an epidemic. Wives were not members but attended with their husbands. A member's presence was obligatory at all meetings, and anyone who did not attend could expect ridicule from other members.

Possibly, there were as many as four leaders, who according to one per-son were called the "dogs." Their identifying adornment was composed of two red and two black bands placed over the left shoulder and under the right arm that trailed on the ground, a headdress of split owl feathers, and sometimes a bunch of owl feathers tied to the shoulders. Each carried a deer-hoof rattle and an eagle-bone whistle. The whistle was mainly to alleviate anger. If some member flirted with another member's wife, the offended husband obtained relief by blowing on the whistle.[25]

The two most distinguishing characteristics of the Tlintidie were its contrary nature, prompting the name Contraries Society, and its abundant use of owl feathers. The following description, given by McAllister, provides a sample of how members were expected to act in the Contraries Society:

> The members talked "backward," as it is usually termed. A command to retreat meant "charge"; to stop meant "to continue." Thus, when they were dancing outside and someone said to them, "Don't dance in that water," they were obliged to go into the creek with full regalia. . . .
>
> In battle they were supposed to be very brave. They would ride up to the thickest of the fight and jump off their pony, slapping it to make it run away. Those wearing the trailing bands would "plant" themselves at a dangerous spot by sticking an arrow through the end of the band. Only another person could release them by pulling out the arrow and telling them "to stay there."[26]

The sacred nature of the society was manifest by its strong association with the forbidden bird, the owl. The owl provided a variety of regalia and unique behavior that characterized the whole society. When the "owl man," or "ghost man," the most prominent of the leaders, shook out his breech-cloth, which resembled an owl, the group was obligated to dance for four days and nights. A hoot from an owl or from someone imitating an owl the morning after a dance meant the members had to continue dancing for one more day. On the battlefield, an owl hoot meant members had to stand their ground. At the dances, the owl man characteristically engaged in antisocial and shocking behavior that could include disrobing or engaging in open sexual behavior. A woman could avoid him by saying "Do it to me," in which case he could not touch her.[27]

Izuwe

About twenty of the oldest women and one old man belonged to the secret Izuwe Dancing Society, the only Dancing Society with an inherited right to membership passed down the female line. Meetings took place when a man returned who had been successful in a war or raiding party and who before he left had asked the old women to pray for him. Upon his return, he erected a tepee for the meeting. When all had gathered, he filled and smoked a peace pipe that was passed and smoked by each of the old women who prayed for him again.[28]

The tepee was curtained near the door so no one could see inside. The old man, who sat on the west, sang and drummed as the old women danced. He drummed by rubbing a dried buffalo hide with something that made a "washboard sound, zuh, zuh, zuh," from which the organization got its name.

157

He covered himself with a blanket so no one could see how he made the sounds. The women wore feathers that resembled horns on each side of their heads, and they painted their faces red and black.[29]

Unfortunately, little else is known about the Izuwe, except that during the Scalp Dance the members bit body parts brought back to the camp as trophies. And sometimes the group prayed for the sick.[30]

Scalp Dance

The Scalp Dance was danced by women holding newly acquired scalps from a raiding or war party, although imitation scalps were sometimes used or sometimes none at all. If all warriors returned to camp, the women decorated themselves and the scalps with red paint and white clay to celebrate. Rose Chaletsin told how the scalp was obtained and described the general reluctance to touch it:

> If a man killed an enemy, he could take one thing off of him so he would be able to show that he had killed this man. . . . They would take the scalp. They would take off a little piece of the hair but not all of it. Then they would tie it on a stick with buckskin. They tied it to short poles. . . . The Apache would carry the scalp on a stick wherever he went. After the Scalp Dance, they would destroy the real scalps. Some of them were afraid of the scalp. Some are just that way. But people who [have] got killed relatives do things to the scalp. Others didn't touch it. The man that brings it back, he don't have to touch it. It's on a stick. After he cuts the scalp off the enemy, he might go to the creek and wash his hands or wash with dirt.[31]

The women's dance started, according to Ray Blackbear, with the women forming a line, each holding a scalp high on a stick. They danced clockwise around the drummers, then reversed and danced counterclockwise while singing a Scalp Dance song. In recent times the Scalp Dance has been danced during the intermission of the War Dance and the Manatidie.[32]

War Dance

The War Dance, Rose Chaletsin maintained, was given to the Apaches as an affirmation of peace by the Pawnees, who reportedly got the songs from the Poncas. The Apaches gave the Pawnees horses. In return, the Pawnees gave the Apaches the War Dance, a drum, and four bois d'arc drumsticks, each topped with a carved man's head. She added, "There wasn't no more war after that."[33]

The War Dance was typical in most Plains tribes, and being tapped for membership was considered an honor no one could refuse. Rose Chaletsin remembered it as the customary ceremonial prior to an Apache war or raid-ing party: "In the older days they dance War Dance—just have arrow and spear. They be naked and have moccasin on. . . . They dance warpath dances when going to war. That's the only time they dance them."[34] In spite of this recollection there is some evidence that after 1890 the War Dance, as a substitute for the banned ceremonies, enjoyed a great swell of popularity. When the elders began dying off in the 1920s, participation declined rapidly, and by the late 1920s no one was left to perform the dance.[35] It gained renewed interest when World War II broke out.

According to Ray Blackbear the dance began with all participants sing-ing a series of songs and ended with a dance by two tail dancers.[36] Rose Chaletsin added that in the later version everybody danced the "chicken dance," so called because of the abundance of feathers worn by participants: "Thirty or forty years ago, that's when feathers came in. Nowadays they never been to war . . . they wear sheep on their ankles, they look like work-horses, they use tennis shoes."[37]

Pipestem Dance

All that is known about the Pipestem Dance came from one person Brant interviewed. The ritual undoubtedly celebrated the sacred nature of the pipe with a more elaborate ceremony than the simple pipe ritual described in Chapter 3, although no stated purpose is known. Joe Blackbear's narrative of the ritual commemorating the pipestem, described simply as "long with buf-falo hair fastened to the end," follows:

> There was a dance that was put on in the spring when the grass is growing, and again in the fall when the leaves are turning. It is called *Isákàs*. That means "pipestem." I saw one held at White Owl's place. Another time was at Whiteman's place. It was before the country opened up. I heard about it two days ahead. . . .
>
> It is held at night and lasts until nearly morning. Then they eat.
>
> The man in charge sits by the door of the tepee. He begins to sing and gets two pipestems from a stick they are hanging on. His wife sits on the west side. He gives a pipestem to someone on the north side and one to someone on the south side. The one on the south side goes to the doorway. They face each other. Each has a gourd rattle in his right hand and the pipestem in his left hand. They dance back and forth past each other. The man in charge drums. His wife is painted red all over her face except for a spot on the forehead above the nose, one on the chin, and on the cheekbones. These places are green. The drum is green in the center.
>
> The pipestems are passed to the next man on each side, and those two dance. When all have danced, the pipestems are hung back up on the

forked sticks on the northwest side. Then a pipe is smoked by the headman and passed around. Then he prays.

All during the dance a small fire is burning in the middle. Outside food is prepared by the women, and they eat when the dance is over.

We stopped having this dance when the country opened up. I think the Kiowas learned this dance from the Comanches. We had it as far back as I can remember, though.[38]

Rain Dance

A four-day rain dance, or the Wild Apache Medicine Dance observed by Thomas Battey, the Quaker, in 1872, was the only Plains Apache ritual ever described in which the participants were masked. Battey noted that with the exception of two lone women, all the dancers "wore hideous masks, some with distorted noses, grotesquely painted." The dancers were "fantastically dressed, with feathers attached to their legs, arms, backs, and head-dresses" consisting of wooden frames, and small bells were attached to their legs. The two unmasked women wore dresses of dark blue and scarlet and draped scarlet capes completely covered by elk teeth around their shoulders. The leg bells jiggled to the beat of the drum while the participants danced. After the fourth day, it rained.[39]

Masks and headdresses of wooden frames on the dancers were important identifying characteristics of Apaches located in the Southwest. Assuming Battey's observation was correct, it would provide another link between the Plains Apaches and Apache tribes in the Southwest.

Sixty-two years later, in 1934, McAllister described an entirely different rain dance, the Geese Dance. This dance was held in the fall or spring, when the geese were flying, for the purpose of bringing the rain. The four-day ceremonial was conducted by the medicine man Dävéko, who had the prerogative of picking nine close male relatives and friends to join him.

All participants wore breechcloths and draped white sheets around their shoulders. Their bodies were painted white and their arms black from elbows to fingertips. Each had a blue-green stripe 1 inch wide across the forehead that continued around the outside of each eye and back to the middle of the cheeks. Five men had a large blue-green circle that looked like rain painted on their chests and sheets. The other four had a green-blue crescent with points up painted on their chests and sheets. Dävéko's body was painted white, and his sheet had a picture of a goose. All of the dancers shook little bells to the accompaniment of a drum.[40]

All participants rode white horses to the first meeting, held southwest of Ft. Cobb. They did not drink or eat. They first sat in the tepee on the east side facing west and sang five or six songs while dancing in imitation of geese.

Dävéko then put ten sticks 2 inches long in a bucket of water. Each participant filled his mouth with the water and, without swallowing, went outside, stood in a circle around the tepee, and blew water toward the tepee to simulate rain. Then each ran back inside as fast as he could. The sticks in the bucket had disappeared and been replaced with ice floating like big hailstones. Each man took a piece of ice and chewed it.[41]

When night fell, the rains came. Dävéko went into the heavy rain and did not get wet. He brought into the tepee a prairie turtle, which he tried to swallow but could not.

After the fourth night the men with white painted bodies and bluegreen markings rode their white horses to an Indian village 6 miles away, honking like geese as they rode.[42]

The only similarities in the two versions of the rain dance were the purpose, length, and dancing with bells to the accompaniment of the drum. They might be different versions of the same dance, or they may have no connection.

Kiowa Sun Dance

The Apaches never had a Sun Dance, but they attended and took part in portions of Sun Dances held by other Plains tribes, most notably those of the Kiowas. Although Apaches had a specified place in the Kiowa camp circle, they were not equal participants with the Kiowas. No evidence supports Apache participation in the planning of the Sun Dance or policing of the hunt, an important activity of the Sun Dance. According to Rose Chaletsin, only two Apaches in the past had ever participated as official dancers.[43]

Chaletsin stated plainly that Apaches were not enthusiastic about other tribes' (excluding the Kiowas') Sun Dances because "it was hard for people to join the Sun Dance. You could go and camp way back somewhere, not in the main circle. If you went to visit them, those people were our enemies in those days, you got to camp away from them."[44]

The annual Kiowa Sun Dance has been described variously by a number of early observers.[45] Because Apache participation was largely passive, for purposes here I describe only briefly its major features in which Apaches participated.

The purpose of the Sun Dance ceremony was to cure illness and secure material benefits from the sun and the *Taime*, or medicine doll, that served as a special fetish for the Sun Dance. Everyone, including the Apaches, was

Sun Dance of 1893 framework and center pole with pieces of good luck material attached. Photo, James Mooney. Courtesy, Museum of the Great Plains.

under the jurisdiction of the Kiowa chief who owned the Taime and directed the activities.

A favorite part of the Sun Dance gathering was the preliminary six-day period of socializing, exchanging gifts, and enjoying sexual license. But it also was a period of serious endeavors given over to (1) raising a medicine lodge made of trees and skins, and (2) procuring the sacred tree to be used for the center pole of the lodge, an activity circumscribed by considerable ritual.

Apaches were most enthusiastic about participating in the construction of the medicine lodge. They learned a new song and several dance steps to accompany the gathering of the willows and cottonwoods, which they bound with a rope and dragged to the site of the earth lodge. The songs and dance steps became so popular that they were adopted for the Brush Dance Apaches performed separately from the Sun Dance. Ray Blackbear, as one of the participants, described the procedure: "They put poles in a circle, bending on the top to a center pole. They use these poles about 4 inches in diameter. We'd go down to the creek after some brush to put on the sides of the arena. You don't cover the top; the sun comes in there. While they go for the brush, they sing songs; that's how the Sun Dance arena is built."[46]

The other activity that was greatly anticipated concerned the sacred tree. The "tree of life," which linked Mother Earth to the sacred Sun, had a hide of the life-sustaining buffalo stretched across its forks and a buffalo head facing east. To mark the beginning of the four-day dance, participants, when the sacred lodge was officially opened, rushed to tie various offerings on the tree of life to be ensured a long life of good health and happiness. After the participants took their designated places in the camp circle, the keeper of the sacred Taime circled the camp with the figure on his back to signal the beginning of the ceremony.

Rose Chaletsin described the excitement she experienced at an Arapaho Sun Dance she believed was just like the Kiowa Sun Dance:

> In the morning when they open up the big tepee, everybody hollers, and
> then they sing. . . . I took my children, Alfred, Gertie, and Raymond.
> This old lady told me to take them out there and touch the leaves
> because it gives you good luck. And [helps] you raise your children.
> Well, that morning they opened that tepee. The sun's coming up. Just as
> the sun comes up, everybody rushes over there with their children. I had
> Alfred's little shoe, it's old and ragged. She said, "You tie it on there."
> And Gertie's old ragged dress and Raymond's old ragged shirt. She said,
> "Take it over there," this old woman. . . . I took all them things and run
> down there, my mother and my aunt, we all run down there . . . and I
> tied it to them cottonwood leaves.[47]

Once all the good luck items were secured on the sacred tree, the old women held a dance, and the pipe circulated. The Buffalo Dance followed, and the "buffalo" were driven into the sacred lodge. Then the soldier societies held a frolic. The last four days and nights were devoted to the public dance. Although the main dancers were young men, women sometimes danced. The Taime owner was painted red and yellow. The four main dancers were also painted, and they danced the whole four-day period without food or water. They appeared in Sun Dances for four consecutive years and then chose their successors, who paid for this privilege with a gift of horses or buffalo robes.

Although Mooney maintained that the Kiowa Sun Dance lacked all elements of self-torture,[48] others observed that although the Kiowas did not suspend dancers by a rope from the center pole tied to a skewer inserted into the chest or shoulder blades—a common feature of the Sun Dance—"they sacrificed their flesh and finger joints to the sun. . . . The sun and moon were painted on the chest and on the back of the dancer; then the skin was cut away as a sacrifice and to make the designs permanent after his [the dancer's] first Sun Dance."[49]

The Sun Dance was of interest to Apaches, but never sufficiently to motivate them to have their own. They were seemingly content to be rather passive participants in Sun Dances of other tribes, which may be explained in part by their small size, as well as by a supposition that they were content with their own unique Apache celebrations.

The ceremonial dances discussed in this chapter were generally more elaborate and more public than other Apache rituals—for example, the curing rituals and the Medicine Bundle rituals—but not necessarily, as the rain dance was private. Within this widely varying group of rituals, each performance was organized around a distinctive set of symbols that embodied Apache values. In full-blown ceremonials a multiplicity of embellished symbols took on increased significance, which invigorated participants and kindled in them a heightened sense of the divine. It put them in touch with the supernatural. The ceremonial dances served three important functions: (1) they provided clusters of symbols from which people derived meaning; (2) they maintained equilibrium by promoting group solidarity; and (3) as Leach reminds us, they provided "a highly efficient way for members of a culture to encode and communicate relevant cultural knowledge through the generations."[50]

Pan-Indian Religion

Roots of Pan-Indianism

The roots of contemporary pan-Indianism, which defines members of different tribes simply as "Indians," can be traced to the Plains in the last quarter of the nineteenth century when tribes began forming political alliances across tribal boundaries. The mobility afforded by the horse and the unobstructed flatness of the Plains fostered intertribal contacts, and tribes began visiting back and forth and camping next to each other. Tribal endogamy, which the Plains Apaches had always practiced, yielded to a system freely permitting marriages to members of other tribes; and under the program of assimilation on the reservation, young children from different tribes were sent to boarding schools where they grew up together—factors conducive to the development of an intertribal nationalism. At a time when Indian despair was at its height, Indians from different tribes found strength and comfort in each other's presence. In pan-Indianism they found a new sense of belonging and hope for a greater identity.

Ghost Dance

Despondent Apaches yearned for and were particularly vulnerable to the promise of supernatural deliverance, which first came to them from several Kiowa prophets and later from a Paiute visionary. In 1882 a Kiowa named Buffalo-Bull-Coming-Out prophesied the return of the buffalo, and six years later another Kiowa named In-the-Middle revived the buffalo prophecy with the added prediction that whites would be destroyed on an appointed day. All Kiowas and presumably a number of Apaches waited on Elk Creek near the western limit of the reservation for the event, but the prophecy was not fulfilled. Although disappointed, they were assured by the prophet of a future coming.

In summer of 1890 word of a Paiute messiah reached the Kiowas, and a Kiowa delegation was sent to the Cheyenne and Arapaho Agency to learn more of the matter. The delegation returned with favorable news and a quantity of sacred red paint, brought from the land of the Paiute messiah, reported to be endowed with miraculous powers. Soon thereafter, at a large gathering of the Kiowas and Apaches at the Anadarko Agency, the Ghost Dance was formally introduced by its leader painting the main participants with the sacred red paint. The movement picked up momentum in October 1890 when Sitting Bull, an Arapaho prophet, appeared and consecrated seven men and women as leaders and teachers of the doctrine by giving each a sacred feather to be worn in the dance as a badge of priesthood. The sacred feather was significant because women had never had the privilege of wearing feathers in their hair.[1]

The Ghost Dance religion that swept the Plains during these years of despair was led by Wovoka, a Paiute visionary from Nevada, who promised destruction of the white man, a return of the buffalo and of old tribal ways, and a new millennium in which the Indian dead would return and all would be free from misery, death, and disease.

Approximately twenty older Apaches—eight or nine men and ten or twelve women—joined the Kiowa Ghost Dance group and attended the regular weekend meetings.[2] Many, however, were skeptical and did not participate except for the special semiannual celebrations held on the Fourth of July and at Christmas. (July Fourth was the expected time for the fulfillment of the Wovoka prophecy.)[3]

Claude Jay recalled: "There were many Apaches who did not belong to it. My grandfather used to say that he didn't believe it was possible to bring the dead people back to life like they claimed, so he didn't belong to the Ghost Dance."[4]

Some people joined because they feared the consequences of not belonging. Claude Jay explained, "I was a member of the Ghost Dance. I was pretty young at the time. I think the reason I joined was that they said only those who were members would survive the wind that was going to blow over the earth, pick people up, and destroy them. I think a lot of people joined because they were afraid of that."[5]

According to Susagossa, the Kiowa Ghost Dance was held in a large tepee that accommodated 300 or 400 people. At the appointed time for the ceremony to begin, the fireman made a fire in the center of the tepee and then summoned everyone with a "Whoo." The men entered the door on the east and formed a rainbow-shaped row opening to the east with the fire in the center, and the women sat behind them. On the west, in front of a cedar tree, was a red cross approximately 5 feet high, and in front of the cross was a hole for burning cedar so participants could envelop themselves with smoke.[6]

Women dressed in plain buckskin, according to Susagossa and Rose Chaletsin, with painted designs of a large half moon and two stars on the front, a star on the back, and a rainbow stripe running down each sleeve. An eagle feather with a cross or sometimes a painted moon was worn at the back of the head. And sometimes they pasted red-painted down to the tip of the feather and marked their foreheads with a cross, star, or moon in different colors. Men, Susagossa remembered, dressed simply in their best shirts and moccasins and wrapped white sheets around their waists. For decoration, they wore eagle feathers in their hair.[7]

Datose was indelibly impressed by the leader who "dressed all in white. He dressed like Jesus. . . . He couldn't see either, but he died and he come back and tell us how it all was."[8]

Participants prayed to him and gave him gifts. In return he promised: "In a certain year you going to see dead father or brother. At certain time I'm going to take the sun down. At the time the plums get ripe, all dead people come and have resurrection." But the skeptical eyewitness, Rose Chaletsin, recalled, "It didn't happen. He lie."[9]

The Ghost Dance ceremony began with the leader placing a mixture of sumac and Granger Twist in a pipe, lighting it, and passing it for all to smoke. The pipe started on the south side, moved clockwise to the northeast, and then reversed, never passing directly in front of the door on the east. Then, according to Susagossa:

> They smoke four times, and four times there's singing in between . . .
> four times four songs. . . . Some have a little bell, and some have cow
> hooves to sing with. . . . The women, when they feel like it, they stand
> up there and dance, and the men, they all sing . . . sometimes they get up

Ghost Dance north of Anadarko, 1891. Inside the big circle exhausted supplicants lie prostrate on the ground. Monte Swett Collection. Courtesy, Museum of the Great Plains.

to dance. They stand in one place, they don't go around, just in one place inside the tepee. . . . On and on all afternoon, Sunday afternoon, they dance and sing and smoke. Well, in the evening when they quit, they got quitting song . . . they go home and cook supper. . . . And Sunday night they come back again and go over [the ritual] again. . . . When it's over they all get up and go home, and they do that every Saturday night and Sunday and Sunday night. They quit about twelve on Sunday night.[10]

Although most of the ritual was Indian, God and Jesus were in the prayers and songs. Susagossa recalled: "People would say, 'I pray to God and medicine,' you know, medicine bag. The medicine bag goes with this ceremony. This old man would put God and Jesus first and then the medicine bag in his prayers."[11] Rose Chaletsin remembered one song that was about Jesus going back to heaven as the clouds turned red, yellow, and gray, "and then everybody just get all holy and shout."[12]

Susagossa described the highly charged atmosphere: "Sometime women get to feeling good inside, just like that 'Holy Roly' you might say. They get that way, some kind of shaking or spell. That's what it is. Sometime they fall and roll around and roll around . . . just like Holiness."[13]

Ray Blackbear witnessed the atmosphere of frenzied participants who passed out, came to, and declared they had been to heaven and seen their relatives:

> They get to singing these songs, and then, you might say, they just pass out. Just feel so good—in a trance, you might say. And then when they wake up, they come to, they tell stories. [They say] "Oh, I been to heaven, and I saw your nephew, and I saw your grandchild and saw your brothers." . . . The music gets so good. Some people just feel so good they just pass on out. . . . They make believe that they've really gone to heaven.[14]

Skepticism began to grow among the Kiowas and Apaches as different messengers reported that Wovoka was a fraud. The Kiowas ended the Ghost Dance for a few years but revived it in September 1894 and, according to Rose Chaletsin, continued it in secret into the second decade of the twentieth century even though "the government said that they couldn't have the Ghost Dance anymore."[15] The government greatly feared that an emergent Indian union, clearly fostered by the intertribal Ghost Dance, would pose a threat to the great white migration. Susagossa, the only living Apache in 1967 who had been a member, was present at the last Ghost Dance when she was twenty-two, which would have been in 1915. She believed it was stopped because "the preachers wanted us to get rid of this kind of doin'. And when this old man [the leader] was dead, the rest just gave up. I guess when this old man died, no one else knew how to do it the right way."[16]

The origins for the myth of the Ghost Dance movement promising the return of dead relatives, according to Brumbaugh, as well as the Devil's Lake myth in Chapter 4, can be traced to the "North American Orpheus Tradition." The Native American legend, with many variants, focused on an Orphic hero who traveled to the Land of the Dead to recover dead relatives. The portal guardian imposed a taboo that was not to be broken if the mission were to succeed. The taboo usually was broken, and the object of the quest was lost forever. Typically, the hero-turned-prophet brought back to his people a ceremonial dance (the Ghost Dance) or a sacred curing fetish (the Water Medicine Bundle), the instructions for which he obtained from deceased relatives or associated supernatural spirits located in the indigenous Land of the Dead. Not by coincidence, the distribution of the Orphic legend replicated the northwestward path of the Europeans across the continent. In Brumbaugh's view, the Ghost Dance was a new paradisiacal religion created to respond to the rapidly rising death rates caused by the invasion of the Europeans and their diseases, a crisis that engendered a yearning for a return to paradise and a reunion with deceased loved ones.[17]

Limited in its distribution and appeal even at its peak, the Ghost Dance had little chance of surviving. Its unrealistic doctrine of revolt against Western culture, rather than one of adjustment and accommodation, almost certainly ensured its failure. Amid the developing intertribal contacts and the activities of tribes located on the Plains and its periphery, however, another movement was quickly spreading that would have a very different fate.

Peyote Religion

The state of heightened pan-Indianism—which fostered closer contact between tribes, a mutual antagonism toward whites, and a unanimity of Indian ideals across tribal lines—was fertile ground for the rapid diffusion of another nativistic movement with broad appeal, the Peyote religion. Contemporaneous with the Ghost Dance, the Peyote religion—variously called the Peyote Cult, the Native American Church, and the Church of the First Born—spread rapidly to become the most significant and widespread pan-Indian religion of the twentieth century.

The new religion centered on the use of the peyote plant as a sacrament, a ritual practice observed as early as 1530 by the historian Herrera in the Cerquin province of Honduras[18] and by Father Sahagun among Aztecs, a Chichimec tribe.[19] Two other Mexican tribes, the Huichols and the Tarahumaras, in particular were also known to have used peyote sacramentally in more recent times. With Mexico as a center of diffusion, the plant and its ritual use spread northward. The Tonkawas, on the Texas-Mexico border, were the first group reported to have utilized it in the United States, and from them the Lipan Apaches adopted it in approximately 1850. It quickly spread to a number of Plains tribes, any one of which could have passed it to the Plains Apaches, but the Plains Apaches claim they obtained it directly from the Lipan Apaches. Bittle maintained that this could not have occurred much before 1870, when the Kiowas were known to have acquired peyote from the Mescalero Apaches.[20]

The Plains Apaches had several peyote origin stories that told how peyote and its ritual came to the Lipans. One version, told by Joe Blackbear and recorded by Brant in 1949, was similar to the following one except: (1) in Joe Blackbear's version the woman's companion was a boy rather than a girl, and (2) his version did not include a role for God.[21] This version, a compilation from several elders, stressed that peyote was a gift from God not only to the Lipans but to all Indians:

THE ORIGIN OF PEYOTE

A very long time ago, a war was raging between the Lipan Apache and the American Army. The soldiers were winning the war, and they had already killed and driven off most of the Lipan. As the Indians fled before the army, an old woman with a small girl at her side was unable to keep up with the group and finally was lost in the mountains. The two wandered about for days, getting more and more hopelessly lost and, of course, hungrier. As they could hear soldiers in the area, they hid themselves during the day and moved along only at night. After many days of extreme hunger, the woman one night heard a voice speaking to her. "In the morning," the voice said, "when daylight comes, you should look under your head where it has been laying, and you will see something growing there. Whatever you find, take it and eat it, and it will alleviate your hunger and enable you to reach your own people again."

When daylight came, the woman looked under her head and found a plant growing there, and this plant was peyote. She took it and ate it and gave some of it to the little girl. And at the same time, they were no longer hungry. Each day from that time on, they found peyote, and both ate of it. Then one night she heard a drum beating away off in the mountains. She thought to herself that there must be people living up there where the drum was beating. She gathered up a great lot of peyote and with the little girl set off in the direction of the drumbeat to determine who was living there and who was playing the drum. As they walked toward the drum, they met a coyote who approached them in a friendly way, wagging its tail. The woman at first thought it was just an ordinary dog, but then she realized it was a coyote. The coyote turned around and started off in the direction of the drum, and the pair followed him, thinking that he could lead them to the encampment.

When night came again, the three of them laid down in the same spot and cuddled together, slept there. In the morning they could still hear the drum, and again they set off in search of it. For four nights and four days they walked in the proper direction. At the end of the fourth day the woman could hear voices talking, and she could understand what they were saying. They did not, however, go into the camp that night but once more lay down to sleep. In the morning they went to the top of a hill and looked beyond, and there they saw an Indian encampment on the banks of a little creek. They went down into the camp, and when they reached it, they saw that the coyote had left them.

On reaching the camp, a relative of the old woman's came up to her and welcomed her, and she told him how it was that they had found their way back to the camp. She also told them about the voice and about what she had found in the mountains. And she told the Indians, "I am a woman, and you are my relatives. This is a good thing. Someone spoke to me in the mountains, and I learned all of this. It is good for all of you."

So she told them what she had learned, and they began to set up a tepee. After this was done they built a fire inside, and all of the people went into the tepee for a meeting. At the first meeting, the woman told them each step of the ceremony, but at the second meeting, they knew themselves what had to be done. They had four such meetings, each time at night.

Then one night while they were having a meeting the communicants could hear someone coming toward the tepee, and they could hear the jingling of little metal spangles on this person's moccasins. All of the people in the tepee sat very quietly, and finally a stranger entered the tepee. He carried a little war club in his hand. When the people saw this man with his weapon, some of them were afraid and ran out of the tepee. But some of the braver people remained in their places. The stranger looked around the tepee at each person and then walked slowly behind them. At each person he struck out with his war club, but each man successfully ducked his head and was not hit.

But finally, the stranger came to a young man sitting beside the peyote leader, and he struck out at him and hit him on the head. The young man fell forward on the ground, his head bleeding profusely, and the stranger walked quietly out of the tepee. The peyote leader didn't know what to do, but finally, after talking it over with others in the tepee, he agreed that they would sit quietly until morning and wait to see what would happen to the young man.

The chief then called for the other people who had run out of the tepee, and after these had returned they again began to eat peyote and to sing. When morning finally came, the young lad regained consciousness and sat up and was all right. The chief made a cigarette out of corn husks and gave it to the lad, who was his nephew, and asked him to tell them what he had learned during the night. When the lad had finished his smoke, he began.

"Whatever happened last night," he said, "I don't know anything. The first thing that I remember is that I followed the stranger out of the tepee. We walked for a ways, and then we came to a high bluff. The stranger pointed over the bluff, and below I saw a tepee just like this one. The stranger walked down to the tepee and I followed him. When we reached the place he cried out, 'Here is your brother, the man all of you wanted.'"

And the men inside told them to come in. The people in the tepee were all Indians with long hair, and there were just a few of them in the circle. The stranger sat on the south side of the tepee where they made the fire.

172

Then the peyote leader said to the young man, "I am glad that you have come. This is our way from a long time ago. The Lord made this way just for the Indians, and I want you to learn to use it and to take it back to your people and tell them how the Lord made it and how he wants us to use it. You tell your people that the Lord made it just for Indians and that this is one of the good things which the Lord put on the earth. It happens that the Indians got it. When you go back to your people, you tell them that you saw the Indians of long ago using this plant and tell them that this is to be the Indian religion."

And then the peyote leader told the young man something so that he could remember. He said, "The blood which flowed from your head fell on the ground, and in the springtime you will see different kinds of flowers growing from that ground. They will be beautiful, and they are made by the Lord. You take any of these pretty colors in the flowers and mark yourself on the face with these to show everyone that the Lord gave them to you."

And then the young man returned in the morning to his people and told them what he had learned. And this is how the Lipan came to know what peyote meant and how they learned to paint their faces for the meeting.[22]

Ray Blackbear, speaking for all Indians, emphasized that "God gave Jesus to the white man and peyote to the red man. Jesus is seated on the right hand of God and peyote on the right hand of Jesus."[23]

Datose reasoned: "Nobody plant it but him. God plant everything, even the grass . . . and this peyote, he plant it, too. That's how come it's for Indians only."[24]

Botanically, peyote, or *Lophophorus williamsii*, is a singularly unique desert plant. A succulent, spineless cactus, it is a green, turnip- or carrot-shaped tuber with only a small circular button appearing above the ground. In its typical form, the button is divided by radial grooves that extend outward from a central tuft from which a flower grows. During reproduction, smaller buttons form around the parent button, and when as many as thirteen appear in a clump, they are symbolic of Christ and the twelve disciples.[25]

Pharmacologically, peyote is quite complex. It combines nine alkaloids, which in terms of their effects on humans are both strychninelike and morphinelike. Both effects operate simultaneously and in opposition to each other on the ingestor of the plant, causing first a feeling of light-headedness, dilated pupils, and a flushed face, followed by muscle spasms, delayed perception, and, finally, hallucinations, which at first are visual and then auditory. Commonly, synaesthesis—the phenomenon of stimulating the receptors of one sense to be interpreted in terms of another—occurs. Sounds become colors and colors sounds.[26]

The ultimate effects on a particular individual will vary not only in accordance with each person's bodily chemistry but also with the number of peyote buttons ingested, an amount that can range from as few as ten or twelve up to an occasional total of a hundred. The larger number is likely to be taken by a person who is seriously ill. Peyote is prescribed for ceremonial use only by the ritual leaders, although there are exceptions.

Its availability to the Plains Apaches is somewhat limited because it does not grow in Oklahoma. Its natural habitat is the Big Bend area of Texas and the northern parts of Coahuila and Chihuahua in Mexico. Periodic pilgrimages are taken to obtain the plant, and its collection is accompanied by ritual. When sighted, one approaches it with reverence, offers a prayer, and smokes a ceremonial cigarette. Joe Blackbear described his first sighting of it as a religious experience:

> When I saw my first one, I called Gregg over. He sat there with me. He took off his hat. I rolled a corn shuck cigarette and lit it. I smoked and prayed. I said, "Our father, you planted everything on earth for my people. I heard that this peyote grown here. It is for my body and my soul. I have eaten it. Now I have seen it growing. I will cut it and take it back so my people can eat it and pray for their relatives who are sick." Then I cut it and ate it right there. The peyote is for us Indians just like the white man eats bread and wine [for the communion ritual].[27]

The Peyote religion today is a harmonious blend of Christian and Indian religions. In its Apache beginnings in the late nineteenth century it was a pan-Indian, purely nativistic religion. It was pan-Indian in the sense that its membership crossed over tribal lines, and it was nativistic in the sense that it was an Indian religion with Indian ritual and symbolism. Joe Blackbear recalled: "In the early days they talked only in Indian languages in the peyote meeting, no English. They didn't mention Jesus or God. They prayed to Blue-White Man."[28]

When the government and missionaries began to express fierce opposition to the peyote ritual, factionalism ensued within the Apache tribe. The medicine man Dävéko, one of four peyote leaders, sought to maintain the Indian purity of the ritual, but the other leaders—in particular Old Man Architah but also Saddleblanket and Apache John—advocated eliminating shamanism and incorporating God and Jesus into the ritual.[29] One of the elders gave this account:

> They used to have contests in there like witchcraft, but they stopped that about three generations ago. The missionaries were coming in here around then. But there were still some people [the medicine men] who wanted to show off their power. They wanted to show off what they had

in there. These fellows made up songs when they ate medicine peyote. Those songs interpreted nature. The old people, they said not to reveal those things. They were kind of superstitious. From that time on, they abolished those bad things in there. They put the white man's God in and made it like a church. In Apache John's day the good people got together and made some rules for a peyote meeting. They kept them medicine men out. Dävéko was one of them. They told him not to put a curse on people because it would hurt their health.[30]

Since this modification of the ritual, which reportedly occurred in approximately 1890, the Peyote religion has incorporated aspects from both religions.

State and federal officials continued to oppose the use of peyote on legal grounds—first on the basis that peyote was a restricted drug in the same category as alcohol and later as an illegal narcotic. As a defensive measure, Apaches, in conjunction with other tribes in southwestern Oklahoma, formed the Native American Church at the state level and obtained an Oklahoma charter in 1918. The federal government's acceptance of the use of peyote within the framework of a religious ritual became official with the granting of a national charter in 1955, and for all tribes the Peyote religion became the Native American Church. Membership today, which is concentrated on the Plains, is estimated to be between 15 percent and 40 percent in many tribes. Since membership is not formalized and the churches are loosely confederated, it is almost impossible to arrive at a reasonable estimate of membership. A communicant might attend once in a lifetime and consider himself or herself a member, or he or she may attend regularly. Although only a small number of Apaches have been actively involved in peyotism from the 1960s up to the present, those who are not show a respectful tolerance of others who are.

Of several accounts of the Apache peyote ritual, the one that follows is taken primarily from Bittle's excellent study published in the early 1950s, with added commentaries from various Apaches.[31]

A peyote meeting was only held in accordance with a vow. When a family wanted a blessing for a child, a cure for a family member who was ill, or a celebration of an achievement (a birthday), a meeting was held so the family's request could be heard. The meeting required a sponsor or sponsors, normally the parents of the child, the children of an older person, or a relative of the person who was ill. The person who made the vow then asked one of the peyote leaders to lead the meeting for him. The people invited to attend were likely to include relatives of the patient, the honored one, the sponsors, and the peyote leader, but friends also were invited.[32]

Inside of peyote tepee on the Kiowa, Apache, and Comanche Reservation in 1892 with peyote crescent in the center. Photo, James Mooney. Courtesy, Museum of the Great Plains.

The meeting was held in a specially erected tepee with a door on the east. A crescent moon–shaped altar was mounded in the center of the tepee, with its tips pointing toward the east. The moon, made of damp earth, measured approximately 4 feet in length, 6 inches in height, and 8 inches in width. A secondary moon, about 1 inch high, was molded directly east of the first moon and connected to it. An arc drawn from tip to tip along the center of the crescent was called the road line, or lifeline, and it represented the journey of the individual through life. The south tip of the crescent was the infancy of man, the center midlife, and the north tip old age. The lifeline thus ran clockwise, or sunwise.[33]

Rose Chaletsin, in the account that follows, confided that the road on the crescent originally represented a rainbow:

> The fireplace represents the moon. It used to be a hole, but now they got a little road on it. My father was the one who made that moon and put the road on it. All the old people know that. That moon with the road on it stands for a rainbow, that's what he said when he put it down there. . . . When my father prayed, he prayed for everything in there, the moon and everything. Some of the Indians now say that's a road, but the man that first made it said it was a rainbow. In wintertime you see the sun going down, and one side has a rainbow on it. That represents sickness or rain or snow. When it's cold outside a cloud or moon might have a rainbow on it, and way back they prayed to it.[34]

Around the inside edge of the tepee, seats were prepared for the communicants. First, leaves of sage were spread on the ground and then covered with a layer of canvas, rugs, and quilts.

Some guests, particularly the older ones, wore elaborate buckskin clothing with special moccasins and headgear. Others wore ordinary street clothes but added a special peyote tie, a commercial tie affixed with a piece of costume jewelry in the shape of a sunburst or a bird. Each participant was required to bring a blanket that ideally was made of heavy European wool broadcloth, was half red and half black, and was decorated along the seam with beadwork. Those who did not have these blankets wore ordinary cotton or wool ones often decorated with bands or medallions.[35]

According to Fred Bigman, women generally did not participate in the ritual except in accessory roles. Exceptions occurred when a woman was the person for whom the vow was made or if a woman was being blessed or cured: "They figure they [the women] don't belong in there. Way back I heard they didn't allow no women in there. They wasn't allowed to be around men then unless they was sick. It was so the men wouldn't smell that strong blood [menstrual flow]. That's why they didn't want them in."[36]

Pinaronit, or Big Looking Glass (Comanche), holding peyote drum; Gonkin, or Apache John, last Plains Apache chief, holding peyote gourd, peyote fan, and wooden whip; and Apiatan, or Wooden Lance (Kiowa), after a peyote meeting, 1894. Photo, J. K. Hillers, Bureau of American Ethnology. Courtesy, Museum of the Great Plains.

Shortly before the meeting began, around eight o'clock but always after dark, the fire chief entered the tepee and kindled a fire directly east and outside the compass of the points of the two mounded moons. The firewood was carefully placed so it formed a V with its angle pointed toward the moons and its open side toward the door. A special stick, used at intervals in the ritual to light cigarettes, was placed on the open side of the V pointing toward the door. After the fire was burning, the fire chief summoned the participants, who formed a line behind the peyote leader.[37]

The leader offered a prayer outside the tepee and then entered. He carried a ceremonial cane or staff about 3½ feet high, all of the peyote to be used in the ceremony, a gourd rattle, a feather fan, and a grip that contained other ritual paraphernalia, a small amount of sage, a sack of dry cedar, Bull Durham smoking tobacco, corn husks or black oak leaves for rolling cigarettes, an eagle bone whistle, an altar cloth, and a chief peyote (a particularly fine specimen that he kept and used in all of his meetings).[38]

Following the peyote leader was the drum chief, also known as the second chief, who carried a carved drumstick and the drum, which was a cast-iron, brass, or steel kettle with a buckskin head made by pressing the buckskin over seven marbles or stones and tying it with a rope fastened on bosses. Inside the drum were twelve pieces of charcoal covered with fresh water. Joe Blackbear told the following story about the marbles' significance:

> A long time ago they used rocks and walnuts. Apache John started to use marbles. The glass one represents hail. Two blue ones represent wild cherries. Two yellow ones represent plums when they are beginning to ripen. He used two pink ones for ripe plums. He wanted red ones but couldn't find them. Apache John studied all this himself and learned it. Nobody knew they were marbles the first time he used them. In the morning when he untied the drum they saw the marbles. He explained it to the people. He said the fruits were what the people liked to eat. He said, "I put these in so our father would bless us and give us fruit. The hail in the springtime makes us glad. We also see ice in the winter. God gave it to us."
>
> I don't know how long they have used the marbles. I think I first saw them in 1895 or 1896. When you press the marbles against your body, it means that you hope you will have fruits to eat and be strong. When the gourd is passed around, you shake it and wish to live a long time.[39]

The entry and placement of various participants, described by Datose, began with the peyote leader who entered and took his place on the west side, facing the moon, followed by the drum chief who sat on his right. The other communicants, some carrying their own peyote ceremonial fans—commonly fashioned of eagle, scissor-tail, or magpie feathers—and personal drumsticks, followed behind the drum chief and seated themselves wherever they wished. The fire chief entered last and sat to the door's left.[40]

Throughout the night, communicants participated in the ritual acts of smoking, drumming, praying, singing, and eating peyote. Each act was perceived as a different form of communicating with God through the chief peyote. Although the prescribed movement of objects and people was clockwise, counterclockwise movement was also permitted to avoid blocking a ritual act with the chief peyote. Prescribed also was a recurring purification of participants and equipment with sage and cedar smoke. All persons who left the ceremony, no matter how briefly, purified themselves with cedar smoke upon returning, as Susagossa recommended, "in case bad spirits might be out there—to keep bad spirits out."[41]

179

To open the meeting, the peyote leader carefully unwrapped the chief peyote and asked the Lord to bless the meeting. He then laid out four sprigs of sage, each pointing to one of the cardinal directions on the midline of the crescent, and placed the chief peyote on the bed of sage. Ray Blackbear spoke of the high regard all had for the chief peyote: "You use it [the chief peyote] for a lifetime. Every time they conduct a meeting, the owner takes it out of a special box. Some of them are fifty or seventy-five or even a hundred years old. They're about the size of a silver dollar. They're a special kind. When you find one it's like a four-leaf clover."[42]

The leader then instructed the participants to rub themselves with leaves of sage stored under their seats and directed the fire chief to make and smoke a cigarette. The leader passed corn husks and Bull Durham to the fire chief, who carefully rolled his cigarette and passed the materials to the person on his left. The smoking materials were then passed left to each in turn until all communicants had cigarettes. The fire chief lit his cigarette with the special stick that again was passed left to each in turn. While everybody was smoking, the chief offered a prayer, after which each person who smoked said a prayer also. After the prayers were finished, the leader placed the remains of his cigarette at the foot of the crescent, and the others put theirs out in front of them.[43]

Each person then purified himself with cedar smoke four times. Peyote was passed, and communicants took two (sometimes four) and consumed them one at a time while moving their hands in clockwise circles in the air. And sometimes, Ray Blackbear added, "you rub your left and right hands alternately over your head, arms, legs, chest. That means if you're sick, somewhere you can brush the sickness off. After that you just sit still and listen."[44]

The drum chief passed the drum to the person sitting left of the fire chief, and the peyote leader passed the staff and the gourd rattle to the fire chief, who sang four songs holding the rattle in his right hand and the staff and his fan in his left hand while the person to his left drummed for him. These items were then moved clockwise to the next singer, who sang four songs while the last singer drummed for him. When all had sung, the ritual ingestion of peyote, praying, smoking, singing, and drumming were repeated until midnight.[45]

When midnight came, the peyote leader called for the drum, staff, gourd, and all of the fans individuals had used. The fire chief collected the cigarette stubs that had accumulated during the evening, placed them in the form of a crescent between the main altar and the fire, and brushed the ashes from the fire onto the new crescent. Then, according to Ray Blackbear:

At midnight, water is brought in by the fireman, and the chief sings four songs. The chief will ask someone to offer a prayer for the water. It's refreshing. He'll have some mountain cedar and throw it on the ashes. The water man will catch the smoke and put it on himself. Everyone else does the same thing. That's for good luck and a long life. After this they pass tobacco to the fireman and then to the chief. The chief lights it, and the fireman . . . smokes and prays and then gives it to the chief who smokes and prays.[46]

Then the fire chief took water from the bucket with a cup he had brought, sang four special water songs, and prayed while he drank. The water bucket passed clockwise around the tepee, with each communicant singing four songs, taking a drink, and praying.

The water songs were the most important songs of the ceremony, with special value placed on their origin. Bittle told of one man who got his water song from his grandfather:

The grandfather, on a particular occasion, was staying away from the camp for a number of days. He felt faint one afternoon and lay down on the prairie. In a dream, he saw a pure white horse standing on a rise in the distance. The horse was galloping about rather aimlessly with his mane blowing in the wind. Although his body was white, his hooves were black and streaked with yellow. This was a sign that he was a nature horse. Suddenly, storm clouds came up, and the wind and the rain began. The horse, unable to stand the storm, rushed off. So the man took this to be a sign and made a water song about it. The marks on the hooves represented clouds, and the white of the horse represented bright skies. The horse thus symbolized the antithetical elements of storm and calm.[47]

After the water bucket was taken out, the chief purified the fans with smoke and passed them back to the participants. The music and the ingestion of peyote continued until the water ceremony, performed at dawn. By then, many participants were experiencing increasingly frequent peyote-induced color visions and auditory hallucinations. The leader called for all of the ritual paraphernalia, which he placed on the altar cloth near the moon. He then took the eagle bone whistle, stepped outside, and while circling the tepee blew the whistle four times each to the east, south, west, and north, after which he threw cedar through the doorway of the tepee and returned to his place.

To start the morning water ceremony, the bucket of water was brought in and placed near the fire. The leader asked a special blessing, dipped his fan in the water, and sprinkled drops over the person being honored or cured. The drum and other paraphernalia were passed to the fire chief, and beginning with him, each person in turn sang four closing songs. The paraphernalia was returned to the leader and drum chief. The leader said a closing blessing and announced that the breakfast would begin. Ray Blackbear described the breakfast ritual:

> When the breakfast is ready, the chief sings a song, and a woman brings the breakfast into the tepee. The breakfast consists of four goods—water, corn, fruit, and pounded meat—that the Indian had before the white man came. Sometimes two kinds of corn, roasted corn and cornmeal mush, are served with the fruit omitted. Fry bread sometimes is served with the meat. The chief sings three more songs, the last being the special quitting song, and then asks the woman to pray for the breakfast.
>
> When she gets through, they untie the drum and rinse it off. They wind the rope up. Pass the gourd and staff around. Everybody takes it and shakes it. The same with the water. It's holy water.[48]

The bosses were passed so anyone who wished could rub the rocks or marbles over a sore area of the body, as doing so could alleviate pain. The drum was passed without the head, and each person took the drumstick, dipped it in the water, and passed it over his hair and face. The drum then went back to the leader, who emptied its contents on the moon altar. The four foods were passed to the communicants, who took only a small portion of each. The food was removed from the tepee, and the ceremony was over.[49]

The curative powers of peyote have been widely attested to by many who have either been cured or observed others cured in varying degrees. Certainly, the expectation of a cure was extremely powerful, just as it was for the patient in the medicine man curing ceremony. But whether the peyote was responsible for the direct physiological cure is not known, although its sedative effect temporarily alleviated pain and undoubtedly made the patient feel better. Fred Bigman likened it to aspirin: "It [peyote] eases the pain. I don't know how—like an aspirin. Gradually, gradually, the pain goes away. When it cures, it goes all over your system, just cures it."[50]

Many cures like the one Susagossa related were common: "I remember one fellow, he was pretty sick. He went to church with church people. Evil spirit touch him and he had a stroke, and he couldn't do anything about it. Some relatives brought him to a peyote ceremony. They had four meetings, and he was well. Chief said when you come four times you will get well, and that's all we want. Then you can go back to church if you want. We just want you to get well."[51]

Ray Blackbear told about one person who was cured by peyote of a disease that had been diagnosed but not cured by Western doctors:

Fred Redbone's wife had TB. They could do nothing at the hospital. So they held a peyote meeting for her. . . . The doctors gave her up at the hospital. Put up the meeting and kept giving her peyotes. [She] vomited, [was] restless, miserable. At daylight she came back to her senses. Somebody will chew it and give it to you [if you are sick]. They tried to give her 100 peyotes, and she is okay today.[52]

One Apache father touted the effectiveness of peyote:

When it comes to real sickness, peyote can do as much for you as penicillin. I've experienced that. I took my boy to the Indian Hospital with double pneumonia. The doctors said that they were afraid he was going to die, so I took him to see a peyote chief. He doctored him. I don't know everything that he did to him, but he took a spoon and gave him some peyote. During the meeting, the chief went to see him ever so often. I was the fireman. The chief came back and said, "Your son is going to be all right." I went into the house the next morning, and he was sitting up. From that day on, he's never been sick.[53]

By adopting the basic tenets of Christian ethics and superimposing them on traditional Indian values, the Peyote religion bridged the gap between the old beliefs and the twentieth-century world. And by uniting peyotists of all tribes in a growing pan-Indian movement, the Peyote religion forged a new identity for Indians and enabled them to retain a distinctive culture by accommodating the old ways and ceremonies to a new alien world.

Apache peyotism has experienced many changes during its time span of slightly more than 100 years. The four meetings per year at the turn of the twentieth century increased to ten between 1915 and 1960 but began a steady decline after 1960, the year the Manatidie was revived. Women who were totally excluded from meetings at first were permitted after 1935. After 1960 there was virtually no participation by the young—anyone under thirty-eight. In his 1971 article on Apache peyotism, Beals noted three broad trends that are valid for today: (1) a declining social importance of peyotism, (2) the elimination of many native elements and incorporation of more Christian elements, and (3) the increased importance of peyotism as a vehicle of pan-Indianism, simultaneous with an increased importance of the Manatidie as a focus of tribal identity.[54]

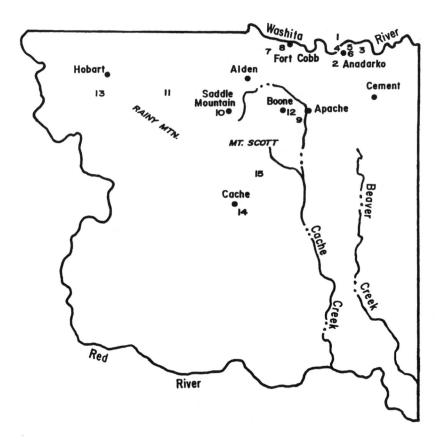

Indian missions, schools, and churches attended by Apaches, 1875–1915:

1. Riverside Indian School (Government)
2. St. Patrick Catholic Indian Mission
3. Mary Gregor Memorial School (Presbyterian)
4. Protestant Episcopal Mission
5. Methvin Institute and Memorial Methodist Church
6. Pentecostal Mission Church of God
7. Apache Indian Baptist Church
8. Fort Cobb Indian Methodist Church
9. Cache Creek Mission (Presbyterian)
10. Saddle Mountain Baptist Mission
11. Rainy Mountain Indian School (Government)
12. Indian Methodist Church
13. Elk Creek Baptist Mission
14. Cache Baptist Mission (Deyo)
15. Quaker Mission School at Ft. Sill

Christianity

Early Missionaries

Land-hungry Americans justified their encroachment on Indian hunting lands in the nineteenth century as fulfilling God's plan. They believed they were a chosen people ordained by God to expand throughout North America and create a model Christian society. They wanted Indian lands, and they wanted Indian souls. As messengers of God, missionaries were sent to win Indian souls and bring the "lightness" of the Christian world to the "darkness" of the heathen world. If the Plains Indians could be Christianized and civilized, it was reasoned, they could be assimilated into American society as agriculturalists and be able to live on considerably less land.

In a thrust that was highly evangelical, missionaries rushed to the Southern Plains to spread the gospel. They emphasized the teachings and authority of the biblical Scriptures and the importance of baptism by the Holy Spirit, or "being born again." They held the Bible to be the sole standard of faith, and they believed the mere acceptance of the Bible by the unenlightened would miraculously produce repentance, conversion, and a new life in Christ.

As missionizing became a matter of great urgency, some Christians soon realized that without literacy in the Indian population, the gospel could neither be understood nor self-propagating. Indian literacy, which was desirable, required teachers and in turn the founding of schools; and schools needed an economic system to support them. That could only come about with civilizing. Debates ensued in the missionary societies of the different denominations over whether first to civilize or Christianize. Although denominations took different sides, on the whole there was a recognition that each depended on the other, and the two became inextricably intertwined.[1] The missionaries' arrival could not have been more opportune, for the highly demoralized Apaches—stripped of their economic base, their freedom, and the right to practice their native religion—were in a spiritual vacuum. At first, their response to the new religion was decidedly mixed, but over the following six decades a majority gradually converted to Christianity, although few made a complete break with the old religion.

The plan for mission endeavors on the Plains actually began with the inauguration of the newly elected president, Ulysses S. Grant, in March 1869. Almost immediately, Grant turned Indian affairs on the Plains over to the Quakers, stating confidently, "If you can make Quakers out of the Plains Indians, it will take the fight out of them."[2] By July, the Executive Committee of the Society of Friends, or Quakers, had appointed Lawrie Tatum, a farmer from Iowa, to be the new Indian agent for the Kiowas, Comanches, and Apaches—in Tatum's words, "the worst Indians east of the Rocky Mountains." Tatum, placed under the dual jurisdiction of the Quakers and the commissioner of Indian Affairs in Washington, was faced with a daunting task. Not only was he expected to build an agency, secure more rations for the starving Indians, instruct them in farming methods, prevent them from raiding livestock and terrorizing others, and act as arbitrator between the Indians and the nearby army to minimize overreaction on both sides, but he was also to instruct them in the teachings of the gospel. It soon became obvious that he would fail to meet most of these expectations. His religious endeavors did not produce any Christians, his withholding of rations from the Indians who made repeated forays into Texas and Mexico did not prove a successful deterrent, and the payment of $100 to Indians for each captive they returned only encouraged more taking of captives. He resigned in 1873.[3]

In 1872 Thomas Battey, a Quaker teacher, arrived to help establish a government boarding school for Indians on the adjacent Wichita Reservation. (It later burned and was rebuilt 1 mile north of Anadarko, Oklahoma, as the Riverside Indian School for all tribes, and it flourishes today.) Battey then went across the Washita River south to do the same for the Kiowas,

Comanches, and Apaches. But they were uncooperative and would not remain in one place. Battey left after one year because of ill health.

In frustration, the Quaker committee sent instructions on additional methods of spreading the gospel and a reminder to preach against multiple wives to the next Quaker agent, James Haworth. After three years, in 1876, Haworth was finally able to report that Indian schoolchildren and "some adult Indians" were attending First day morning services at one of the ten worship places on the reservation and the eleven Scripture schools with daily Bible studies. Although he could report no Indian conversions, he believed he had made some advance in Christianizing the Indian.[4] Certainly, his leadership in the establishment of a school on the Ft. Sill army post in 1875 was an important accomplishment for the Quakers. Haworth resigned in 1878 for health reasons, and the Quaker influence at the agency ended. Overall, the Quakers did not accomplish what they had planned during their nine years with the Indians, but they clearly made the way easier for those who followed.[5]

In September 1898 the Kiowa, Comanche, and Apache Agency consolidated with the Wichita Agency to become the Anadarko Indian Agency responsible for Comanches, Kiowas, Apaches, Wichitas and affiliated bands, and Caddos.[6]

Apaches at one time had been grouped into five gonkas, or local bands, in separate geographical areas near the latter-day Oklahoma towns of Ft. Cobb, Boone, Alden, Cement, and Anadarko; but by 1900 they were clustered into three groups near Ft. Cobb, Boone, and Apache.[7] Readily accessible to them were six mission schools and churches established in the Anadarko, Apache, and Ft. Cobb areas from 1881 to 1907. Missions located in other parts of the reservation ministered mainly to Comanches and Kiowas but sometimes to Apaches also.

Following the Quakers were Episcopalians who established a mission in Anadarko in 1881. The Reverend John Bartlett Wicks, a priest from Paris Hill, New York, who trained young Indians for missionary work, brought two of them—David Pendleton Oakerhater (Medicine Maker) and Paul Zotom—with him to Indian Territory to serve as missionaries among their fellow tribesmen. Both young men had been U.S. government military prisoners in Pensacola, Florida. Oakerhater, who was a Cheyenne, went to the Darlington Agency for Cheyennes and Arapahos; and Zotom, a Kiowa, went to the Anadarko Agency. Wicks worked with whites and Indians at both places and built a chapel in Anadarko in 1883. His religious endeavors were directed mainly to Indian children. He suffered a breakdown in health in 1884 and left Indian Territory. Soon thereafter, the Reverend Paul Zotom

Christmas tree for Indians at Episcopal Chapel, 1898. Phillips Collection. Courtesy, Western History Collections, University of Oklahoma Libraries.

ceased his ministerial efforts and returned to his native religion. He was officially defrocked by the Episcopal ministry in 1894.[8]

From 1896 to 1903, Miss Ida Roff conducted a lace-making school under the auspices of the Protestant Episcopal Church and taught Sunday School in the chapel Wicks had erected. More than fifty women participated in the school. Indian women were able to sell their lacework easily and received about ten cents an hour for their work. In 1898 a Christmas worship service at the school brought together Christian Comanches, Kiowas, Apaches, Delawares, and Caddos. Roff married an Episcopal priest in 1903 and left Anadarko.[9]

In 1887 the Reverend John Jasper Methvin, a Methodist, arrived in Anadarko and started a mission and church. An energetic evangelist, Methvin began visiting the Indians in their tepees and after about two years succeeded in converting To-hou-sin, a popular Kiowa chief. When To-hou-sin and his wife joined Methvin's church, some Kiowas, Apaches, and other Indians also joined. The Kiowas gave Methvin citizenship in the Kiowa tribe and granted him an allotment of land on which he built a parsonage with a church annex for regular services. In spring of 1890 he established the

Miss Roff, Episcopal missionary, visiting Kiowas on the Kiowa, Apache, and Comanche Reservation. She taught lace making to Indian women. Courtesy, Archives and Manuscripts Division, Oklahoma Historical Society.

Methvin Institute with the opening of a school for Indian youth. Fifteen pupils attended the first year, and by 1901 that number had increased to 120.[10]

Methvin was strongly committed to the boarding school concept because he believed it would be a quick path to assimilation. He announced, "All along a double task has been set the Church, both of Christianizing and civilizing the Indian, both of changing him and his condition."[11] To achieve those goals, Indian children were literally whisked from their parents' homes and put in boarding school where they could be supervised around the clock. After each was given a new Christian name and Western clothes and the boys received drastic haircuts, the children were immersed in the teachings of the gospel and all the civilities of white Christians. Methvin later had to rescind his policy of taking children without their parents' support because he could not keep those children from leaving the school.

Throughout his ministry Methvin was outspoken about the evils of the native religion. He believed nature worship was of the lowest order, nothing but idolatry—in his words, "a wall of darkness that God alone can penetrate"—and

189

he called the Ghost Dance a "Messianic craze" and the peyote ceremonies "a drug habit under the guise of religion."[12] Susagossa remembered Brother Methvin saying: "Don't you go to that tepee and sit there all night tom, tom, tom. You go to church and learn how to pray to Jesus. . . . God don't like it if you worship some image, some idol."[13]

In 1907, after seventeen years of educating Indian children, the Methvin Institute closed because of a lack of financing from the Methodist Women's Missionary Society. Methvin retired one year later.[14]

Two Presbyterian missionaries came to Anadarko in successive years after Methvin's arrival. The first was the Reverend Silas V. Fait from the Home Missions of the Northern Presbyterian Church, who established a school and mission east of Anadarko in 1888. The second was the Reverend W. W. Carrithers of the synod of the Reformed Presbyterian Church in Pennsylvania, who established the Cache Creek Mission southwest of Apache in 1889[15]—a mission that remained in continuous use from the time of its construction to the present, becoming the oldest mission in the Kiowa-Comanche-Apache area.

Students, nuns, and priests at St. Patrick's Indian Mission, 1912. Sooner Catholic Magazine Collection. Courtesy, Western History Collections, University of Oklahoma Libraries.

Father Isadore Ricklin, from the Order of St. Benedictine, arrived in Anadarko in spring of 1891 to establish a Catholic mission. He lived with the Indians to learn their language and customs and after five months was adopted by the Comanches. He shared their love of horses and always chose the most fiery steed to ride, which soon won him the title "Chief Thunderbolt." He built St. Patrick's Mission southwest of Anadarko, which opened in November 1892 with 35 Comanches, Apaches, and Kiowas enrolled. By 1899 a chapel and three new buildings had been added, and enrollment had increased to more than 100. By 1902 enough funds had been raised to build the Holy Family Church in Anadarko.[16]

On a Sunday in 1909, when Father Isadore was saying mass in Ft. Sill, St. Patrick's burned to the ground. Undaunted, he traveled to the eastern United States to raise funds for a replacement. His entertainment as "Chief Thunderbolt, the Comanche priest," in which he sang, acted, and whooped in Indian regalia, was a roaring success, and he came back with $25,000 for a new brick building. In 1911, when the building was complete, the federal government assumed financial responsibility for the mission until 1932, when it was turned back to the Benedictine fathers.[17]

On January 11, 1921, after thirty years of mission work, the illustrious Father Isadore Ricklin died. Father Aloysius Hitta, who had been ordained in the mission chapel in 1901, became principal of the school. In 1927 Father Al, as he was known, constructed the Isadore Memorial Chapel. High on the chapel wall was a frieze that depicted the life and struggles of Father Isadore during the early history of the Catholic school. The frieze was painted by five young Kiowa artists who were students at the mission. The now famous five were Spencer Asah, Stephen Mopope, Monroe Tsa-Toke, James Auchiah, and Jack Hokea.[18]

In 1892 the American Baptists started a mission at Elk Creek (4 miles south of the present town of Hobart). Although six or seven active and influential Baptist missionaries were at the mission during the next decade, one of the earliest and most popular was Miss Isabel Crawford, who arrived in 1893. She worked for three years at the Elk Creek Mission and then volunteered to go to Saddle Mountain, 40 miles to the southeast, to start another mission. After six years, with the help of Paul Zotom, she organized and built the Saddle Mountain Mission Church. Zotom, the deacon previously defrocked by the Episcopal Church, was baptized once more, this time by the Baptists. He became Crawford's interpreter and was very influential in recruiting new members. But again, after several years Zotom abandoned the Baptists and went back to his old religion. Crawford spent ten years with the Indians and another twenty years on the Baptist Mission board. After retiring, she lived to age ninety-five, deaf and almost blind, in Ontario, Canada. When she died in November 1961, at her request she was brought back to Oklahoma and buried at Saddle Mountain.[19]

From 1907 to 1912 the Reverend Harry H. Treat served at Saddle Mountain. He established the Apache Baptist Church south of Carnegie, which he later moved to Ft. Cobb. During his ministry he converted many Apaches. He was well liked and was remembered as sincere and never inconvenienced by Indian requests.

Mission boards from other denominations established missions in succeeding years, some missions that had previously closed were reopened, and several local white churches sponsored Indian missions. Some flourished; others did not, dissolving for lack of support. Eventually, the sponsoring churches relinquished their efforts to educate Indian children, and the government assumed responsibility for Indian education thereafter.

Churches, however, kept up their evangelistic efforts, especially with adults, and by 1949 a majority of Apaches could be found on the rolls of the Baptist and Methodist Churches. By the 1960s the Holiness Church had gained considerable ground and was almost as well attended as the Baptist and Methodist Churches. The policy of using lay preachers of Indian descent to replace white missionaries who had been formally trained was adopted by most Protestant churches and carried out when committed candidates were found. Although the policy was effective overall, complaints were occasionally made about some Indian preachers, the most common being that they were overly zealous and threatened too much hell, fire, and brimstone. Other lay preachers, however, were extremely tolerant of their parishioners' persistence with the old ways and did not perceive the native religion to conflict with Christian teachings.

Missionary Impact

Fred Bigman remembered the good impression the early missionaries made on the Apaches:

> They [the Apaches] had no objections. They just took it right in. The missionaries got to preaching down there, preaching the Lord's word. Some of the older people took a notion to join. The interpreter translated into Apache, and they liked it. They said, "Well, I'll join this church I guess." The older Indians didn't know what the missionary was, just thought he was some kind of preacher.[20]

Ray Blackbear pointed out that many Apaches were indifferent: "In the early days some of the Apaches didn't like the missionaries and their work. The missionaries would go around to the camps to preach even when they knew the people were against them. There were times when they would be preaching, and the men would go right on smoking and telling stories."[21]

Some persons joined the church without really understanding the church or its precepts. Fred Bigman wanted to join because others did:

> I decided to join. I sat in one of those vacant chairs. I went forward, you might say. Preacher asked me questions, like why I came up, who sent me, did I believe in Christ, would I work for Christ. I told him I didn't want to join, but my uncle told me to join. . . . Preacher asked me, "Did I know anything about Christ?" And I said, "No." When he asked me why I came up I say, "Just because I wanted to." He asked me if I was going to be a good church member, and I said, "Yes." But I didn't know what Jesus was. . . . They accept me. They take me to the creek and baptize me that afternoon. They didn't sprinkle me like the Methodists. They ducked me—the Baptists. I was a church member then.[22]

Christianity's appeal to and success with Apaches varied considerably from one denomination to another and depended on a number of factors, some more important than others. In general, they fell into four broad categories: (1) the communication skills of the missionaries; (2) the concrete symbols of a church's generosity—icons, gifts, and other material benefits; (3) the extent to which concepts and rituals of Christianity were analogous to those of native religions; and (4) the degree of tolerance the particular denomination had for the integration and continuance of indigenous beliefs.

The lack of communication skills was a major stumbling block for missionaries. The inability to speak or understand the Apache language, and a halfhearted effort to learn it, caused the missionaries to be heavily dependent on interpreters to deliver the Lord's message. Inevitably, much was lost in the translation, and much was misunderstood. One example was seen when the missionaries handed out Bibles. The Apaches could not read, but as one man explained: "They liked them because the paper was thin, and they could use the pages to roll cigarettes. They didn't know the Bible contained good words."[23]

Father Daniel, the priest at St. Patrick's Mission in the 1960s, blamed the language barrier for many of the difficulties of the early missions: "If when the missionaries first came here they would have interpreted the hymns into some of the native languages and presented some of the religious teachings in the native language, the change would have been easier. Also, if part of the Catholic service had been in the vernacular, it would have had more appeal."[24]

Susagossa, who learned English at Cache Creek Mission School, expressed her frustration with the Bible's vocabulary: "Lot of things I can't understand in the Bible. Some words hard for me."[25]

The words were hard because the Apache language did not have equivalent terms for many Christian concepts—angels, Trinity, baptism, resurrection, and hell, among others. And when an interpreter translated English into Apache, there was often confusion over the meaning of the sermon, as in the case of the Reverend J. J. Methvin, who very early in his ministry converted a surprising number of Apaches. Although some of his initial success could be attributed to his conversion of the popular Kiowa chief, as noted earlier, the Apaches' misunderstanding of what his "promise of eternal life" meant played an important part also. In 1949 a man recalled his childhood memory of the event:

> The people around camp were talking about how this man was going to show them how they could come back after they died. They thought that he was some kind of medicine man. What he meant was that if you led a good life, your soul would have eternal life. But the Indians thought that he could bring the dead back to life. Everybody started sending their children to that church. My mother told me that if I should die, I wouldn't be gone forever but would come back to life. . . . Later on I began to understand that they meant that when you die you don't return to earth but go up to heaven.[26]

Another complex concept was baptism. The minister from the Indian Capitol Baptist Mission believed:

> The hardest thing for them is baptism. The Baptists don't believe that it is of saving value. It's just a symbol. It's hard for them to understand that baptism is not salvation. I am not sure why this is so. It may be because they only see the tangible things. They will say, "I was baptized in thus and so," meaning that they were saved. If you press them they will say they were saved when they took Christ as their personal savior, but they'll always come back to that salvation.[27]

Apaches did not worry about being saved in the old religion because they had no concept of hell. They believed everyone would share in the afterlife and that no matter how evil or incapacitated someone might be, that person would be redeemed and made whole and join relatives and friends in the afterlife. If Christianity required its communicants to be saved, an Apache reasoned, the perfunctory baptism should suffice.

Interpretation difficulties also arose when in literal translation to Apache a Christian concept became a word with an entirely different meaning than what was intended. A case in point was the Christian concept of Holy Spirit, which summoned Apache ghost fears. A puzzled American Baptist minister, the Reverend J. L. Treat, remarked, "They find it hard to understand the concept of the Holy Spirit. They will use the term *Holy Ghost* in a spooky, kind of Halloween sense. Maybe they had a ghost or spirit concept, and this is a carryover."[28]

A second set of factors contributing to missionary appeal had to do with giving and exchanging material objects or gifts. As Father Daniel noted:

They are very good as far as having something to which they can contribute money or effort. When they have the Indian dances, they spread a blanket out there, and that's where they leave their contributions. One of the good qualities that the Indians have—well, their charity toward one another. If one has something, the other one has it too. There's something good about that. They have a strong sense of loyalty.[29]

Apaches had always shared with each other and automatically assumed that others would share also. Persons who have more than others are, in fact, obligated to share with those who have less, an ethic that has enabled Apaches to survive difficult times in the past. Consequently, they were inclined to trust missionaries who handed out gifts or provided something free and to mistrust those who did not. One man remembered how excited he was to receive a rosary from one of the Catholic sisters:

They told me to wear mine all the time. I felt proud of it. I never took it off. I wore it when I slept and even when I was swimming. People would go back every Sunday . . . just to get a rosary with beads on the chain. A lot of them didn't believe in it, but they wanted those beads.

We knew them [the nuns] by their robes and because they gave us rosaries with beads on them. The Indians said the others were no good because all they wanted was money and gave us nothing. . . . The old people knew that when they prayed in the Indian way they didn't have to give anybody any money, and that was why they disliked the churches that asked for money.[30]

Father Daniel believed it was easier for Indians to conceptualize Roman theology when "they had something concrete—something on a material level. If you go into the Indian homes, you will find statues, crucifixes, rosaries. This may be one of the appeals of the church."[31]

A third factor affecting missionary success was the degree to which rituals and beliefs in both religions were alike. Clearly, the most conspicuous likeness was the practice of praying. An elderly man described the impact of observing Catholic nuns at prayer when he was a child:

This man who was with the sisters prayed. . . . He took out a . . . Bible. He started reading from it. I didn't understand at that time. The only thing he was doing that I knew was good was the praying because we had always had praying in the Indian way. Every now and then I could understand a little bit, like when he talked about "our Father," but the rest of the time I didn't know what he was talking about.[32]

Another similarity was the favorite Indian form of group entertainment, which for Apaches was storytelling around the campfire. Early in the Christianization process, storytelling became a choice pastime at the missions. The Apaches never seemed to tire of hearing Bible stories. Ray Blackbear remembered them as special:

> I still remember her, Miss Allen was her name [the matron], lined up by our beds at night. She was stern in a way. We had a book there, a picture book, a book about Christ. I remember it taught about David and Goliath and the good Samaritan, and there's a few that stands out in my mind even today. It sure wrought a lot of inspiration in me spiritually. Even today when I think of the good done by others, it comes back, the good Samaritan. Another is Christ and the sheep.[33]

The Christian denomination that probably had the most rituals analogous to those of the native religions was the Pentecostal Holiness Church. Apaches found the healing, visions, and intense fervor of the ministers appealing. The Reverend Ann Palmer, the Holiness preacher, observed that the Indians were no longer suspicious of her work after "they had either been healed in a special Holiness service or had a vision of the Lord vouchsafed to them."[34] Certainly, the Holiness healing experience harked back to the old healing ceremonies conducted by the medicine man, and seeking a vision of the Lord evoked memories of the old Indian vision quest and the visionary experience in the Peyote church. The highly emotional, speaking-in-tongues service was a good facsimile of the Ghost Dance, and a number of Apaches were drawn to it while simultaneously scoffing at the preacher's threat of eternal damnation.

The last and most important factor contributing to mission success was the degree to which the church or pastor allowed Apaches to keep their native beliefs. Officially, church policies did not permit tolerance of any facet of native religions, but in practice the Catholic priests and some Protestant preachers—especially those who came in the mid-twentieth century—viewed religious indoctrination as a matter that required flexibility. The Baptist, Pentecostal Holiness, early Methodist, and Presbyterian missions were, on the whole, intolerant of native beliefs; the Catholic and Dutch Reformed Churches were tolerant; and the American Baptist Church regarded Indian religions as "incomplete." The Reverend J. L. Treat was confident that "when they [the Apaches] have more light, they will come to the regular church."[35] In general, the most successful missions were those that tolerated or endorsed at least some elements of the indigenous religion,

Indian boys and girls at Riverside School in Anadarko, Oklahoma, learning to launder by machine clothes washed in the creek at home, 1901. Phillips Collection. Courtesy, Western History Collections, University of Oklahoma Libraries.

whereas those that followed strict church directives tended to have more limited success.

Some denominations concentrated on religious indoctrination to the exclusion of everything else, emphasizing Bible reading, regular attendance at religious services, and abandonment of the native religion. Others, however, sought to totally change the culture of the Indian. They broadened their religious endeavors with education—the teaching of English, reading, agricultural and domestic skills, proper dress, and manners.

The strictest mission was the Pentecostal Holiness Mission, a late arrival to the Apache area, where the threat of hell and damnation for all nonbelievers was declared routinely in services. It frightened some Indians, intrigued some, but persuaded others to convert. Rose Chaletsin described her Holiness experience:

> Today, Holiness is taking over. . . . They have some kind of little bells [tambourines and] thing you play this way [refers to playing an accordion], on their neck. They sing one song right along, scream, hit floor, clap. I sit there and I listen. When they get over, the minister get up. He calls himself a minister. They put us in the front row. This man—talks

kind of broken English. He says, "Come on, come on." He point to my daughter and say, "You're guilty." I believe, I pray, but it's just too much. He says that if you don't believe in Jesus, you're going to hell. He pointing at us. He say, "Move, move. You got devil on your back, and he can't move." How can I move? Who's going to make me move? I ain't got no Holy Spirit in me. He talk, "If you don't have Jesus, the Holy Ghost's not going to talk to you." Next day at the breakfast table, my boy come in. "Well good morning. You look tired." "Yeah," I say, "we got too much Holy Spirit last night."

Now, these people talk against the old way. They say, "You Indian people don't know nothing. You're going to hell if you don't go to church. We got one way, your way's over." That's what they . . . say to the old people. But some of the old people don't believe what they say. . . . These ministers, they talk pretty bad. Just like tonight, the preacher talks to us like we don't know nothing. They say we gone the devil's way.[36]

The Presbyterian Mission at Cache Creek was also strict but less so than the Pentecostal Holiness Church. Former students remembered it as a school that taught a lot of Bible. Most of the students, Susagossa recalled, seemed to regard the Reverend Carrithers as a pretty good man, but "he preach about image or idol. He preached where people make a golden calf and worshiped that. He said not to do that."[37]

Boarding there was a traumatic experience for some but was generally an accepted necessity. The government's annuity payments to parents were withheld if the children were not in school, a strong incentive for the parents to get them there. Rose Chaletsin told about the beginnings of the mission and her curriculum:

The church been built since 1887 [1889], that's the first church built on the Indian reservation—at Cache Creek Mission. It's there today. The Apaches built it. I was baptized in 1908, and I learned to go to church. . . . I just learned to read the Bible, to memorize it, what page to study—Old Testament and New Testament. . . . We had geography, reading, and spelling. We study every night—Monday night, Tuesday night, Wednesday we have prayer meeting. . . . We go to church Saturday night and Sunday morning, noon, and night. Sing, memorize, read Bible, all the kids.[38]

Susagossa stressed the strictness of the school and questioned the practicality of keeping the Sabbath:

They're very particular down there. You have to say "Sabbath," not Sunday. We don't even get to have nothing to do with another kind of book besides the Bible. We can't play, and we have to keep the Sabbath day holy. They taught us to pray. . . . Sometime if I do something wrong, I pray for forgiveness in Jesus name. I always think God so precious, bright. . . . He labor six days but rest the seventh. We not supposed to labor on the seventh, but sometime I have to. I say "ox in a ditch." If ox is in a ditch, you have to get him out no matter when it is. If I have to work, I got to work. He won't want me to suffer 'cause I work on a Sunday. He forgive me several times.[39]

Ray Blackbear, who attended Cache Creek in his youth, never forgot being punished for speaking Apache at the school. The three years he spent at the school "seemed just like 300 years—a prison." His best memories were of "the Christmas holidays—we'd all camp around that church. There'd be around sixty, seventy, eighty tents around that church. Camp there Christmas, New Year's—something to look forward to each year."[40] The tents held visiting parents and relatives who had not seen their children for many months.

The Catholics were more accommodating to the native religion. They arrived on the Plains with considerably more experience in missionizing Indians than any of the Protestant missionaries and knew they had to win Indian hearts before they could win their souls. Through the use of Christian "charms"—rosaries, crucifixes, sacred images, and relics—an abundance of food, and elaborate rituals, they gained the early trust of many Indians. With the added charisma of Chief Thunderbolt, Catholicism was difficult to resist. Many Apache children attended the mission school and liked it, and they often joined the church in groups. One person complained about the Catholic Bible because it did not have Genesis and Exodus, which the other Bible had, and others complained about having to kneel too much; but in general the Apache elders did not regard St. Patrick's as having been strict and remembered living at the school as a positive experience.

Father Daniel concluded that most of the Indians he came in contact with had no legalistic (ritualistic) conception of religion: "The church says, 'Mass on Sundays and Holy days of obligation.' The Indians' concept is 'Yes, we should worship God, but when and where I please.'"[41]

Many Apaches showed no particular loyalty to any specific church or denomination. If an urgent need for spiritual help arose, they commonly took a pragmatic approach and found a church that was accessible, which could be any one of the Indian missions, white Christian churches, or the Peyote church. Rose Chaletsin explained, "A lot of people go to the white man's church. They have their own church, but if they can't reach it, you have to go to another church. I couldn't wait for another peyote meeting, so I have to go to another church."[42]

Datose verbalized her general lack of concern about the importance of denominations: "We Methodist. We got Duke Tsootl. He's our preacher. I don't know which it is—Methodist or Baptist. We go under the water—which is that? Well, it doesn't matter."[43]

Paradoxically, Christianity meant something different for Apaches than it did for non-Indians. The precepts and laws of the Christian churches did not permit any compromise with Indian religion. A belief in Jesus Christ as the savior was exclusionary for a non-Indian Christian and did not allow worship of other gods or beliefs. But as Susagossa stated defiantly: "Sure, it's [the powwow] against the church, but me, [if] I think it's wrong to go to the dances I'll go anyway, even though I know it's wrong to go, even though I'm an old Indian. My people to begin with didn't know what was wrong, and we go to kill, steal. But later we know better. I know it's wrong to go, but I'm a pretender."[44]

The Apaches also embraced Christianity to expand their spiritual options and social dimensions. A majority could not accept or understand the exclusivity of the new religion and commonly belonged to a Christian church while continuing to attend the Peyote church. Fred Bigman explained:

> They [Apaches] think about it in this way. Why should they give up the old religion when they worshiped the same person? That's the way I did. When I joined the church I didn't do away with nothing. That's the way I do in my Native American Church. I smoke, and I go on praying—tell him what I'm here for. . . . I like it [the Native American Church] better. I'm used to it. Then too, I get acquainted with people I ain't never seen before. People outside my tribe like the Caddo, Wichita, and Arapaho. The same people go all the time to the white church.[45]

Susagossa affirmed her lack of conflict between the two religions:

> I believe in both. . . . I believe that the church does more, the white church. Course, I take that medicine [peyote] when I need it. When you take that medicine, it sure helps you pray. I feel like my prayers got there. . . . I go to church over there, but sometimes I don't like the preacher. That's when I don't like to go to church. . . . The preacher say, "Here's your feet. If you go to some other church, you have your feet on both sides. I think God don't like that. You should pick up your feet and take the right path." But preachers tell you anything. Sometimes I just don't believe it.
>
> I go to the Peyote church and the Methodist Church. I like both churches. Of course, sometimes I kind of get scared 'cause the Bible says not to have two masters. But I look at it this way. God made me an Indian. That's [peyote] an Indian way. I talk to God in the meetings, and

that's the same God. I say to him that I'm sorry if I'm mistaken and ask him to forgive me.[46]

Rose Chaletsin summed up her frustration with white Christian opposition to all things Indian:

> Most of the church people are against peyote. They say it's bad if somebody eats peyote. We used to pray to bags and smoke on the ground a long time ago. The church people talk all against that. They talk against any Indian way. They even talk against the [Blackfeet] dance. . . . Cecil Horse [a Kiowa preacher] talked to us at Boone. He got a bad mouth. He talks bad to Apaches. He said, "They dance too much. They eat peyote. Lord, they're lost. Let God forgive them." He was praying like that in church, at the Apache Baptist Church.[47]

In 1969, after 100 years of evangelization, the names of most Apaches could be found on the rolls of the local Christian churches, but only a few of those Apaches had made a complete break with their native religions. The most common pattern was a compartmentalization of religion that allowed Apaches to adhere to the old beliefs and rituals while also accepting certain aspects of Christianity. Apaches tended to be pragmatic about religion. Each person took what he or she wanted from any one, two, and, often, all three religions—native, Christian, and Peyote. They regarded religious beliefs as a personal matter, and although some accepted the exclusivity of Christianity, the majority simply regarded Christianity as one more path to the supernatural.

Apaches are a deeply spiritual people who have a complex system of beliefs in the supernatural. In the native religion they were not concerned about being saved or condemned to eternal damnation but were open to new religious ideas if the ideas had some counterpart in the old religions. And when they needed urgent spiritual help, they were inclined to go to the nearest sacred place to communicate with the supernatural, which might be a peyote meeting as well as any of the Christian church services. Denominations were not important to the average Apache and often were chosen according to the personality of the minister, friends expected to be there, quantity and quality of food served, time and length of service, good stories, and good Apache songs.

What was the overall effect of the missionaries? Clearly, the missionaries improved the quality of Apache life by teaching needed language and writing skills and, in general, helping to soften the Indian adjustment to an alien way of life. Missionaries performed many humanitarian services and were usually spoken of kindly by the elders in later years. But missionaries were generally insensitive to Indian culture, never entertaining the thought that they might learn something from the Indians in return.

Evangelizing Christians often regarded the Indian as inferior, and even after Indians became Christians, their Indian dress and crude manners were viewed with distaste, as Lawrie Tatum divulged regarding evangelistic endeavors on the adjacent Wichita Reservation in the 1870s:

> About fifteen or twenty Indians were converted [Wichitas]. . . . The agent, his wife, and all of the friends connected with the agency were thankful for the change of heart that had taken place. At this point a grave difficulty was presented. What shall be done with these uncouth Christian Indians? The agent and his wife were educated, refined Philadelphia Friends. It would hardly seem consistent to take these Indians, some dressed in citizen's clothes and some wearing blankets, into church membership with those living in the City of Brotherly Love although equally, so far as they appeared, the children of God. In addressing them we could call them brothers because we were all created by the same Supreme Being, and his love extended to all.[48]

Today, approximately half belong to Christian churches, and of that half, some have accepted the exclusivity of Christianity. Others have not because they find the Native American Church and the worship of the medicine bundles still relevant to their lives. The Blackfeet Dance, sacred at one time, is now a secular celebration, and attending it does not interfere with Christian beliefs. Whatever the religious preference of individual Apaches, they are respectful of other religions.

Conclusion

The essential element enabling the Plains Apaches to cope and even prosper as nomads on the vast, uncharted Great Plains was their heavy reliance on an all-encompassing sense of oneness with nature and its spirit beings, which could be invoked frequently for any matter, large or small. When enemies, disease, famine, or internal strife threatened, Apaches rallied around to respond and, hoping for the best outcome, called on the supernatural and the spirit beings to gain strength and courage.

Apaches routinely offered prayers, self-sacrifice, and pledges to the spirit beings in exchange for their help and blessings. If the crisis was especially calamitous, that is, if an advancing enemy seriously outnumbered them, all came together in a full-fledged ceremonial to evoke supernatural forces through prayer, songs, dance, and symbols.

Symbols are important in all societies, but in native religions, in which analogical thinking predominated, symbols took on extraordinary importance. People viewed the natural world as analogous to the human world, which allowed them to endow animal and bird beings with souls and perceive them as spirit beings. The Apache trilevel world was made up of a middle level, the inhabited part where the human beings and animals lived and interacted; an upper level, the uninhabited sky; and a lower level, a source of medicine power that incorporated the Land of the Dead and the sacred lakes. Good and bad spirits could be found anywhere in this trilevel universe.

The upper level, the sky, was generally perceived to be the most sacred. Its shrouded mystery, vastness, and inaccessibility combined to inspire a belief in the supernatural. The sky was where the gods lived, the gods with names like Blue-White Man, Creator, and Man-Up-There. The sky was where the sun, the moon, and the stars directed life on the earth below. The sun in particular was recognized as a life-giving force, and its circular shape and red and yellow colors were replicated many times in Apache clothing, shield, and tepee designs.

The sky provided infinite space for the freedom-loving birds with admirable qualities Apaches especially desired to possess. The strength and power of the eagle; the swiftness of the prairie falcon; the intelligence of the woodpecker; the beauty of the scissor-tailed flycatcher, magpie, and male pheasant were desirable characteristics believed to be transferable through their feathers. Hence, feather symbols, or "good feathers," took on exaggerated importance in all rituals, from the relatively small curing rituals to full-blown tribal ceremonials.

Birds regarded as anomalous because they ate carrion, stayed awake at night, or had a scary look were scrupulously avoided. They were never eaten, and their feathers were never used. The owl was an exception, and it was regarded ambiguously. In spite of its negative attributes, which included being an omen of death and an incarnation of the dreaded ghost, it was also considered a source of wisdom for those who had special owl knowledge, and its otherwise forbidden feathers were required finery for members of the Tlintidie Contraries Society.

In the animal kingdom, Apaches found a wealth of symbols to which they applied analogical thinking to improve their health and well-being. From the buffalo—their powerful Master Animal—the liver, kidney, and tripe imparted strength to persons who consumed them; and buffalo hide, horns, hooves, and the tail conveyed sacred power to participants in ceremonies. Horns and antlers of the antelope, symbolizing swiftness and new life, sometimes decorated the peyote drum. The white tails of the ermine, symbolizing adaptability, were placed on each side of a war bonnet; and the otter's hide, as a source of good luck, was required to wrap the four staffs in the Manatidie Dancing Society.

Anomalous animals were avoided. They were nocturnal, foul-smelling, weird-looking, or scavengers; and the most abominated were those that exhibited characteristics from more than one Apache classification—human, bird, animal, and reptile. For example, the bear was an abomination because it was an animal, but it walked upright like a human; the bat because it had fur but flew like a bird.

Supernatural power was concentrated in the medicine bundles, and although today only one is given ritual care, it is still an important source of power for the very traditional Apaches. This power in varying degrees was also held by medicine men and medicine women who had actively sought and obtained it in a vision quest or accepted it passively in a dream. But the power always came from some animal, bird, or atmospheric phenomenon— the symbols of which were used ceremonially to effect a cure, bring the rain, or keep the enemy at bay.

Not only did the supernatural embolden the warrior and hunter, it also cured the sick, and it helped enforce the strict code of social control by creating a sense of potential retribution. For example, the rule prohibiting all contact or discourse between affines and a rule dictating that all aggressive behavior, especially between family members, be repressed were adhered to closely. Not to do so threatened the peace and goodwill of family members toward each other, and no one wanted to be visited by a ghost. The spirit beings, which came in many forms, were charged with the moral order, and they functioned to prevent internal strife from developing and threatening the tribe. Coyote casually reinforced the code of behavior while providing comic relief. He constantly warned others of the inherent risk of attempting to cross forbidden boundaries and aspiring to be something or someone the rules did not allow. Throughout the book he sounded a cautionary note about overdependence on the supernatural and reminded people of the importance of being self-reliant.

The sacred symbols on which preliterate Apaches focused are still used in the Blackfeet Dance today. One cannot say the symbols have completely lost their sacred meanings, but they now also provoke a nostalgic feeling and remind Apaches of their rich heritage. The symbols hark back to a time when the tribe enjoyed full economic, religious, and political freedom—a freedom they will unlikely ever have again. But the world has drastically changed since then, and many Apaches—Alonzo Chalepah estimates more than 50 percent—today belong to Christian churches. Some belong to the Native American Church, and others still look to the medicine bundle for divine inspiration. Few, though, worship in any one church exclusively, preferring a Christian church that embraces the Apache culture and uses Indian hymns with Apache words, the Peyote church that uses Christian elements, or the Medicine Bundle ritual that has some Christian concepts. In all three, the power of the supernatural still predominates, and many Apaches believe all religions are inspired by one and the same God. Syncretic manifestations of religion are appealing to Indians because they allow them to retain part of their culture while accommodating themselves to an alien, industrialized world. The Plains Apaches' ability to experience the wonders of nature in much greater depth than others and to find a solace not found elsewhere underlies the explanation of why the Apache supernatural is so powerful.

Notes

In citing reference works and names of contributors in the notes, I have generally used short titles and abbreviations. References and contributors frequently cited are identified with the following abbreviations.

ARCIA: Commission of Indian Affairs, *Annual Reports*

Bittle, "HKA": William E. Bittle, "A Brief History of the Kiowa Apache," *University of Oklahoma Papers in Anthropology* 12, no. 1 (1971): 1–34.

Bittle, "PRKA": William E. Bittle, "The Peyote Ritual of the Kiowa Apache," *Oklahoma Anthropological Society*, Bulletin II (1954): 69–78.

D: Datose, or Connie Mae Saddleblanket

DDC: Doris Duke Collection

FB: Fred Bigman

JB: Joe Blackbear

Jordan, "EKA": Julia A. Jordan, "The Ethnobotany of the Kiowa-Apache." Master's thesis, University of Oklahoma, 1962.

McAllister, "KASO": Gilbert J. McAllister, "Kiowa-Apache Social Organization," in *Social Anthropology of North American Tribes*, ed. Fred Eggan, 97–169 (Chicago: University of Chicago Press, 1937).

McAllister, "KAT": Gilbert J. McAllister, "Kiowa Apache Tales," in *The Sky Is My Tipi*, ed. Mody Boatright, 1–141. *Publications of the Texas Folklore Society* XXII (Dallas: Southern Methodist University Press, 1949).

Opler and Bittle, "DPKA": Morris E. Opler and William E. Bittle, "The Death Practices and Eschatology of the Kiowa Apache." *Southwestern Journal of Anthropology* 17, no. 4 (1961): 383–394.

RB: Ray Blackbear

RC: Rose Chaletsin

S: Susagossa, or Louise Saddleblanket

TB: Tennyson Berry

All field notes without the name of the interviewer were recorded by Bittle in the 1950s and 1960s or by one of his students in the 1961, 1963, or 1964 field schools. Some field notes identify Bittle as the interviewer, but most have no identification. In general, scholars who are interviewing do not write their names on each sheet they are transcribing. One cannot conclude that only those with Bittle's name are his and the others belong to his students. Lacking definite identification of the interviewer in the years 1961, 1963, and 1964, I therefore have omitted the interviewer's name on each of these entries.

Introduction

1. RB, int., June 10, 1961.
2. Mooney, "Calendar History"; McAllister, "KASO," "KAT," "Dävéko," "Four Quartz"; Brant, "Cultural Position," "Kiowa Apache Indians," "Kiowa Apache Culture History," "Peyotism," *Jim Whitewolf*, ed. Brant.
3. Bittle, "Kiowa-Apache," "PRKA," "Manatidie," "HKA"; Opler and Bittle, "DPKA"; Jordan, "Ethnobotany"; Bross, "Kiowa-Apache Body Concept"; Beals, "Kiowa Apache Peyotism."
4. Nelson, *Make Prayers to the Raven*; Anderson, *Peyote*.
5. Geertz, *Interpretation of Cultures*, 234.
6. Geertz, *Works and Lives*.
7. Tyler, "Post-Modern Ethnography," 130–131.
8. Clifford, "Introduction," 15.
9. Tyler, "Post-Modern Ethnography," 126.
10. Geertz, *Local Knowledge*, 58.
11. Levi-Strauss quoted in Geertz, *Works and Lives*, 46.
12. Bittle, letter to the author, November 16, 1992.
13. Bittle, "Position of the Kiowa Apache," 6; Krauss, "Plains Apache Language"; Young, "Apachean Languages," 400.
14. Levi-Strauss, *Savage Mind*, 15.
15. Godelier, *Perspectives in Marxist Anthropology*, 204–220.
16. Durkheim, *Elementary Forms*, 34–35; Eliade, "Methodological Remarks," 95; Eliade, *Sacred and Profane*.
17. Douglas, *Purity and Danger*.
18. Geertz, "Religion as a Cultural System," 85.
19. Ibid., 84; Malinowski, "Role of Magic and Religion," 45.
20. Geertz, *Islam Observed*.
21. Eliade, *The Quest*.

22. Irwin, *Dream Seekers*, 233.
23. Bierhorst, *Mythology of North America*, 5.
24. Ibid., 20.
25. Ibid.
26. Brumbaugh, "Quest for Survival," 189–190.

Chapter 2

1. Gunnerson, "Southern Athapaskan Archeology," 162, places the arrival of Apacheans in the Southwest at A.D. 1525. Forbes, *Apache, Navajo, and Spaniard*, xiv–xxiii, believes it was several centuries earlier, and Opler, "Apachean Culture Pattern," argues that A.D. 1400 is a more reasonable date.
2. Hoijer, "Chronology of Athapaskan Languages," "Position of Apachean Languages," 3–6.
3. Gunnerson, "Southern Athapaskan Archeology"; Opler, "Apachean Culture Pattern," 384; Brugge, "Navajo Prehistory," 489.
4. Gunnerson, "Southern Athapaskan Archeology"; Brugge, "Navajo Prehistory," 489–490.
5. Ibid.
6. Ibid.; Bittle, "Kiowa-Apache."
7. Davis, "Cultural Preadaptation Hypothesis," *Ecology*.
8. Mooney, "Calendar History," 245.
9. Ibid., 248–251.
10. Lange, "Relations of the Southwest."
11. ARCIA 1904, 490; Mooney, "Calendar History," 169.
12. Bittle, "HKA," 3–4.
13. Ibid.
14. ARCIA 1849, 1071–1072.
15. ARCIA 1852, 67.
16. Bittle, "HKA," 13.
17. Ibid., 12.
18. Mooney, "Calendar History," 297–299.
19. ARCIA 1904, 601.
20. ARCIA 1860, 139.
21. ARCIA 1863, 7.
22. ARCIA 1865, 530.
23. Ibid., 517–527.
24. Ibid., 533.
25. Bittle, "HKA," 28.
26. Mooney, "Calendar History," 180.
27. Bittle, "HKA," 28.
28. Mayhall, *The Kiowas*, 288.
29. Brant, "White Contact," 10.
30. Allen, "Health and Medical Care," 196–200.
31. Bittle, "HKA," 28.
32. ARCIA 1902, 64–66; 1907, 63–64.
33. Brant, *Jim Whitewolf*, 60, 183.

34. Alonzo Chalepah to author, September 13, 2001.
35. Kehoe, *North American Indians*, 565–566.
36. Meadows, *Kiowa, Apache, and Comanche*, 395.
37. Bittle, "HKA," 30.
38. Alonzo Chalepah to author, September 13, 2000.
39. Meadows, *Kiowa, Apache, and Comanche*, 249.
40. Brant, "Kiowa-Apache Indians," 148.
41. Bittle, "Kiowa-Apache," 76.
42. Oklahoma Indian Affairs Commission, 18.
43. Krauss, "Plains Apache Language Documentation."
44. Ibid.
45. Alonzo Chalepah to author, September 13, 2000.
46. Parsons, *Kiowa Tales*.

Chapter 3

1. FB, int., June 19, 1963.
2. JB, int. by Brant, March 21, 1949.
3. RC, int., June 12, 1961.
4. Ibid.
5. S, int., July 5, 1963.
6. S, int., June 25, 1964.
7. D, int., July 15, 1963.
8. RB, int., June 10, 1961.
9. Stewart Klinekole, int., July 26, 1961.
10. RB, int., June 10, 1963.
11. McAllister, "KASO," 162–163; Brant, *Jim Whitewolf*, 5; JB, int. by Brant, March 12, 28, 1949.
12. TB, int. by Brant, February 19, 1949.
13. RC, int., June 12, 1961.
14. Gertie Chalepah, int., July 21, 1964.
15. RB, int. by Bittle, March 25, 1956.
16. Solomon Katchin, int. by McAllister, in "KAT," 17–19.
17. RB, int. by Bittle, April 3, 1956.
18. Katchin, int. by McAllister, in "KAT," 24–25.
19. Ibid., 25–26.
20. RB, int. by Bittle, March 29, 1956.
21. McAllister, "KASO," 22–25.
22. JB, int. by Brant, March 28, 1949.
23. McAllister, "KASO," 137.
24. RC, int., June 9, 1961; JB, int. by Brant, March 3, 1949.
25. S, int., June 10, 1961.
26. Ibid.
27. S, int., June 29, 1964.
28. TB, int., May 2, 1953.
29. McAllister, "KAT."
30. Bierhorst, *Mythology of North America*, 157.

31. Quoted in Hultkrantz, *Religions of the American Indians*, 39.
32. RB, int. by Bittle, March 29, 1956.
33. RB, int. by Bittle, April 3, 1956.
34. RB, int., July 18, 1961.
35. Ibid.
36. RB, int., July 28, 1961.
37. RB, int., July 11, 1963; RC, int., June 12, 1963; D, int., June 17, 1961.
38. JB, int. by Brant, March 16, 1949.
39. RB, int., June 29, 1961.
40. McAllister, "KASO," 167–168.
41. JB, int. by Brant, March 17, 1949.
42. JB, int. by Brant, April 3, 1949.
43. McAllister, "Dävéko," 45–46.
44. RB, int. by Jordan, June 26, 1967, DDC, vol. 40, T-233, 17.
45. S, int., April 22, 1964.
46. RB, int., July 27, 1961.
47. S, int., April 22, 1964.
48. Helen Blackbear, int. by Bittle, June 26, 1967, DDC, vol. 3, T-53-3, 3.
49. RC, int., June 9, 1961.
50. S, int., July 14, 1964.
51. RB, int. by Bittle, April 19, 1956.
52. RC, int., June 6, 1963.
53. RB, int., July 27, 1961.
54. S, int., June 27, 1961.
55. RC, int., June 12, 1961.
56. FB, int., July 5, 1963.
57. RC, int., June 12, 1961.
58. S, int., June 27, 1961.

Chapter 4

1. RB, int. by Bittle, October 4, 1966.
2. McAllister, "Four Quartz," 215.
3. JB, int. by Brant, March 16, 1949.
4. S, int., June 17, 1961.
5. McAllister, "KASO," 167.
6. JB, int. by Brant, March 17, 1949.
7. S, int., June 23, 1961.
8. McAllister, "Four Quartz," 213.
9. FB, int. by Bittle, June 26, 1967, DDC, vol. 39, T-56-1, 13.
10. JB, int. by Brant, March 12, 1949.
11. Alfred Chalepah, int. by Brant, March 1, 1949.
12. McAllister, "Four Quartz," 213.
13. Ibid.; RB, int. by Bittle, April 4, 1956, April 3, 1959; Apache Ben Chaletsin, int. by Brant, March 17, 1949.
14. S, int., July 26, 1961.
15. McAlllister, "Four Quartz."

16. Brumbaugh, "Quest for Survival," 185–186.
17. Quoted in McAllister, "Four Quartz," 220.
18. Apache Ben Chaletsin, int. by Brant, March 17, 1949.
19. McAllister, "Four Quartz," 213.
20. FB, int. by Bittle, June 26, 1987, DDC, vol. 39, T-56-1, 12–13.
21. Ibid., 17.
22. RC, int., July 27, 1961.
23. Bittle, "Manatidie," 154.
24. Ibid.

Chapter 5

1. For this chapter I have relied heavily on John Terres, *The Audubon Society: Encyclopedia of North American Birds,* and Roger Tory Peterson, *A Field Guide to the Birds of Texas and Adjacent States,* for information on habitats and characteristics of Apache birds.
2. RB, int., June 28, 1961.
3. RC, int., June 12, 1963.
4. RB, int., July 11, 1963.
5. S, int., July 1, 1963; RB, int., June 29, 1964.
6. S, int., July 1, 1963.
7. RC, int., June 22, 1961.
8. RB, int., July 11, 1963.
9. RC, int., June 22, 1961.
10. S, int., June 24, 1963; RC, int., June 12, 1963.
11. *Encyclopaedia Britannica,* 15th ed., s.v. "Falconiformes."
12. RB, int., July 11, 1963.
13. RB, int., July 12, 1963.
14. RB, int., July 22, 1961.
15. RC, int., June 12, 1963.
16. FB, int., June 25, 1964.
17. RB, int., July 1, 1964.
18. S, int., June 10, 1961.
19. RB, int., July 1, 1964; FB, int., June 26, 1964.
20. RB, int., July 12, 1963.
21. Ibid.
22. RB, int. by Bittle, March 26, 1956.
23. RB, int., July 1, 1964; S, int., July 14, 1964.
24. RC, int., June 22, 1961.
25. RC, int., July 3, 1964.
26. RB, int., June 5, 1963.
27. RC, int., June 15, 1964.
28. S, int., June 10, 1961.
29. RC, int., July 20, 1961.
30. S, int., June 10, 1961.
31. RC, int., July 20, 1961.
32. S, int., July 14, 1964.

33. McAllister, "KASO," 154–155.
34. RC, int., July 21, 1961.
35. RB, int., July 21, 1963; S, int., July 14, 1964.
36. RC, int., July 3, 1964.
37. RB, int., July 1, 1964.
38. RB, int. by Bittle, March 29, 1956.
39. RC, int., July 3, 1964; RB, int., June 29, 1964.
40. S, int., July 14, 1964.
41. RB, int., June 29, 1964.
42. JB, int. by Brant, March 3, 1949.
43. RB, int., July 22, 1961.
44. FB, int., June 25, 1964.
45. RB, int., July 22, 1961.
46. RC, int., July 3, 1964.
47. RB, int., July 1, 1964.
48. JB, int. by Brant, March 3, 1949.
49. RC, int., July 3, 1964.
50. JB, int., October 18, 1952. For another version of this story, see *The Sky Is My Tipi*, ed. Mody C. Boatright, *Publications of the Texas Folklore Society* 22 (Dallas: Southern Methodist University Press, 1949).
51. RC, int., June 22, 1961, July 3, 1964; S, int., July 14, 1964.
52. RB, int. by Bittle, March 29, 1956.
53. Ibid.
54. RB, int. by Bittle, April 19, 1956.
55. RC, int., July 3, 1964.
56. RB, int., July 1, 1964.

Chapter 6

1. D, int., June 15, 1964.
2. Battey, *Life and Adventures of a Quaker*, 16–19.
3. McAllister, "KAT," 52–53.
4. RB, int., June 20, 1961.
5. RB, int. by Bittle, April 19, 1956.
6. RB, int., July 12, 1963.
7. RB, int., June 28, 1961.
8. RC, int., June 21, 1961.
9. S, int., July 11, 1963.
10. Ibid.
11. JB, int. by Brant, March 3, 1949.
12. *Tlintidie* is a more correct linguistic rendering of McAllister's *Klintidie*, used in "KASO," 153–157. According to Bittle in letter to author dated November 16, 1992: "The first consonant is the affricated voiceless 'ł,' orthographically, a barred lambda. . . . The word [should be] spelled *Lintidie*, or even better, *Tlintidie*."
13. RB, int., June 20, 1961.
14. RB, int. by Bittle, April 3, 1956.

15. McAllister, "KAT," 97–101.
16. Ibid., 51–52.
17. S, int., July 11, 1961.
18. RC, int., June 20, 1961.
19. Johns-Stands-in-Timber and Liberty, *Cheyenne Memories*, 89, 113.
20. D, int., July 21, 1961.
21. Bittle, "Kiowa-Apache Raiding Behavior," 40–41.
22. *Grzimek's Encyclopedia of Mammals*, 1990 ed., s.v. "Pronghorns."
23. RB, int., July 18, 1961.
24. S, int., July 13, 1964.
25. Ibid.
26. Stewart Klinekole, int., July 28, 1961.
27. RB, int. by Bittle, March 29, 1956.
28. S, int., June 30, 1961.
29. JB, int. by Brant, March 12, 1949.
30. Mrs. Bigman, int. by Brant, February 14, 1949.
31. S, int., July 13, 1964.
32. RB, int., June 16, 1964.
33. Ibid.
34. FB, int., June 23, 1964.
35. RC, int., July 2, 1964.
36. Personal communication with Alfred Chalepah, October 9, 1996.
37. RC, int., July 2, 1964.
38. Ibid.
39. S, int., June 27, 1961.
40. JB, int. by Brant, April 2, 1949.
41. S, int., June 16, 1961.
42. D, int., July 17, 1963.
43. *Grzimek's Encyclopedia of Mammals*, 1990 ed., s.v. "Mustelids."
44. Kehoe, *North American Indians*, 255; Brasser, "Mahican," 200.
45. RB, int., June 28, 1961.
46. RC, int., July 2, 1964.
47. McAllister, "KAT," 80–81.
48. RC, int., July 17, 1963.
49. RB, int. by Bittle, March 29, 1956. For another version of this story, see *The Sky Is My Tipi*, ed. Mody C. Boatright, *Publications of the Texas Folklore Society* 22 (Dallas: Southern Methodist University Press, 1949).
50. FB, int., June 23, 1964.
51. JB, int. by Brant, March 16, 1949.
52. Alonzo Chalepah, int. by Brant, n.m., n.d., 1949.
53. Jordan, "EKA," 18–19.
54. RC, int., July 2, 1964.
55. Roots, *Animals of the Dark*, 82.
56. D, int., July 25, 1961.
57. RB, int., June 29, 1964.
58. RB, int. by Bittle, March 29, 1956.

59. *Grzimek's Encyclopedia of Mammals,* 1990 ed., s.v. "Hares and Rabbits"; Caire, *Mammals of Oklahoma,* 166–168.
60. RC, int., July 2, 1964.
61. D, int., June 17, 1964.
62. RB, int., June 29, 1964; Roots, *Animals of the Dark,* 121–122.
63. RC, int., July 2, 1964.
64. RB, int. by Bittle, March 29, 1956.
65. RB, int., June 16, 1964; D, int., June 17, 1964.
66. RC, int., June 22, 1961.
67. RC, int., August 14, 1961.
68. Ibid.
69. Ibid.; JB, int. by Brant, March 3, 1949.
70. JB, int. by Brant, April 3, 1949.
71. RB, int., June 23, 1961.
72. S, int., July 15, 1964.
73. RC, int., August 14, 1964.
74. TB, int., November 22, 1955.
75. TB, int., March 3, 1953.

Chapter 7

1. Opler and Bittle, "DPKA."
2. Bittle, "Life Cycle," 89.
3. Bittle, "Camp Organization and Daily Routine," 2–3.
4. McAllister, "Dävéko," 36; Hoig, *The Kiowas,* 236.
5. McAllister, "KASO," 93–94.
6. Ibid., 103–136.
7. Ibid., 124.
8. RC, int., June 19, 1961.
9. Ibid.
10. Bittle, "Life Cycle," 92.
11. Ibid., 96.
12. Ibid.
13. S, int., June 21, 1961; McAllister, "KASO," 137.
14. RB, int., June 17, 1961.
15. S, int., June 21, 1961; Bittle, "Life Cycle," 8.
16. Bittle, "Life Cycle," 11.
17. RB, int. by Bittle, November 10, 1959.
18. RB, int. by Bittle, April 30, 1956.
19. TB, int. by Brant, February 17, 1949.
20. RB, int. by Bittle, April 30, 1956.
21. RB, int. by Bittle, November 10, 1959.
22. RB, int. by Bittle, April 30, 1956.
23. RB, int. by Bittle, November 10, 1959.
24. Opler and Bittle, "DPKA."
25. D, int., July 21, 1961.
26. S, int., June 19, 1964; RB, int., November 10, 1959.

27. S, int., July 1, 1961.
28. D, int., July 26, 1961.
29. D, int., June 21, 1961.
30. JB, int. by Brant, February 18, 1949.
31. RB, int. by Bittle, November 10, 1959.
32. JB, int. by Brant, February 18, 1949.
33. D, int., June 24, 1964.
34. TB, int. by Brant, February 17, 1949.
35. S, int., July 14, 1964.
36. D, int., June 24, 1964.
37. S, int., June 17, 1961; FB, int., July 3, 1964, June 20, 1963.
38. D, int., June 17, 1961.
39. D, int., June 24, 1964.
40. Bittle, "Life Cycle," 108.
41. McAllister, "KASO," 158.
42. RB, int. by Bittle, April 30, 1956.
43. Opler and Bittle, "DPKA," 389.
44. S, int., July 10, 1963.
45. Bittle, "Life Cycle," 115.
46. RC, int., July 26, 1961.
47. Ibid.
48. S, int., July 10, 1963.
49. RC, int., June 17, 1961.
50. D, int., June 17, 1961.
51. RC, int., July 20, 1963.
52. Opler and Bittle, "DPKA," 386.
53. Mayhall, *The Kiowas*, 167.
54. RC, int., July 26, 1961.
55. S, int., July 1, 1963.
56. Wallace Redbone, int., June 17, 1961.
57. RC, int., June 20, 1961.
58. Bittle, "Life Cycle," 117.
59. RB, int. by Bittle, November 10, 1959.
60. Ibid.
61. RB, int., June 24, 1961.
62. RB, int., June 10, 13, 1961.
63. RB, int. by Bittle, April 30, 1956.
64. RB, int. by Bittle, November 10, 1959.
65. Opler and Bittle, "DPKA," 388; D, int., June 17, 1961.
66. D, int., July 15, 1963.

Chapter 8

1. Gertie Chalepah, int., July 21, 1964.
2. RB, int., July 18, 1964.
3. D, int., July 28, 1961.
4. JB, int. by Brant, March 3, 1949.

5. McAllister, "Dävéko," 38.
6. RC, int., June 6, 1963.
7. RC, int., June 10, 29, 1961.
8. RB, int., June 28, 1961.
9. FB, int., June 13, 1963.
10. D, int., June 10, 1961.
11. Blackwood, "Native American Genders," 293.
12. Jacobs, "Is the Berdache a Phantom?" 30.
13. Alonzo Chalepah to author, September 13, 2000.
14. RB, int., June 27, 1963.
15. FB, int. by Bittle, June 26, 1967, DDC, vol. 39, T-56-1, 6.
16. D, int. by Brant, March 2, 1949.
17. S, int., July 12, 1961.
18. RC, int., June 29, 1961.
19. JB, int. by Brant, March 3, 1949.
20. RC, int., June 29, 1961.
21. FB, int. by Bittle, June 26, 1987, DDC, vol. 39, T-56-1, 3–4.
22. RC, int., June 27, 1961.
23. RB, int., July 5, 7, 1961.
24. S and D, int., June 12, 1961.
25. RB, int. by Bittle, April 26, 1956.
26. RC, int., June 29, 1961.
27. RB, int. by Bittle, April 26, 1956.
28. RC, int., June 9, 1961.
29. RB, int. by Bittle, April 26, 1956.
30. Gertie Chalepah, int., October 14, 1964.
31. RC, int., June 30, 1961.
32. Gertie Chalepah, int., July 21, 1964.
33. D, int., July 19, 1961.
34. RC, int., June 6, 1963.
35. JB, int. by Brant, March 3, 1949.
36. RB, int., June 10, 1961; RC, int., June 14, 1961.
37. RC, int., June 12, 1961.
38. Jordan, "EKA," 133.
39. RB, int. by Bittle, April 26, 1956.
40. Jordan, "EKA," 116.
41. RB, int., June 20, 1961.
42. RC, int., July 27, 1961.
43. Jordan, "EKA," 112.
44. Ibid., 107–108.
45. RC, int., August 14, 1964.
46. Jordan, "EKA," 118–120; D, int., June 12, 1961.
47. FB, int. by Bittle, June 26, 1967, DDC, vol. 39, T-56-1, 1–3.
48. JB, int. by Brant, February 18, 1949; Bross, "Kiowa-Apache Body Concept," 94.
49. Jordan, "EKA," 109–134; RB, int., April 20, 26, 1956; RC, int., June 30, 1963.

50. RB, int. by Bittle, April 26, 1956, July 5, 1961; Jordan, "EKA," 129–130.
51. D, int., July 25, 1961.
52. S, int., July 8, 1961.
53. Ibid.
54. FB, int., June 20, 1963; RB, int., July 5, 1961.
55. S, int., July 8, 1961.
56. D, int., June 28, 1961.
57. S, int., July 11, 1963.
58. S, int., July 8, 1961.
59. RB, int., July 26, 1961.
60. D, int., July 8, 1961.
61. RB, int., July 26, 1961.
62. S, int., July 11, 1961.
63. Wolf, "Bradycardia of the Dive Reflex," 192–197; Wolf, "End of the Rope," 1022–1024.
64. "Bell's Palsy," in 2001 Mayo Foundation for Medical Education and Research file (database online) cited February 7, 2000; "Stroke," in Mayo Foundation for Medical Education and Research File (database online) cited February 3, 2000.
65. RB, int., July 7, 1961.
66. Jones, *Sanapia*, 86–87.
67. S, int., July 8, 1961.

Chapter 9

1. Singer quoted in Geertz, *Interpretation of Cultures*, 113.
2. Ibid., 92, 216.
3. Quoted in Meadows, *Kiowa, Apache, and Comanche*, 216.
4. Bittle, "Manatidie."
5. McAllister, "KASO."
6. RC, int., June 14, 1961.
7. Claude Jay, int. by Brant, March 31, 1949.
8. McAllister, "KASO," 141.
9. Ibid.
10. Ibid.
11. Ibid., 166.
12. Brant, *Jim Whitewolf*, 57.
13. McAllister, "KASO," 151.
14. RC, int., June 27, 1961.
15. RB, int., June 14, 1961.
16. McAllister, "KASO," 152.
17. RC, int., June 27, 1961; June 10, 1964.
18. Ibid.
19. RC, int., June 11, 1964.
20. RC, int., July 29, 1961.
21. RC, int., June 27, 1961.
22. Bittle, "Manatidie," 156.

23. Ibid., 158.
24. Ibid., 160–162.
25. Bittle, Field Notes, July 21, 1963.
26. McAllister, "KASO," 154.
27. Ibid., 154–155.
28. Ibid.
29. Ibid.
30. Ibid., 156.
31. Ibid., 156–157.
32. RC, int., June 24, 1961.
33. RB, int., June 14, 1961.
34. RC, int., June 27, 1961.
35. RC, int., June 12, 1963.
36. Meadows, *Kiowa, Apache, and Comanche,* 219.
37. RB, int., June 5, 1963.
38. RC, int., June 12, 1963.
39. JB, int. by Brant, March 18, 1949.
40. Battey, *Life Among the Indians,* 127–129.
41. McAllister, "Dävéko," 58.
42. Ibid.
43. Ibid., 58–61.
44. RC, int., June 23, 1961.
45. Ibid.
46. Scott, "Sun Dance of the Kiowa," 343–379; Mooney, "Calendar History," 439–445; Spier, "Kiowa Sun Dance," 433–450.
47. RB, int., July 25, 1961.
48. RC, int., July 22, 1961.
49. Mooney, "Calendar History," 242.
50. Mayhall, *The Kiowas,* 150.
51. Leach, "Ritualization in Man," 229.

Chapter 10

1. Mooney, *Ghost-Dance Religion,* 17, 162–167.
2. S, int. by Bittle, June 27, 1967, DDC, vol. 39, T-56, 3.
3. Mooney, *Ghost-Dance Religion,* 68.
4. Claude Jay, int. by Brant, March 30, 1949.
5. Ibid.
6. S, int., June 27, 1961.
7. Ibid.; RC, int., July 24, 1961.
8. D, int., July 22, 1961.
9. RC, int., July 24, 1961.
10. S, int. by Bittle, June 27, 1967, DDC, vol. 39, T-56, 1–4.
11. S, int., June 27, 1961.
12. RC, int., July 24, 1961.
13. S, int. by Bittle, June 27, 1967, DDC, vol. 39, T-56, 2.
14. RB, int. by Jordan, June 26, 1967, DDC, vol. 40, T-223, 8.

15. RC, int., July 24, 1961.
16. Mooney, *Ghost-Dance Religion*, 175; RC, int., July 24, 1961; S, int., June 27, 1961.
17. Brumbaugh, "Quest for Survival."
18. Brinton, *Nagualism*.
19. Anderson, *Peyote*, 4–9.
20. La Barre, *Peyote Cult*; Bittle, "PRKA," 70.
21. Brant, "Joe Blackbear's Story."
22. Bittle, "PRKA," 71–72.
23. RB, int., June 12, 1961.
24. D, int., July 16, 1963.
25. Bittle, "PRKA," 70.
26. Ibid., 71.
27. JB, int. by Brant, March 7, 1949.
28. JB, int. by Brant, March 16, 1949.
29. Beals, "Kiowa Apache Peyotism," 47–52.
30. Ibid., 51.
31. Bittle, "PRKA."
32. Ibid., 73.
33. Ibid.
34. RC, int., July 15, 1964.
35. Bittle, "PRKA," 73–74.
36. FB, int., July 1, 1964.
37. Bittle, "PRKA," 74.
38. Ibid.
39. JB, int. by Brant, March 7, 1949.
40. D, int., July 25, 1961.
41. S, int., June 14, 1961.
42. RB, int., June 26, 1964.
43. Bittle, "PRKA," 74.
44. RB, int., June 27, 1961.
45. Bittle, "PRKA," 75.
46. RB, int., June 17, 1961.
47. Bittle, "PRKA," 75.
48. RB, int., June 25, 1961.
49. Bittle, "PRKA," 76.
50. FB, int., June 12, 1964.
51. S, int., June 14, 1961.
52. RB, int., June 17, 1961.
53. Beals, "Kiowa Apache Peyotism," 46.
54. Ibid., 77–88.

Chapter 11

1. Berkhofer, "Protestant Indian Missions."
2. Tatum, *Our Red Brothers*, xvii–xviii.
3. Buntin, "Quaker Indian Agents"; Corwin, "Missionary Work," 41–43.

4. ARCIA 1876, 82.
5. Hoig, *The Kiowas*, 236; Buntin, "Quaker Indian Agents."
6. Mitchell, "Early Days of Anadarko," 391.
7. Meadows, *Kiowa, Apache, and Comanches*, 189–190.
8. Petersen, *Plains Indian Art*, 186–190.
9. Ibid.
10. Ibid.; Babcock, "John Jasper Methvin."
11. Forbes, "John Jasper Methvin," 61.
12. Ibid., 70–71.
13. S, int., July 3, 1963.
14. Forbes, "John Jasper Methvin," 72–73.
15. Hume, "Pioneer Missionary Enterprises," 115.
16. "'Chief Thunderbolt' Founded Anadarko Mission," Souvenir number, *Southwest Courier* 34, no. 42. Golden Diocesan Jubilee 1905–1955 (October 8, 1955).
17. Ibid.
18. Ibid.
19. Corwin, "Missionary Work," 49–51, "Saddle Mountain Mission"; Petersen, *Plains Indian Art*, 189–190.
20. FB, int., June 2, 1963.
21. RB, int., July 1, 1963.
22. FB, int., June 20, 1963.
23. Brant, *Jim Whitewolf*, 135.
24. Father Daniel, int., July 23, 1963.
25. S, int., July 20, 1964.
26. Brant, *Jim Whitewolf*, 45.
27. Reverend Joe Prickett, int., June 15, 1963.
28. Reverend J. L. Treat, int., July 11, 1963.
29. Father Daniel, int., July 23, 1963.
30. Brant, *Jim Whitewolf*, 44–45, 135.
31. Father Daniel, int., July 23, 1963.
32. Brant, *Jim Whitewolf*, 45.
33. RB, int., July 1, 1963.
34. Reverend Ann Palmer, int., June 22, 1963.
35. Reverend J. L. Treat, int., July 11, 1963.
36. RC, int., June 25, 1963.
37. S, int., July 3, 1963.
38. RC, int., June 25, 1963.
39. S, int., July 3, 1963.
40. RB, int., July 1, 1963.
41. Father Daniel, int., July 23, 1963.
42. RC, int., July 15, 1963.
43. D, int., June 24, 1964.
44. S, int., July 5, 1963.
45. FB, int., June 29, 1964.
46. S, int., July 6, 1963.

47. RC, int., July 14, 1964.
48. Tatum, *Our Red Brothers*, 207–208.

Bibliography

Allen, Virginia Ruth. "Health and Medical Care of the Southern Plains Indians." Ph.D. diss., Oklahoma State University, 1973.

Anderson, Edward F. *Peyote: The Divine Cactus*. Phoenix: University of Arizona Press, 1996.

Babcock, Sidney H. "John Jasper Methvin 1846–1941." *Chronicles of Oklahoma* 19, no. 2 (1941): 113–118.

Battey, Thomas C. *The Life and Adventures of a Quaker Among the Indians*. Williamstown, Mass.: Crown House, 1972.

Beals, Kenneth. "The Dynamics of Kiowa Apache Peyotism." *University of Oklahoma Papers in Anthropology* 12, no. 1 (1971): 35–89.

Berkhhofer, Robert F. "Protestant Indian Missions." In *The Indian in American History*, ed. Francis Paul Prucha, 75–84. American Problem Studies. Hinsdale, Ill.: Dryden, 1971.

Bierhorst, John. *The Mythology of North America*. New York: Quill William Morrow, 1985.

Bittle, William E. Unpublished Plains Apache field notes, 1953–1956, 1961, 1963, 1964, 1966.

———. "The Peyote Ritual of the Kiowa Apache." *Oklahoma Anthropological Society*, Bulletin 2 (1954): 69–78.

———. "The Position of the Kiowa Apache in the Apachean Group." Ph.D. diss., University of California at Los Angeles, 1956.

———. "The Manatidie: A Focus for Kiowa Apache Tribal Identity." *Plains Anthropologist* 7, no. 17 (1962): 152–163.

———. "Kiowa-Apache." In *Studies in the Athapaskan Language*, ed. Harry Hoijer and others, 76–101. *University of California Publications in Linguistics* 29. Berkeley, 1963.

———. "A Brief History of the Kiowa Apache." *University of Oklahoma Papers in Anthropology* 12, no. 1 (1971): 1–34.

———. "Kiowa-Apache Raiding Behavior." *University of Oklahoma Papers in Anthropology* 20, no. 2 (1979): 33–47.

———. "Camp Organization and Daily Routine." William E. Bittle field notes, n.d.

———. "Life Cycle." William E. Bittle field notes, n.d.

Blackwood, Evelyn. "Native American Genders and Sexualities." In *Two-Spirit People*, eds. Sue-Ellen Jacobs, Wesley Thomas, and Sabine Lang, 284–294. Chicago: University of Illinois Press, 1997.

Botkin, Sam L. "Indian Missions of the Episcopal Church in Oklahoma." *Chronicles of Oklahoma* 36, no. 1 (1958): 40–46.

Brant, Charles S. Unpublished Plains Apache field notes. Archives of Western History Collections, University of Oklahoma, Norman, 1949.

———. "The Cultural Position of the Kiowa-Apache." *Southwestern Journal of Anthropology* 5, no. 1 (1949): 56–61.

———. "Peyotism Among the Kiowa-Apache and Neighboring Tribes." *Southwestern Journal of Anthropology* 6, no. 2 (1950): 212–222.

———. "The Kiowa Apache Indians: A Study in Ethnology and Acculturation." Ph.D. diss., Cornell University, 1951.

———. "Kiowa Apache Culture History: Some Further Observations." *Southwestern Journal of Anthropology* 9, no. 2 (1953): 195–202.

———. "Joe Blackbear's Story of the Origin of the Peyote Religion." *Plains Anthropologist* 8, no. 21 (1963): 180–181.

———. "White Contact and Cultural Disintegration Among the Kiowa Apache." *Plains Anthropologist* 9, no. 23 (1963): 8–13.

———, ed. *Jim Whitewolf: The Life of a Kiowa-Apache Indian*. New York: Dover, 1967.

Brasser, T. J. "Mahican." In *Handbook of North American Indians*, ed. William C. Sturtevant. Vol. 15, *Northeast*, ed. Bruce Trigger, 198–212. Washington, D.C.: Smithsonian Institution Press, 1978.

Brinton, Daniel O. *Nagualism: A Study of Native American Folklore and History*. Proceedings of the American Philosophical Society 33. Philadelphia: McCalle, 1894.

Bross, Michael G. "The Kiowa-Apache Body Concept in Relation to Health." Master's thesis, University of Oklahoma, 1962.

Brugge, David M. "Navaho Prehistory and History to 1850." In *Handbook of North American Indians*, ed. William C. Sturtevant. Vol. 10, *Southwest*, ed. Alfonso Ortiz, 498–501. Washington, D.C.: Smithsonian Institution Press, 1983.

Brumbaugh, Lee. "Quest for Survival: The Native American Ghost-Pursuit Tradition ('Orpheus') and the Origins of the Ghost Dance." In *Folklore Interpreted: Essays in Honor of Alan Dundes*, eds. Regina Bendix and Rosemary Lévy Zumwalt, 183–198. New York: Garland, 1995.

Buntin, Martha. "The Quaker Indian Agents of the Kiowa, Comanche, and Wichita Indian Reservation." *Chronicles of Oklahoma* 10, no. 2 (1932): 204–218.

Caire, William, et al. *Mammals of Oklahoma*. Norman: University of Oklahoma Press, 1989.

Clifford, James. "Introduction: Partial Truths." In *Writing Culture: The Poetics and Politics of Ethnography*, eds. James Clifford and George Marcus, 1–26. Berkeley: University of California Press, 1986.

Commissioner of Indian Affairs, Department of the Interior. *Annual Report*. Washington, D.C.: Government Printing Office, 1849–1865, 1902–1907.

Corwin, Hugh D. "Saddle Mountain Mission and Church." *Chronicles of Oklahoma* 36 (1958): 118–124.

———. "Protestant Missionary Work Among the Comanches and Kiowa." *Chronicles of Oklahoma* 46 (1968): 41–57.

Davis, Michael G. "The Cultural Preadaptation Hypothesis: A Test Case on the Southern Plains." Ph.D. diss., University of Oklahoma, 1988.

———. *Ecology, Sociopolitical Organization, and Cultural Change on the Southern Plains*. Kirksville, Mo.: Thomas Jefferson University Press, 1996.

Douglas, Mary. *Purity and Danger: An Analysis of the Concepts of Pollution and Taboo*. London: Routledge and Kegan Paul, 1966.

Durkheim, Émile. "The Elementary Forms of the Religious Life." In *Reader in Comparative Religion: An Anthropological Approach*, 4th ed., eds. William A. Lessa and Evon Z. Vogt, 27–35. New York: Harper & Row, 1979.

Eliade, Mircea. *The Sacred and the Profane: The Nature of Religion*. New York: Harcourt Brace Jovanovich, 1959.

———. "Methodological Remarks on the Study of Religious Symbolism." In *The History of Religions*, eds. M. Eliade and J. M. Kitagawa, 86–107. Chicago: University of Chicago Press, 1959.

———. *The Quest: History and Meaning in Religion*. Chicago: University of Chicago Press, 1969.

Forbes, Bruce David. "John Jasper Methvin: 'Methodist Missionary to the Western Tribes.'" In *Churchmen and the Western Indians 1820–1920*, eds. Clyde A. Milner II and Floyd O'Neil, 41–73. Norman: University of Oklahoma Press, 1985.

Forbes, Jack D. *Apache, Navaho, and Spaniard*. Norman: University of Oklahoma Press, 1960.

Geertz, Clifford. *Islam Observed: Religious Developments in Morocco and Indonesia*. New Haven: Yale University Press, 1968.

————. *The Interpretation of Cultures*. New York: Basic Books, 1973.

————. "Religion as a Cultural System." In *Reader in Comparative Religion: An Anthropological Approach*, 4th ed., eds. William A. Lessa and Evon Z. Vogt, 78–89. New York: Harper & Row, 1979.

————. *Local Knowledge: Further Essays in Interpretive Anthropology*, 3d ed. New York: Basic Books, 1983.

————. *Works and Lives: The Anthropologist as Author*. Stanford: Stanford University Press, 1990.

Godelier, M. *Perspectives in Marxist Anthropology*. Cambridge: Cambridge University Press, 1977.

Gunnerson, James H. "Southern Athapaskan Archeology." In *Handbook of North American Indians*, ed. William C. Sturtevant. Vol. 9, *Southwest*, ed. Alfonso Ortiz, 162–169. Washington, D.C.: Smithsonian Institution Press, 1979.

Hoig, Stan. *The Kiowas and the Legend of Kicking Bird*. Boulder: University Press of Colorado, 2000.

Hoijer, Harry. "The Chronology of the Athapaskan Languages." *International Journal of American Linguistics* 22, no. 4 (1956): 219–232.

————. "The Position of the Apachean Languages in the Athapaskan Stock." In *Apachean Culture, History, and Ethnology*, eds. Keith H. Basso and Morris E. Opler, 3–6. *Anthropological Papers of the University of Arizona* 21. Tucson, 1971.

Hultkrantz, Ake. *The Religions of the American Indians*. Berkeley: University of California Press, 1979.

Hume, C. Ross. "Pioneer Missionary Enterprises of Kiowa, Comanche, and Wichita Indians." *Chronicles of Oklahoma* 29, no. 1 (1951): 113–116.

Irwin, Lee. *The Dream Seekers: Native American Visionary Transitions of the Great Plains*. Norman: University of Oklahoma Press, 1994.

Jacobs, Sue Ellen. "Is the 'North American Berdache' Merely a Phantom in the Imagination of Western Social Scientists?" In *Two-Spirit People*, eds. Sue Ellen Jacobs, Wesley Thomas, and Sabine Lang, 21–43. Urbana: University of Illinois Press, 1997.

John-Stands-in-Timber and Margot Liberty. *Cheyenne Memories*. Lincoln: University of Nebraska Press, 1967.

Jones, David E. *Sanapia: Comanche Medicine Woman*. New York: Holt, Rinehart, and Winston, 1972.

Jordan, Julia A. "The Ethnobotany of the Kiowa-Apache." Master's thesis, University of Oklahoma, 1962.

————. Unpublished field notes. March 21, 1971.

Kehoe, Alice B. *North American Indians: A Comprehensive Account*, 2d ed. Englewood Cliffs, N.J.: Prentice-Hall, 1992.

Krauss, Michael. "Plains Apache Language Documentation." Reports, Alaska Native Language Center, University of Alaska, Fairbanks, September 1999.

La Barre, Weston. *The Peyote Cult*, 5th ed. Norman: University of Oklahoma Press, 1989.

Lange, Charles H. "Relations of the Southwest with the Plains and Great Basin." In *Handbook of North American Indians*, ed. William C. Sturtevant. Vol. 9, *Southwest*, ed. Alfonso Ortiz, 201–205. Washington, D.C.: Smithsonian Institution Press, 1979.

Leach, Edmund. "Ritualization in Man in Relation to Conceptual and Social Development." In *Reader in Comparative Religion: An Anthropological Approach*, 4th ed., eds. William A. Lessa and Evon Z. Vogt, 229–233. New York: Harper & Row, 1979.

Levi-Strauss, Claude. *The Savage Mind*. London: Weidenfeld and Nicolson, 1966.

Malinowski, B. *Magic, Science, and Religion and Other Essays*. London: Souvenir, 1974 [1925].

———. "Role of Magic and Religion." In *Reader in Comparative Religion: An Anthropological Approach*, 4th ed., eds. William A. Lessa and Evon Z. Vogt, 91–97. New York: Harper & Row, 1979.

Mayhall, Mildred P. *The Kiowas*, 2d ed. Norman: University of Oklahoma Press, 1971.

McAllister, Gilbert J. "Kiowa-Apache Social Organization." In *Social Anthropology of North American Tribes*, ed. Fred Eggan, 97–169. Chicago: University of Chicago Press, 1937.

———. "Kiowa Apache Tales." In *The Sky Is My Tipi*, ed. Mody Boatright, 1–141. *Publications of the Texas Folklore Society* 22. Dallas: Southern Methodist University Press, 1949.

———. "The Four Quartz Rocks Medicine Bundle of the Kiowa-Apache." *Ethnology* 4, no. 2 (1965): 210–224.

———. "Dävéko: Kiowa-Apache Medicine Man." *Bulletin of the Texas Memorial Museum* 17: 1–61. Austin: University of Texas Press, 1970.

Meadows, William C. *Kiowa, Apache, and Comanche Military Societies*. Austin: University of Texas Press, 1999.

Mitchell, Sara Brown. "The Early Days of Anadarko." *Chronicles of Oklahoma* 28, no. 4 (1950): 390–398.

Mooney, James. "Calendar History of the Kiowa Indians." In *Seventeenth Annual Report of the Bureau of American Ethnology, for the Years 1895–96*, pt. 1, 129–445. Washington, D.C.: Smithsonian Institution Press, 1898.

———. *The Ghost-Dance Religion and the Sioux Outbreak of 1890*, ed. Anthony F.C. Wallace. Classics in Anthropology. Chicago: University of Chicago Press, 1965.

Nelson, Richard K. *Make Prayers to the Raven: A Koyukon View of the Northern Forest.* Chicago: University of Chicago Press, 1983.

Oklahoma Indian Affairs Commission. *Oklahoma Indian Nations Information Handbook,* 2001.

Opler, Morris E. "The Apachean Culture Pattern and Its Origin." In *Handbook of North American Indians,* ed. William Sturtevant. Vol. 10, *Southwest,* ed. Alfonso Ortiz, 401–418. Washington, D.C.: Smithsonian Institution Press, 1983.

————. *Myths and Tales of the Chiricahua Apache Indians.* Reprint, with an appendix of Apache and Navaho comparative references by David French. Lincoln: University of Nebraska Press, 1994 [New York: American Folk-Lore Society, 1942].

Opler, Morris E., and William E. Bittle. "The Death Practices and Eschatology of the Kiowa Apache." *Southwestern Journal of Anthropology* 17, no. 4 (1961): 383–394.

Parsons, Elsie Clews. *Kiowa Tales.* Memoirs of the American Folklore Society 22. New York: G. E. Stechert, 1929.

Petersen, Karen Daniels. *Plains Indian Art from Fort Marion.* Norman: University of Oklahoma Press, 1971.

Peterson, Roger Tory. *A Field Guide to the Birds of Texas and Adjacent States.* Boston: Houghton Mifflin, 1963.

Roots, Clive. *Animals of the Dark.* New York: Praeger, 1974.

Scott, Hugh Lenox. "Notes on the Kado, or Sun Dance of the Kiowa." *American Anthropologist* 13, no. 3 (1911): 345–379.

Spier, Leslie. "Notes on the Kiowa Sun Dance." In *Sun Dance of the Plains Indians,* ed. Clark Wissler, 433–450. American Museum of Natural History, *Anthropological Papers* 16, pt. 6. New York, 1921.

Tatum, Lawrie. *Our Red Brothers and the Peace Policy of President Ulysses S. Grant.* Lincoln: University of Nebraska Press, 1970.

Terres. John K. *The Audubon Society: Encyclopedia of North American Birds.* New York: Alfred A. Knopf, 1980.

Tyler, Stephen A. "Post-Modern Ethnography: From Document of the Occult to Occult Document." In *Writing Culture: The Poetics and Politics of Ethnography,* eds. James Clifford and George Marcus, 122–140. Berkeley: University of California Press, 1986.

Wolf, Stuart. "The Bradycardia of the Dive Reflex: A Possible Mechanism of Sudden Death." *Transactions of the American Clinical and Climatological Association* 76 (1964): 192–200.

————. "The End of the Rope: The Role of the Brain in Cardiac Death." *Journal of the Canadian Medical Association* 97 (1967): 1022–1025.

Young, Robert W. "Apachean Languages." In *Handbook of North American Indians,* ed. William C. Sturtevant. Vol. 10, *Southwest,* ed. Alfonso Ortiz, 393–400. Washington, D.C.: Smithsonian Institution Press, 1983.

Index

Page numbers in italics indicate illustrations.